# Counseling and Teaching Across the Life Span

# Counseling and Teaching Across the Life Span

## A Humanistic Perspective

*First Edition*

Written and edited by
Noréal F. Armstrong, Ph.D.
Emma Borens, M.A.
Sharon Bowles, M.A.

cognella®
SAN DIEGO

Bassim Hamadeh, CEO and Publisher
Amy Smith, Senior Project Editor
Jeanine Rees, Production Editor
Abbie Goveia, Junior Graphic Designer
Alexa Lucido, Licensing Manager
Natalie Piccotti, Director of Marketing
Kassie Graves, Vice President of Editorial
Jamie Giganti, Director of Academic Publishing

Cover image copyright © 2018 iStockphoto LP/serts.

Printed in the United States of America

 cognella | CUSTOM
3970 Sorrento Valley Blvd., Ste. 500, San Diego, CA 9212

# Contents

**CHAPTER 3**    **CROSS-CULTURAL APPLICATION TO LIFE SPAN DEVELOPMENT**    32

*Kimberly N. Frazier, PhD*

**CHAPTER 4**    **LGBTQ+ AND HUMAN DEVELOPMENT**    43

*Stacy Speedlin Gonzalez, PhD; Chelsea Barron Davila Conaway, MS; and Aneesa Anderson, MS*

# Foreword

In the world abroad and near, there lies a common link that threads us all together. It is not the world of "I" or "Me." It is not country, race, sexual orientation or designation, or any other labels we use to separate us. What ties the world together is self-realization—having the power to identify, acknowledge, and respond to circumstances as one who can do something about the situation. We must be responsible for this vital power we each possess. Too often, we go through life ignoring this fact. The impact of neglecting it results in narratives that justify our neglect and spiral to lower depths of presence titled "Survival," "Defend and Protect," "Acquire and Hoard," "Manipulate," "Imitate," "Right and Wrong," "Bad and Good," "This will never happen to me again!"

I dare to call this narrative a "reaction." From this narrative, we have written our ethics and laws, constructed societies, and assigned worth and priority. We explain our impulses, actions, and justifications that provide us a sense of restitution. These reactions, however, will never allow us to address our claim to self-realization. Reactions may explain the who, what, how, or when, but they leave the why to a summarized conclusion. In service of 'why,' enters the counselor. A counselor's insight focuses on the hard questions and challenges needed for individuals to acquire the goal of self-realization.

Counselors courageously investigate these questions to create processes and approaches for individuals to discover the answers to questions for themselves. Individual discovery provides assurances (for all who pursue them) to know for themselves the "why" in self-discovery. Having the answer to "why" then becomes of service to "who I Am," "what I choose," "how I respond to circumstances," and "when I know that I can do something about it."

In service to the world, skilled counselors educate and structure programs in all areas and walks of life, including early education, school academics and curriculum, career development, social work, social relationships, etc. This influence shapes a counselor's perception for a continuous practice of assessing and addressing personal beliefs again and again, helping people discover why they believe what they believe. This continual analysis is in service of their words, thoughts, and ideas, providing a unique contribution for humanity.

Humanity is why the call to be a counselor compels the question, How do we (as counselors and educators) teach, communicate, demonstrate, recognize, and advocate for all people? The answers provided in the following pages are in service of your personal discovery and development. Through the lives, experiences, and perspectives gained from a wide range of professionals who have dedicated their lives to this pursuit and have answered the requests of so many colleagues and students to expand their contribution beyond lecture and mentorship to publication, you will reap the benefit in preparation for your future in helping professions.

Knowing the intent of the writers serves how to listen and what to expect from these pages. For the fulfillment of those who have contributed to this book, I invite you to courageously investigate your narratives of life and boldly pursue your inner truth. Allow the writings to be a guide through introspection to discovery. Prepare yourselves to answer the larger call to service that the world desires to reach now—"Universal Humanity." Educating, advocating, and inspiring our world to own our truth as we realize together the answer to the world's question: Since we are all able to do something about our circumstances and what we do impacts others, how will we express and acknowledge our Humanity?

Best wishes on your journey,
John Milton Borens
Counseling Advocate

# Preface

*Life can only be understood backward; but it must be lived forwards.*
— *Soren Kierkegaard*

For years, we have searched for the perfect textbook to quench the thirst of our ambitious students pursuing an interest and/or career that requires knowledge and study of human development across the life span. Finding the right balance of historical, scientific, and psychosocial information and the application of the related material to real-life situations in one affordable textbook has always been a struggle to overcome. Several years ago, it came to our attention that the remedy to this age-old issue was to create a textbook that meets the needs of our ever-changing universe of learners. With a sense of eagerness, a willing publishing company, and a team of inspiring writers, our ambitious project took root. We hope you find this compilation of written work useful and inspiring as you reach out to educate those who will come after us.

The complexity of our fluid universe forces us to broaden our understanding of human development at all stages of day-by-day life. The deadly COVID-19 pandemic, racial struggles, and economic deficiencies have left so many of our fellow humans barely hanging onto life as we navigate a new normal, while others have succumbed to these battles and melted from existence. Encouraging research and the study of human growth at a time such as today is a vital component of understanding the developing person, while providing wind beneath our wings as we move into the light of the new beginnings.

Our textbook includes the most recent material from an interdisciplinary perspective across the life span as we consider preconception and all of life's stages, including the end of life and beyond. We conceptualize the related aspects of biological, cognitive, emotional, and environmental segments that contribute to the making of a person. Discussions on the influence of heredity, genetics, attachment, nutrition, neuroscience, spectrum disorders, addictions, cultural and ethnical differences, spiritual, religious, and diversity considerations, the "ISM" factors (an attitude of prejudice against a given group), gender, sexual orientation, and the effects of immigration will be infused throughout chapters of the textbook as they relate to each stage of life and their effects on human development.

As Kierkegaard tells us, we live life looking forward. We must set our goals for the outcome we want to accomplish at each stage of the process. In order to reach our goals, it will be necessary to look back, evaluate our progress, and make adjustments as needed if we are to appreciate the journey and arrive safely at our desired destination.

## Acknowledgment

We wish to acknowledge our project editor, Amy Smith of Cognella Publishing, for her outstanding support of the coeditors and contributing authors. Thank you, Amy.

# About the Author–Editors

Dr. Noréal Armstrong earned her PhD in counselor education and supervision from the University of Texas at San Antonio's CACREP-accredited program. She is a licensed clinical mental health counselor supervisor (LCMHCS), nationally certified counselor (NCC), licensed chemical dependency counselor (LCDC), and a licensed professional counselor supervisor (LPC-S, TX). Dr. Armstrong has taught secondary and postsecondary students in addition to owning a private counseling practice. She also has a passion for working with the deaf population. Dr. Armstrong demonstrates her passion  through service work, presentations, and workshops on today's current issues.

Dr. Armstrong, tenured Associate Professor, is the former department chair of the clinical mental health counseling program at Montreat College in North Carolina. During her time at Montreat, she has been instrumental is attaining CACREP accreditation, restructuring the course delivery format, and creating new master's programs. Dr. Armstrong has served the counseling profession for 11 years and in that time has given more than 30 professional presentations at the local, state, and national levels. She has three peer-reviewed publications, two book chapters, and numerous newsletter publications. Dr. Armstrong is active in her community, providing mental health training and services to local churches. She is the Executive Director and CEO of A Therapist Like Me, a non-profit organization providing counseling and other mental health services to BIPOC and marginalized communities.

She is an active member of the American Counseling Association (ACA), Association for Multicultural Counseling and Development (AMCD), Association for Counselor Education and Supervision (ACES), Southern Association for Counselor Education and Supervision (SACES), and the North Carolina Counseling Association (NCCA). As a member of these organizations, she has served in leadership roles. Dr. Armstrong currently serves as the AMCD vice president of the Women's Concern Group and was AMCD secretary for the 2019–2020 year. In February 2020, she was awarded Administrator of the Year by the NCCA in recognition for her many accomplishments as department chair.

Dr. Armstrong has a strong research agenda in multiculturalism, deaf populations, substance abuse, adolescent development, and women in the professorate. She is passionate about advocacy, mentoring, and educating future counselors. She believes mentorship is key to her success and the success of those new to the profession. Dr. Armstrong uses her platform to share knowledge, tips, and networks for the next generation of counselors. She is very active in the community, serving as a Resource for Resilience board member and member of Delta Sigma Theta Sorority Inc.

A Texas native, Noréal is an avid sports fan who enjoys using her creativity to write, draw, bake, and create art. She loves reading and using her skills and knowledge of American Sign Language to help others. Noréal attributes much of her success to the support, guidance, and influence of her family, mentors and close friends.

Emma Borens is a native of Shreveport, Louisiana, and a graduate of Bethune Junior/Senior High School, where she was an honor scholar and first chair French hornist. She received her BA with honors from Talladega College in Alabama. She taught 7th and 9th grade World and U.S. History for a year and directed the Dixon Middle school choir before moving to Durham, North Carolina, where she worked as an eligibility specialist and later social worker for the Department of Social Services. These working experiences prompted her to recognize the need for counseling services to address the wider needs of the public and to interrupt the generational cycles of poverty and miseducation she observed. While working, she entered the Master of Education program with

Copyright © 2019 by California Counseling Association Cruise 2019. Reprinted with permission.

a major in Guidance and Counseling at North Carolina Central University and received her MA degree with honors. Emma is a retired school counselor, having served the students of the Oakland public schools in California for more than 30 years. She holds a lifetime pupil personnel services credential. During her tenure, she served on several district and school committees and developed many innovative programs and policies to enhance the development of the entire school community. She continues to volunteer in several programs to help young people develop.

For the past 15 years, she has been an adjunct professor in the Department of Counseling in the Master of Counseling Program and the Child and Adolescent Development Department at San Francisco State University, retiring in August 2020. Emma developed a passion for professional development and continues her membership in several counseling associations, including the American Counseling Association, the Association for Multicultural Counseling and Development (AMCD) and its California division (CAMC), the Association for Spiritual and Religious Values in Counseling and its California division (CARVIC). She is often a California representative for the ACA Western Region and currently serves as president of the California School Counselor Association and as governing board member of the California Counseling Association. Among her many public service activities, she holds membership in Delta Sigma Theta Sorority, Inc.

Emma was inducted into the H. B. McDaniel Hall of Fame for outstanding contributions to professional counseling in April 2015 at Stanford University. Along with her co-teacher, Sharon Bowles, Emma received the 2016 Professor of the Year award from the SFSU Counseling Student Association.

Emma is the author of the *Student Study Guide: How to Study and Take Tests*. She was also a contributing writer for the original *High School Success Guide* for the Oakland Unified School District in California and coeditor for a life span development book.

The proud mother of five adult children and nine grandchildren, Emma has enjoyed singing since childhood. Gifted with a wide vocal range, she is most often heard singing the top soprano parts in many Bay Area choirs and churches. Keeping spirituals—the songs of her ancestors—alive is one of her passions. She has sung in and directed several choirs over the years and has performed in concert at many churches around the Bay Area, across the United States, and internationally.

Sharon Bowles received a bachelor's degree from Mills College in Oakland, California, majoring in mathematics and history, and received a master's degree in secondary education with an emphasis in school counseling from the University of San Francisco. She also holds a lifetime secondary teaching credential and a lifetime pupil personnel service credential. A 34-year veteran math teacher and school counselor (retired), Sharon has been a leader in many capacities. She served as chair of the math department for Frick Junior High School before becoming a school counselor there. Transferring to high school, Sharon served as chair of the counseling

department for 22 of the 27 years she was a counselor in the Oakland Public Schools District. During that time, she served for 3 years on the Selection Committee for the National Merit Scholarship Corporation and 8 years on the Grant Advisory Committee (GAC) of the California Student Aid Commission, including distinction as GAC vice chair and parliamentarian.

Sharon served on several district and school committees, making valuable contributions to the establishment of programs and policies that benefited the students of the entire district. She was a contributor to the original publication of the *High School Success Guide*. After her retirement, she has continued to serve as a consultant for counselors. For the last 15 years, Sharon has served as co-teacher with Emma Borens as a professor in the Department of Counseling in the Master of Counseling program and in the Child and Adolescent Development Department at San Francisco State University, retiring from those positions in August 2020.

In 2008, Sharon was inducted into the H. B. McDaniel Hall of Fame at Stanford University for outstanding contributions to professional counseling. In 2016, she received the Professor of the Year award from the SFSU Counseling Student Association.

Over her years of membership in the American Counseling Association (ACA), Sharon has served in many leadership positions. She is past president of California School Counseling Association, the California Counseling Association and past chair and past treasurer of the ACA Western Region. Currently, she serves as the executive director of the California Counseling Association, Western Regional representative for the Association for Multicultural Counseling and Development, president of the California Association for Religious Values in Counseling, and Northern Region representative for the California School Counselor Association.

Among her many civic activities she counts her services on the Neighborhood Community Council, her volunteer activities as church trustee and choir director, and her membership in the Oakland chapter of Delta Sigma Theta Sorority, Inc., where she has served as parliamentarian and scholarship chair.

The coeditors and contributors offer our thanks to Sharon as a prime mover in making this life span development book a reality.

# About the Contributors

**Aneesa Anderson** is a counselor education and supervision doctoral student at the University of Texas, San Antonio. She received her MS in clinical mental health counseling from Lipscomb University in Nashville. Ms. Anderson has experience providing counseling services in integrative health care and nonprofit crisis services. Her research and advocacy interests reside under the multicultural umbrella with an emphasis on race-based trauma, LGBTQIA issues, and intersectionality of identities.

Ms. Anderson is a member of the counseling honor society, Chi Sigma Iota, and a part of the illustrious Alpha Kappa Alpha Sorority. Community advocacy drives her personal and professional goals. She hopes to obtain her counseling license and become an adjunct professor post-graduation.

**John Milton Borens** is a musician, consultant, and counselor advocate who attended Langston University of Oklahoma and Heald College Schools of Business & Technology in California with an emphasis in Electronics. John shares his innate skills with Landmark Worldwide, Amos Temple Christian Methodist Church and Redeemer Lutheran Church both of Oakland, California in addition to supporting personal growth among individuals throughout the Bay Area.

**Dr. Kaye W. Cole, PhD, LMHC, NCC, BC-TMH,** is co-owner/senior consultant of The Cole Group, LLC, a consultation practice that addresses mental health and programming gaps in services for the athlete population. In this role, she provides consulting services designed to address complex behavioral issues, clinical mental health interventions, educational evaluation and programming, academic/vocational concerns, and challenges associated with athletic transitioning. She also holds an adjunct lecturer appointment in the Department of Rehabilitation and Counselor Education at the University of Iowa, and in clinical mental health counseling at Montreat College in North Carolina. Additionally, Dr. Cole is a licensed mental health therapist and school counselor and provides individual counseling services ranging from conflict resolution to trauma-informed interventions.

Dr. Cole currently serves on the University of Iowa's College of Education Advisory Board for the Baker Teacher Leadership Center; the University of Iowa's Athletic Diversity, Equity, and Inclusion Accountability Board; conference chair for the Association for Multicultural Counseling and Development, a division of the American Counseling Association; national ambassador for Diversity, Equity, Inclusion, Access; co-chair and Advisory Board committee member for the Food Allergy Research and Education (FARE) organization; and as a "connector" to services for the Women of the NFL group. She has used her platform as an educator, philanthropist, and advocate to establish partnerships with community groups and organizations to tackle societal ills; served on leadership councils for three NFL teams (Green Bay Packers, Seattle Seahawks, Carolina Panthers); served as chair and co-chair of many service and fundraising projects; served as a spokesperson for various causes; and shares her knowledge on numerous panels.

Dr. Cole enjoys spending time with her family, traveling, cycling, and working out. She lives with her husband of 15 years, former 13-year NFL defensive tackle Colin Cole, their three beautiful children—Karys, Colin, Jr., and Cassius—and English bulldog Cleopatra. Her oldest son, Drez, lives in Los Angeles.

Chelsea Barron Davila Conaway is a queer, first-generation, Mexican American doctoral student in counselor education and supervision at the University of Texas, San Antonio. She earned a Bachelor of Science in Psychology and Bachelor of Arts in Philosophy from the University of Houston, Downtown, and her Master of Science in Clinical Mental Health Counseling from the University of Texas, San Antonio. Chelsea is currently a licensed professional counselor intern working with low-income children and families. Chelsea's scholarly interests include academic coloniality and decolonization, Latinas' educational attainment, and indigenous approaches to thinking, learning, and knowing. A native of the Rio Grande Valley, Chelsea came to Anzaldúa's work in a quest to understand her experiences of physical and psychological borders.

Jordan Elliott is a doctoral student at the University of Texas, San Antonio (UTSA), studying counselor education and supervision. She graduated in May 2018 with a Master's in Clinical Mental Health Counseling from UTSA. Her research interests include moral distress in the supervisory relationship, the correlation between substance abuse and trauma, social advocacy and counseling, and the effect of family violence on communities.

Dr. Kimberly N. Frazier received her PhD in counselor education from the University of New Orleans. She holds licensure in the state of Louisiana as a professional counselor (LPC), licensed marriage and family therapist (LMFT), and certification as a nationally certified counselor (NCC). She is an associate professor in the Department of Clinical Rehabilitation and Counseling at Louisiana State University Health Sciences Center–New Orleans (LSUHSC-NO). Her research areas of interest include counseling pediatric populations, cultured centered counseling interventions and training, and systemic oppression and trauma with families and children. Dr. Frazier has conducted training, workshops, and presentations on cultural competency in counseling, cultural competency in the workplace, culturally competent interventions when working with children and families, and mentoring African American female counselors in training. Many of her published works can be found in the *Journal of Multicultural Counseling and Development*, the *Journal of Counseling and Professional Psychology*, and other national journals and book chapters.

Dr. Frazier serves on the editorial board of the *Journal of Multicultural Counseling and Development*. She also served on the American Counseling Association Governing Council and as chair of the mentoring program for the Association of Multicultural Counseling and Development, where she is also a past president of the association. She is most proud of the work she does mentoring graduate students and writing about issues affecting Black families. Dr. Kimberly Frazier is the president elect of the American Counseling Association and will serve as the 71st ACA President from July 1, 2022, to June 30, 2023. She will be the sixth African American woman to serve in this position. Dr. Frazier has also been awarded the American Counseling Association's most prestigious distinction of ACA Fellow.

Brittany Hudson (she/her/hers) is a doctoral candidate in counselor education and supervision at the University of Texas, San Antonio. Brittany currently works at a Victims of Crime Act grant-funded counseling center providing trauma and grief counseling services to rural communities. She is the director of communications for LPC Associates of Texas and a student member of the American Counseling Association Human Rights Committee. Her scholarly interests include chronic pain, social justice advocacy, relational-cultural theory, and critical feminist research. Brittany has co-led various professional and social justice advocacy projects throughout her doctoral studies.

Tora Kincaid is an adjunct faculty member in the adult undergraduate studies psychology program at Montreat College in North Carolina, maintains a private practice, and works in community mental health. She is a licensed clinical mental health counselor (LCMHCA) and a licensed clinical addictions specialist (LCASA) in North Carolina. As a national certified counselor (NCC), Tora believes certification shows unity among counselors and advances professional identity. Her research interests include the African American experiences with discrimination within the cosplayer fandom and advancing clinical understanding of participants who engage in cosplayer and LARPing activities. She is currently pursuing her doctorate in Capella University's counselor education and supervision program.

Jacqueline Kroemer is a recent graduate of the Montreat College master's program in Clinical Mental Health Counseling in North Carolina. While studying, she was part of the Chi Sigma Iota–Mu Chi honors society. Her undergraduate degree in psychology is from Iowa State University. She has numerous years of experience working with children and adolescents at various developmental stages. During her 2 years working as a graduate assistant in the clinical mental health counseling program at Montreat College, she assisted in various administrative and research tasks and was given the amazing opportunity to be a part of this project. Her research interests involve the interactions between neurological, cognitive, and behavioral in psychopathologies such as depression, post-traumatic stress disorder, and related symptoms in personality and psychotic disorders. Her research interests also include various theories and concepts such as rational emotive behavior therapy, acceptance and commitment therapy, dialectical behavior therapy, and radical acceptance. Away from the office, she enjoys sketching, gardening, exercising, and spending time in nature.

Dr. Dianne Logan-Parr, PhD, LPC, currently practices as a licensed professional counselor, with certifications in telehealth mental health and anxiety for Wired Brain. She was destined to be a counselor, and while growing up her family and teachers identified her helping skills at an early age. Dianne majored in psychology as an undergrad and served as a practicum worker for an abuse and neglect hotline, foster care, and adoption agencies. As a deputy juvenile officer for family court, she worked with at-risk youth and children. A former educator, Dianne earned a master's degree in counseling and began school counseling for the Hazelwood School District in Missouri, where she practiced most of her career. As a school counselor, Dianne was a leader in the field as president of the Missouri School Counselor Association and served many years as a governing board member in numerous positions, including program conference chair, career chair, journal editor, and elementary vice president. Dianne's education continued during those years as she completed 30-plus hours in education leadership and administration and continued to earn her doctorate in Educational Leadership: Curriculum and Instruction from the University of Phoenix. Dianne has written curriculum for the Missouri Department of Secondary and Elementary Education and the Hazelwood School District and provided numerous professional workshops for school counselors, administrators, educators, and others both locally and internationally. Dianne's goal is to always do her best to make a difference in the lives she touches.

Jessica Pourhassanian is a biracial Iranian American woman from Southern California who transplanted to Oakland, California, in 2009. Jessica earned her master's degree from San Francisco State University in marriage, family, and child counseling, with an emphasis in clinical mental health counseling. Jessica focuses most of her work on supporting LGBTQ+ and diverse communities through an anti-oppressive, strength-based, relational-cultural framework. Jessica enjoys taking time for self-care by hiking in nature, nurturing her garden, and kayaking around the bay.

Zdravko Rozic was born in the former Yugoslavia and is a refugee of the Bosnian civil war. Having lived in various places throughout the world has informed his interest in multiculturally competent practice. Zdravko earned his bachelor's degree in psychology from the University of North Florida and earned his master's degree in marriage, family, and child counseling from San Francisco State University. His volunteer experience includes working at San Francisco-based TALK Line, whose focus is to reduce child abuse by addressing parents' emotional needs and stressors. While writing this chapter Zdravko became a parent and gained firsthand experience in the challenges of raising an infant.

Dr. Stacy Speedlin Gonzalez, PhD, is a licensed professional counselor (LPC), a licensed chemical dependency counselor (LCDC), and a nationally credentialed counselor (NCC). Dr. Speedlin Gonzalez is currently an assistant visiting professor at the University of Texas, San Antonio, where she teaches a crisis, grief, and trauma course and a course on the biopsychosocial aspects of addiction. Additionally, Dr. Speedlin Gonzalez has a small private practice in which she sees clients with substance use disorders as well as contracts her services to an intensive outpatient treatment center in San Antonio.

Dr. Speedlin Gonzalez has been published multiple times in peer-reviewed journals on the topics of addiction, mentorship, LGBTQ clients and their needs, and how social media affects relational connectivity. She also coauthored five chapters on addiction in a medical book that serves as an educational textbook for medical doctors. Dr. Speedlin Gonzalez is passionate about working with clients with substance use disorders and improving the quality of services they receive.

Dr. Christopher Townsend, PhD, LPC, is an assistant professor at the Texas Tech Health Sciences Center, serving in the Department of Clinical Counseling and Mental Health. He is a faculty member in the master of addiction program. Dr. Townsend serves as director of the developing counseling clinic within the department. He is a licensed professional counselor, specializing in addiction and trauma work with children and adults. Dr. Townsend is both a domestic and international trainer in various mental health topics. He most enjoys his work in Africa, helping those countries suffering from the ills of war and genocide.

# Introduction

Our book begins with the key aspects of human development. We start by asking, what is human development. This topic is introduced and explained throughout several chapters with examples of how to apply concepts in the counseling and teaching professions.

We explore a study of new ideas, strategies, and methods that have emerged from the powerful scientific exploration that serves to undergird cultural, ecological, and humanistic perspectives. We examine leading theories and approaches as they affect the understanding of human development.

I (Emma) received a wall plaque that stated, "Just as the caterpillar thought the world was over, it became a butterfly." The phrase suggests that every ending is a new beginning. Life energy is dynamic; it is always changing. Cells are dying constantly, while others are created. Life is created and ends in every stage of development. Too often, we talk about the process of development without discussing the ending of life, which is also a part of that development. We do not think about life ending until the end of the book when we start to consider the phase of old age. I believe this failure to acknowledge the fact that endings are continual and to accept them as a natural part of life is a major cause of mental health issues for many people. As the saying goes, "An ounce of prevention is worth a pound of cure." Therefore, we want you to consider the effect of loss at each stage and its effect on the lives of those remaining at their various ages.

As we consider the various stages of development, we encourage you to think about the endings that are a part of the progression of life. Considering the myriad of changes that must occur for babies to grow in utero, it is little wonder that many lives end before we even knew that life was present. Other lives end after months of anticipation of birth. Depending on the duration of the pregnancy, we call it a miscarriage or a stillbirth. It is a death that we know about, but often we do not respect the grieving process the family experiences after it happens. Our relationship with death is as varied as the many cultures and belief systems that exist. The great thing about humans is our ability to reflect, learn, and decide how we will proceed in order to create a better future outcome. Our hope is that the knowledge you gain and your application of this information to your relationship with loss will become a cushion for the often negative responses we have to the process of loss and grief. We submit that we can change our relationship with death, and in so doing, change how we explain it to future generations as they experience these natural endings, thereby building in protective thought systems during their earliest stages of development.

As you read the chapters, we suggest you keep a journal of your thoughts about the significant beginnings and endings of each phase of development. Ask yourself; *what changes happened during this time? What attitudes toward life would I like to keep or renew as I continue my life journey? How does knowing this information influence my actions going forward? How can I use this information to prepare myself and my clients for what lies ahead, or inspire them in ways to think about their relationships with beginnings and endings?*

Students and instructors are encouraged to use Chapter 14 as a resource for suggested supplementary materials provided to support and promote learning. We suggest the employment of interactive and Socratic methods of learning to promote excitement and challenge. Recent case studies researched or experienced by the coauthors of this book will be shared.

You are about to embark upon a voyage of life-span development like none other produced for those entering the mental health and educational profession. Roll up your sleeves, sharpen your curiosity, and jump into a wonderful world of reading and discovery. Ask yourself, *what's in this book for me?*

—Noréal F. Armstrong, PhD; Emma Borens, MA; and Sharon Bowles, MA

# The Human Development Process

Sharon Bowles, MA; Emma Borens, MA; Noréal F. Armstrong, PhD; and Jessica Pourhassanian, MS

*If you clearly want something to change, then your ACTIONS will be different.* —*Emma Borens, 2019*

As we traverse the course of life, we notice the physical, cognitive, biological, and psychosocial influences on human development throughout all stages of life. Nothing is more constant than change itself as we transition from one state of development to another, regardless of how small a change actually occurs.

Plato tells us that the unexamined life is a life not worth living. Think for a moment about changes you have experienced both recently and in an earlier time of your life. What circumstances were present during that time of change? Were there contextual influences present in the physical, cognitive, emotional, and psychosocial sphere? What developmental elements sparked the change? We are all unique human beings with unique life circumstances that affect our everyday existence and personal growth. We are the result of many forces acting upon us—environmental, hereditary, cultural, and sociological influences. The counseling and teaching professions are closely related as we impart knowledge to individuals in an effort to effect sustainable change in their lives. It is imperative that practitioners in fields requiring knowledge of human development build an arsenal of information and resources to meet the needs of humanity across the life span.

## How and Why Do We Study Human Development?

According to Stauffer and Capuzzi in their book, *Human Growth and Development Across the Lifespan,* human development is defined as "the physical, cognitive, emotional, and social changes that occur in a person's life." The interconnectedness of humans and other species obviously reflects universality in certain facets of development. This complex idea is often noticed through the genetic composition. There is little wonder that some species are taught to pronounce audible words that mimic the human species, like parrots and the dog that plays the piano and howls with a closeness to the pitch of the musical note being played.

Counselors and educators must also be aware of the cultural, ethnic, social, and racial identities that vary among humans and that often have a tremendous influence on their development. For example, in some cultures it is considered inappropriate for children to look an adult in the eyes while the elder is speaking to them. Meanwhile, other cultures consider that same action of not looking someone in the eyes disrespectful to elders or an indication of deceit. Imagine the number of ways this misunderstanding could affect human relationships in negative ways, causing dire consequences for the misunderstood person. Little wonder that confusion may exist between and among the interactions of humanity. Although we are unique and different in cultural ways within a group, we are alike in many other cultural ways, especially between groups (Chial, 2008).

Additionally, clinicians must have a deep understanding of the individual and the footprint of life each person is developing. We must continue to place the client in the forefront of our actions to achieve positive outcomes. It has been noted that clinicians should strive diligently to "work ourselves out of a job" to promote the success of clients (E. Borens, personal communication, November 12, 2018).

## Key Concepts and Research Methods

### THE SCIENTIFIC METHOD

When we understand that the study of human development is a science, it becomes clear that people are viewed by the parameters of their development, which can be *multidirectional, multicontextual, multicultural, multidisciplinary, or plastic.* Scientists use theories and various approaches to information—from researching to analyzing data and asking questions to seeking answers—that will lead them to sound conclusions.

Throughout the book, various theories will be discussed and their applications considered.

The routine steps used in the scientific method are the following:

1. Based on curiosity about the reason for a particular occurrence, form a question.
2. Develop a theory or a hypothesis.
3. Create research methods to obtain data for empirical evidence.
4. Consider the evidence and evaluate the validity of the hypothesis.
5. State the conclusions.
6. Replicate the study, and try it out on many different groups to determine its conclusiveness.

Replication is extremely important for scientific progress as it may reveal the effectiveness or limitation of a hypothesis, particularly if it is used with different groups of people.

Some challenges and limitations exist in our application of scientific methods. Robert Gates made comments discussing some possible limiting components in scientific methods:

## OBSERVATION

Scientific **observation** is a method of testing hypotheses by unobtrusively watching and recording behavior, either in a laboratory or in a naturalistic setting.

Scientific observation can expose **correlations** (a relationship between two things such that one is more likely or unlikely to occur when the other occurs). Correlations are not cause-and-effect relationships, but can be used to predict behavior. Correlations always have the possibility that the correlation's direction is the opposite of that proposed, or that a third variable may be the cause of the changes.

## THE EXPERIMENT

The **experimental** method involves the deliberate change in one variable (the independent variable) to monitor the resulting change in some other variable (the dependent variable). This is done using an experimental group. At the same time, a fake (placebo) change is made to a control (comparison) group to ensure that results are not due to the participants' expectations. Experiments are designed to expose cause-and-effect relationships.

## OTHER RESEARCH METHODS

- The Survey—vulnerable to bias.
- The Case Study—intensive study of one individual.

## Key Concepts

- **Cross-Sectional:** A research method comparing groups of people who differ in a specific characteristic (e.g., age) but share other important characteristics.
- **Longitudinal:** A research method studying the same individuals over a long period.
- **Cross-Sequential:** A hybrid research method combining cross-sectional and longitudinal. This can be categorized as "the best way."

The purpose of a **quantitative** approach is to describe the current environment, investigate relationships, and to study cause and effect. Quantitative research involves analysis of numerical data.

The purpose of a **qualitative** approach is to provide a focused, interpreted, and detailed study of the participants and their environment. Qualitative research involves analysis of data such as words (interviews), pictures (video), or objects (artifacts). It is important to focus on how these techniques can be integrated.

## NATURE VERSUS NURTURE

The controversy of nature versus nurture has puzzled many scientists for years and probably will continue to do so. **Nature** in development refers to the traits, capacities, and limitations that each individual inherits genetically from his or her parents at conception (Berger, 2018). **Nurture** in development includes all the environmental influences that affect the individual after conception (Berger, 2018).

Many factors such as heredity and environment, sex, and gender contribute to the nature versus nurture discussion. Some people believe that traits are inborn and genetically produced. Others consider some traits the result of nurture as the environment and other manifestations act upon it. Regardless of your beliefs, nature and nurture have interchangeable effects that vary for individuals. Those concerned with human development and considering interventions must always be very careful to address the needs of clients when the nature or nurture question may be a factor in their presenting issues. Indeed, because these two elements are so closely connected, nature and nurture should always be considered together. Therefore, the question is not one versus the other, but more often, how are they connecting to create the observed phenomenon?

## GENETICS

Have you ever stopped to consider the differences and similarities we have as humans? Basic genetic principles explain why our behaviors and appearances are often strikingly different in some ways and yet similar in other ways. It is remarkable how nature and nurture work together to comprise this phenomenon called human development.

The observable characteristics of our human makeup are called **phenotypes**. The blend of genetic material that determines our species and influences our own unique characteristics and traits are commonly known as **genotypes,** which refers to all of the genes a person has inherited. A phenotype is how these genes are actually expressed, and can include physical traits, such as height and color of eyes, and nonphysical traits, such as shyness and extroversion (Cherry, 2020).

The study of genetics is an important study, as genes are inherited from generation to generation in our human development process.

The genes contained in these chromosomes are made up of a chemical structure known as DNA (**deoxyribonucleic acid**) that contains the genetic code, or instructions, that make up all life. Except for the sperm and ova, all cells in the body contain 46 chromosomes (Cherry, 2020). According to the National Human Genome Research Institute, genetic code is the term we use for the way the four bases of DNA—the A, C, G, and T—are strung together so that the cellular machinery, the ribosome, can read them and turn them into a protein. In the genetic code, each three nucleotides in a row count as a triplet and code for a single amino acid (Brody, n.d.).

The formation of sex cells is a central part of human reproduction: In fertilization, an egg cell and a sperm cell combine. Each egg cell and sperm cell has 23 **chromosomes,** which are threadlike structures housed in the nucleus that contain genetic material (Kail & Cavanaugh, 2016). The first 22 pairs of chromosomes are called **autosomes,** and the 23rd pair is known as the **sex chromosomes** because they determine the sex of the child (Kail & Cavanaugh; Berk, 2014; InformedHealth, 2019). A child born with an X and Y chromosome is a boy, and one born with two X chromosomes is a girl. Sex cells are also called **reproductive cells or gametes.** Sperm cells are produced in men's testicles and egg cells are produced in women's ovaries. Sex cells differ from other cells in one special way: They only have one half of the total amount of human genetic information. When a sperm cell fertilizes an egg cell, the resulting cell has a full set of genetic information again (InformedHealth, 2019). Sex cells are formed through a particular kind of cell division called meiosis. Unlike normal cell division (mitosis), the genetic material of the original (parent) cell is divided twice. Development of a child starts when the male reproductive cell, or sperm, penetrates the protective outer membrane of the female reproductive cell, or ovum. The chromosomes contained in each act as a blueprint for human life (Cherry, 2020).

Whether or not a gene is expressed depends on two factors: the interaction of the gene with other genes and the continual interaction between the genotype and the environment.

**Genetic Interactions.** Genes can sometimes contain conflicting information, and in most cases, one gene will win the battle for dominance. Some genes act in an additive way. For example, if a child has one tall parent and one short parent, the child may end up splitting the difference by being of average height. In other cases, some genes follow a dominant-recessive pattern. Eye color is one example of dominant-recessive genes at work. The gene for brown eyes is dominant, and the gene for blue eyes is recessive. If one parent hands down a dominant brown-eye gene while the other parent hands down a recessive blue-eye gene, the dominant gene will win out and give the child brown eyes.

**Gene-Environment Interactions.** The environment a child is exposed to, both in utero and throughout the remainder of his or her life, can influence gene expression. For example, exposure to harmful drugs while in utero can have a dramatic effect on later child development. Height is a good example of a genetic trait that can be influenced by environmental factors. While a child's genetic code may provide instructions for tallness, the expression of this height might be suppressed if the child has poor nutrition or chronic illness (Cherry, 2020).

## ABNORMALITIES

The vast majority of newborns, both boys and girls, have at least one X chromosome. In about one in every 500 births, children are born with either a missing X chromosome or an additional sex chromosome. Klinefelter syndrome, Fragile X syndrome, and Turner syndrome are all examples of abnormalities involving the sex chromosomes. The most common type of chromosomal disorder is known as trisomy 21, or Down syndrome. In this case, the child has three chromosomes at the site of the 21st chromosomes, instead of the normal two (Cherry, 2020).

## INHERITANCE

The basic laws of inheritance are important in understanding patterns of disease transmission. The inheritance patterns of single gene diseases are often referred to as Mendelian because Gregor Mendel first observed the different patterns of gene segregation for selected traits in garden peas. He was able to determine probabilities of recurrence of a trait for subsequent generations. If a disease affects a family, an accurate family history will be important to establish a pattern of transmission. In addition, a family history can even help to exclude genetic diseases, particularly for common diseases in which behavior and environment play strong roles (Genetic Alliance, 2010; Chial, 2008).

Genetic heterogeneity is a common phenomenon with both single-gene diseases and complex multifactorial diseases. It should not be surprising that multiple affected family members may experience different levels of disease severity and outcomes. This effect may be due to other genes influencing the disease phenotype or different mutations in the same gene resulting in similar, but not identical, phenotypes.

There are five basic modes of inheritance for single-gene diseases: **autosomal dominant, autosomal recessive, X-linked dominant, X-linked recessive, and mitochondrial.**

## PATTERNS OF INHERITANCE

- **Autosomal Dominant**
  - Each affected person has an affected parent
  - Occurs in every generation
- **Autosomal Recessive**
  - Both parents of an affected person are carriers
  - Not typically seen in every generation
- **X-linked Dominant**
  - Females more frequently affected
  - Can have affected males and females in same generation
- **X-linked Recessive**
  - Males more frequently affected
  - Affected males often present in each generation
- **Mitochondrial**
  - Can affect both males and females, but only passed on by females
  - Can appear in every generation

TABLE 1.1    Five Basic Patterns of Inheritance

| INHERITANCE PATTERN | DISEASE EXAMPLES |
| --- | --- |
| Autosomal Dominant | Huntington's disease, neurofibromatosis, achondroplasia, familial hypercholesterolemia |
| Autosomal Recessive | Tay-Sachs disease, sickle cell anemia, cystic fibrosis, phenylketonuria (PKU) |
| X-linked Dominant | Hypophosphatemic rickets (vitamin D-resistant rickets), ornithine transcarbamylase deficiency |
| X-linked Recessive | Hemophilia A, Duchenne muscular dystrophy |
| Mitochondrial | Leber's hereditary optic neuropathy, Kearns–Sayre syndrome |

## TERATOLOGY

**Teratology** is the scientific study of birth abnormalities, especially on causes of biological disabilities and impairments. These structural abnormalities are present at birth, although they may not be diagnosed until later in life. They may be visible on the body or internal. Congenital malformations account for approximately 20% of deaths in the perinatal period. A **teratogenic agent** is a chemical, infectious agent, physical condition, or deficiency that can alter fetal development or subsequent function. A **teratogen** is any agent that can induce or increase the incident of a congenital malformation. Recognizing the existence of teratogens offers the opportunity to prevent exposure at critical periods of development and prevent certain types of congenital malformations. There are a variety of causes of congenital malformations including 1) genetic factors (chromosomal abnormalities as well as single gene defects); 2) environmental factors (drugs, toxins, infectious etiologies, mechanical forces); and 3) multifactorial etiologies, which include a combination of environmental and genetic factors. The greater the number of minor malformations, the greater is the likelihood of an associated major malformation. The more severe and the greater the number of major malformations, the greater the likelihood of a spontaneous miscarriage or shortened life span.

In general, drugs, food additives, and pesticides present the majority of possible exposures that should be avoided during pregnancy. Therefore, women of childbearing age must be careful at all times to limit their exposure to teratogens, either ingested or environmental, to prevent the effect upon a possible pregnancy because they may find themselves pregnant after it is too late to begin preventive measures (Chung, 2015).

In addition to regular preventive measures, regular good health measures should be instituted before pregnancy—good nutritional intake, adequate exercise and sleep, etc.

## EPIGENETICS

**Epigenetics** explores the many ways environment (nurture) acts upon genetic expression (nature) beginning with **methylation** at conception and continuing for the entire life span. For example, biological and hereditary forces (nature affecting nurture) along with social and environmental forces (nurture affecting nature) are some of the influences that direct genes in brain development. This thought leads us to make note of **differential susceptibility or sensitivity.** Berger defines differential susceptibility or sensitivity as the idea that people vary in how sensitive they are to particular experiences (Berger, 2018). Some people are tough and forthright, while others are mild and meek. Inherited genes and/or the life experiences affecting the individual's sensitivity to certain provoking criteria often shape these responses to different circumstances. An example may be shown in the fact that different individuals in the same family will respond very differently to an event or situation. For some, the conditions must be just right for them to grow. For others, they will thrive no matter the circumstances. Berger describes this as the "orchid or dandelion" principle. Orchids require a perfect soil and temperature mixture to thrive, whereas dandelions will thrive even through cracks in the concrete.

## Designing the Science of Human Development: Multidirectional, Multicontextual, Multicultural, Multidisciplinary, and Plasticity

### MULTIDIRECTIONAL

Another area that requires attention in the study of human development is **continuity** and **discontinuity. Continuity** refers to successive life-span development stages, and **discontinuity** refers to significant shifts in development (Capuzzi & Stauffer, 2016).

Continuity in the development stages may lead to a progression of steps that are seen as formative and predictable with learning and developmental theorists; however, shifts may occur in this progression and a person may get "stuck or regress" in a stage, whereby discontinuity may develop instability. Change can occur rapidly or over a long period or not at all. Consider a change during your lifetime or the lifetime of someone close to you when continuity and discontinuity were both evident, such as during puberty. We will discuss Erickson's psychosocial stages of development in more detail in later chapters.

Some physical interruptions during gestation may be traumatic and damaging to human development. For example, nature may be profoundly disrupted and cause permanent deformities to the embryo by drugs taken during pregnancy (nurture from the mother's bloodstream) such as thalidomide (a drug prescribed to prevent excessive morning sickness) during a **critical period** (a limited time during development when a specific formation must occur) (Berger, 2018). Other events may cause a delay in development when they occur during a **sensitive period** (a specific period when development is optimal but does not prevent future development). I (Sharon) distinctly remember learning to walk as a child long after I learned to talk. Perhaps that was tied to my cultural influences of being the first child in the family in 14 years. Everyone was eager to transport me from one place to another. I was never allowed to crawl. Some attribute my difficulty in learning left from right to this lack of early patterning that would have developed during the crawling period. I tend to think I enjoyed being carried from one place to the next, which indeed required little effort on my part. On the other hand, unlike the need to walk, talking felt natural as all the adults talked to me, read to me, listened to me, and encouraged my speech formation.

## MULTICONTEXTUAL

> *Human development is fundamentally contextual.*
> —*Pluess, 2015; Berger, 2018*

Many effects on development are physical and possibly related to parental and family relations, community, access to money (or not), ethnicity, cultural aspects, traditions, and so on. Each of the contacts we encounter daily could influence our thinking and actions in later life. Sometimes the contextual exposure we receive occurs sooner rather than later.

**Ecological Systems:** Urie Bronfenbrenner (1917–2005) refined the necessity of considering contexts in the study of human development. He created an ecological systems approach.

**FIGURE 1.1**    Urie Bronfenbrenner's Ecological System

Bronfenbrenner believed every individual was affected by overlapping systems, providing the context of development. Those systems include **microsystems**, which include social contexts (i.e., family, peers); **mesosystems**, or the interaction and connection among the other systems; **exosystems** (i.e., local affiliations, educational and religious); **macrosystems** (i.e., social, cultural, economic, and political standing); and **chronosystems**, or the historical context. Just before the end of his life, he renamed his system the **bioecological theory** to include the internal sexual reproductive and cardiovascular systems.

Bronfenbrenner's approach includes the context of **socioeconomic status**, commonly known as **SES** and the context of **cohort**. The SES concept, also referred to as social class, is used to describe the economic, occupational, and educational status of individuals. It determines the position a person holds in society. This can be limiting in some cases or advantaging in others.

The term cohort is part of the historical context of this approach. This includes people who may be close in age, travel through life circumstances together, and experience similar cultural changes together. An example might be the shared reactions of people in a certain age range to experiences encountered in a particular world war or a global pandemic.

## MULTICULTURAL

Culture is defined as a system of shared beliefs, norms, behaviors, and expectations that persist over time and prescribe social behavior and assumptions (Berger, 2018). Clinicians must be open and respectful of cultural differences in individuals and groups of people lest we create and allow assumptions and stereotypes to guide our actions. Difference does not mean deficit. We are all multicultural and hold beliefs and traditions that often differ within our embraced cultures and ethnicities. Remember that the definitions of the following terms act upon human development in varying ways: **ethnic groups**—people whose ancestors are from a common region and who generally share a common language, culture, and religion; **ethnicity**—a social construction that is a product of social context; and **race**—a social construction, usually based on similar external physical characteristics. It does not indicate biological, cultural, or ethnic foundation. In fact, scientists report more differences within constructed racial groups than between them.

These socially constructed racial divisions persist because they were constructed for political (power hierarchies) social interactions. The rules of interactions were developed by the group in power for their economic and social benefit. Those without the power suffered the deficits caused by their subjugated positions, creating permanent hindrances that began to affect their growth and development due to the environmental disparities. Now it has become important to identify the different racial groups to provide for political, social, economic, and educational funding in an effort to restore equity for those disadvantages ingrained in the society by the original divisions that have existed for hundreds of years.

## MULTIDISCIPLINARY

As we study human development and consider genetic analysis, it is apparent that we should seek to understand the *whole person*. Research done with a multidisciplinary perspective shows that many influences from multiple traits make a person who they are, uniquely individual. The three domains of human development generally do not function exclusively; rather, they are interrelated.

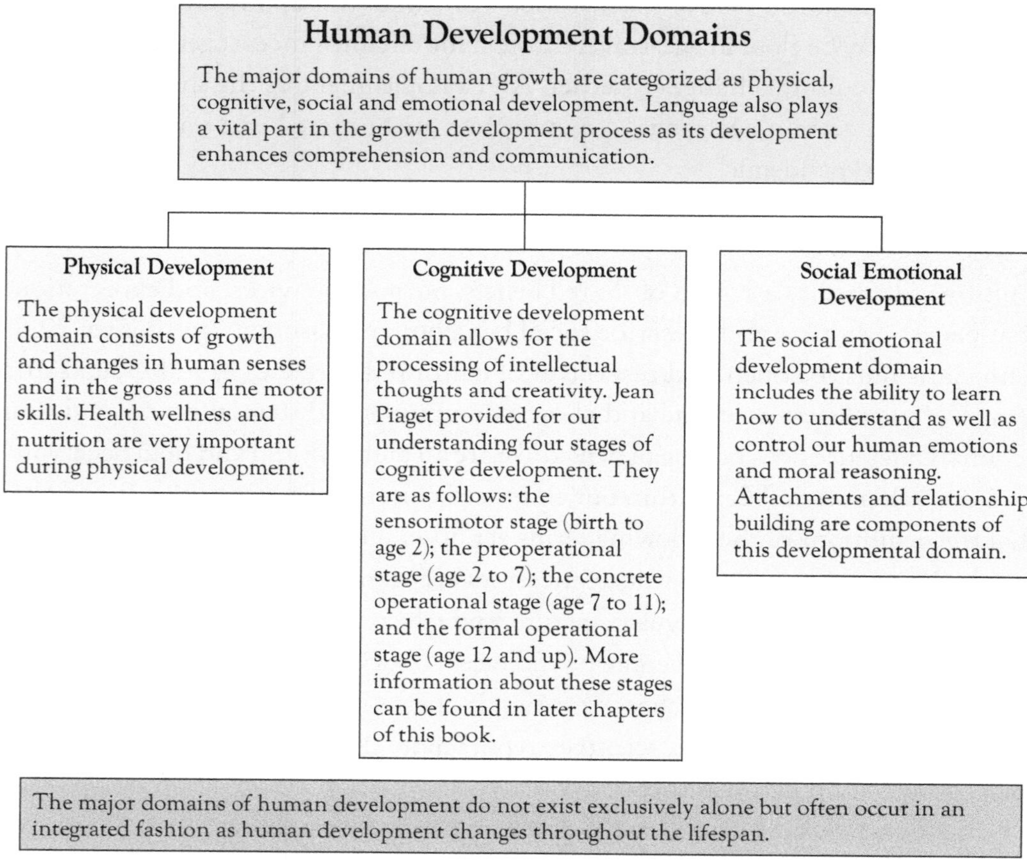

### Human Development Domains

The major domains of human growth are categorized as physical, cognitive, social and emotional development. Language also plays a vital part in the growth development process as its development enhances comprehension and communication.

### Physical Development

The physical development domain consists of growth and changes in human senses and in the gross and fine motor skills. Health wellness and nutrition are very important during physical development.

### Cognitive Development

The cognitive development domain allows for the processing of intellectual thoughts and creativity. Jean Piaget provided for our understanding four stages of cognitive development. They are as follows: the sensorimotor stage (birth to age 2); the preoperational stage (age 2 to 7); the concrete operational stage (age 7 to 11); and the formal operational stage (age 12 and up). More information about these stages can be found in later chapters of this book.

### Social Emotional Development

The social emotional development domain includes the ability to learn how to understand as well as control our human emotions and moral reasoning. Attachments and relationship building are components of this developmental domain.

The major domains of human development do not exist exclusively alone but often occur in an integrated fashion as human development changes throughout the lifespan.

FIGURE 1.2    Domains of Human Development

## PLASTICITY

The early years of a child's life are very important for later health and development. One of the main reasons is how fast the brain grows starting before birth and continuing into early childhood. Although the brain continues to develop and change into adulthood, the first 8 years can build a foundation for future learning, health, and life success.

Plasticity is the idea that abilities, personality, and other human characteristics can change over time (Berger, 2018). Plasticity in human development provides room for change, which in turn promotes hope out of despair. Plasticity is the basis upon which we make the claim that change is the only constant; we are always in the process of change. An important approach that uses the plasticity concept is the **dynamic-systems approach**. This approach views human development as a cycle of continuous changing actions among the physical (biosocial), cognitive, and psychological influences.

## ETHICS

As counselors and educators in training, and as practicing clinicians and instructors, it is extremely important to follow the code of ethics established by our national organizations, such as the American Counseling Association (ACA). The 2014 ACA Code of Ethics is available on the ACA website at counseling.org. Familiarize yourself with the appropriate code of ethics for your discipline. Our overarching goal is to **Do No Harm**. You will face hundreds of questions as you prepare for your career in the helping profession. Remember, the profession is one that honors confidentiality, holds integrity and honesty as ideals, and respects our clientele. Many of us have strong opinions, but we also must know when to hold and when to fold. A counselor and educator's middle name is and always will be *FLEXIBLE*.

## Points to Remember

1.  Human development is studied as a science to explore how people change—or don't—over time. The scientific method consists of the continuous process of asking questions, developing hypotheses, and gathering and evaluating data to make conclusions. These experiments must be replicated to establish the validity of the conclusions.

2.  Scientific **observation** is a method of testing hypotheses by unobtrusively watching and recording behavior either in a laboratory or in a naturalistic setting.

3.  **Nature** in development refers to the traits, capacities, and limitations that each individual inherits genetically from his or her parents at conception (Berger, 2018).

**Nurture** in development includes all of the environmental influences that affect the individual after conception (Berger, 2018).

4. The **experimental** method involves the deliberate change in one variable (the independent variable) to monitor the resulting change in some other variable (the dependent variable).

5. **Continuity** refers to successive life-span development, and **discontinuity** refers to significant shifts in development (Capuzzi & Stauffer, 2016).

6. **Epigenetics** explores the many ways environment acts upon genetic expression beginning with **methylation** at conception and continuing for the entire life span as internal and external environmental changes affect gene and chromosomal expression in biological development.

7. **Ecological systems** was an approach created by Urie Bronfenbrenner (1917–2005). He refined the necessity of considering contexts in the study of human development and formed the bioecological theory of development.

8. The three domains of human development—physical (biosocial), cognitive, and psychological influences—generally do not function exclusively; rather they are interrelated.

9. As counselors, educators, nurses, psychologists, social workers, etc. in training, and as practicing clinicians and instructors, it is extremely important to follow the code of ethics established by our national organizations, such as the American Counseling Association (ACA).

10. Our overarching goal is to "**Do No Harm.**" Every situation needs to be viewed from a multicultural lens as we seek to help individuals reach their growth goals. *FLEXIBLE* must become the middle name of those working in fields based on knowledge of human development.

## Reflections and Targeted Discussion Questions

1. How does the scientific method help progress the study of human development?

2. What are some of the strengths of using qualitative research? What are some of the weaknesses?

3. Explain how the nature versus nurture question may be relevant in an individual's life-span development.

4. How does knowledge of teratogens help people accept the will of nature for spontaneous abortions resulting in miscarriage, or external or internal defects that may present over the life span?

5. Reflect on a change in your lifetime when continuity was evident. Reflect on a change in your life when discontinuity was evident. Compare and contrast these moments in your life and their effect on you.

> *A Brand New Day: "Be hopeful but remain vigilant. Nothing says freedom like being alive."*   —Johnathan Capehart

## References

Berger, K. S. (2018). *The developing person: Through childhood and adolescence* (11th ed.). Worth Publishers.

Berk, L. E. (2014). *Development through the lifespan* (6th ed.). Pearson Education.

Brody, L. C. (n.d.). *Genome.* National Human Genome Research Institute. https://www.genome.gov/genetics-glossary/Genetic-Code

Capehart, J. (Host). (2021, May 16). The Bye Line [Television Program]. In Natalie Johnson (Segment Producer). *The Sunday Show.* New York, NY: MSNBC.

Capuzzi, D., & Stauffer, M. (2016). *Human growth and development across the lifespan: Applications for counselor* (1st ed.). Wiley Publishing.

Cherry, K. (2020). How genes influence child development. *In Very well mind.* https://www.verywellmind.com/genes-and-development-2795114

Chial, H. (2008) Rare genetic disorders: Learning about genetic disease through gene mapping, SNPs, and microarray data. *Nature Education, 1*(1), 192.

Chung, W. (2015, September 11). Hunting down genes that cause human disease. https://www.peoplebehindthescience.com/dr-wendy-chung/

Genetic Alliance. (2010, February 17). District of Columbia Department of Health. Understanding genetics: A District of Columbia guide for patients and health professionals (Appendix B, Classic Mendelian Genetics, Patterns of Inheritance). https://www.ncbi.nlm.nih.gov/books/NBK132145/

InformedHealth.org. (2019, April 11). Germany: Institute for Quality and Efficiency in Health Care (IQWiG); 2006–. How are sex cells made (meiosis)? https://www.ncbi.nlm.nih.gov/books/NBK541152/

Kail, R. V., & Cavanaugh, J. C. (2016). *Human development: A lifespan view* (7th ed.). Cengage Learning.

Pluess, M. (2015). Individual differences in environmental sensitivity. *Child Development Perspectives,* 1–6. DOI: 10.1111/cdep.12120

## Credit

# Child Developmental Theories

Dianne Parr, PhD; Noréal F. Armstrong, PhD; and Emma Borens, MA

*At the beginning of all growth, everything imitates. All of us, when we were children, also only imitated. But children grow up and begin their own development.* —Pramoedya Ananta Toer

## Learning Objectives

After reading this chapter, you should be able to

1. Understand the basic beliefs behind the five major theoretical perspectives on human development.
2. Define key concepts related to development across the life span.
3. Analyze and discuss cultural, social, and environmental influences of each theoretical perspective, along with limitations.

# Introduction

"Development is seen as the emergent product of many decentralized and local interactions that occur in real time" (Smith & Thelen, 2003, p. 343). So development does not know where it is going from birth and depends on the individual's systems to process the demands, expectations, or needs of the environment of the individual during various times of life. Moreover, child development theories attempt to explain how individuals grow and change during childhood, including social, emotional, and cognitive growth to adulthood. Theories of child development provide a structure for thinking and researching human growth and learning. Children were considered smaller versions of adults until the early 20th century when psychologists began to study and research child development (Thomas, 2000). Further, child development theorists base their viewpoints on various developmental processes, which influence the research and investigation process to create the theory. The theorists' perspectives may question what factors affected the individual's development.

# Key Concepts

- **Libido:** The psychosexual energy functioning as the driver for the behavior.
- **Assimilation:** Acquiring new knowledge and integrating it into existing cognitive constructs.
- **Accommodation:** Changing the cognitive structure to include the new knowledge.
- **Stages of Child Development:** Explained human growth and development using various theories describing this process.
- **Psychosexual Development Theory:** Addressed children's means of fulfilling sexual drives from one stage of childhood to another.
- **Reality Principle:** Protecting the individual by opting for more appropriate methods of meeting needs.
- **Person-Context-Process-Time Model:** Defined as the biological organism's development within the framework of environmental systems that support or stifle its growth.
- **Sociocultural Theory:** Posits that children learn through collaborating and interacting with those in their environment.

The process of human development is complicated, complex, and contextual depending on the perspective of the theorists. Moreover, the theorists provide a framework for studying and understanding the process of how humans develop. Each theorist's perspective is supported by basic beliefs of the processes involved in human development. Psychoanalysis theories are based on children's changes in various domains of development and are addressed in stages of unconscious urges or social context. The learning theorists focused on how human behavior development is influenced by environment, experience, and learning. Behaviorists focused on learning, psychoanalysts emphasized the unconscious, and cognitive theorists emphasized conscious thought, including processing, storing, retrieving, and using information. The evolutionary and sociological theorists studied human development from the perspective that human development is inherited with the species. The contextual theorists hypothesized human development occurs within a context or setting of the individual's life (Broderick & Blewitt, 2020). These theories will be revisited throughout the book.

TABLE 2.1    Five Theoretical Perspectives on Human Development

| PERSPECTIVE | IMPORTANT THEORIES | BASIC BELIEFS |
|---|---|---|
| Psychoanalysis | **Freud**'s psychosexual theory<br>**Erikson**'s psychosocial theory | Behavior controlled by powerful unconscious urges.<br>Personality influenced by society and developed via crisis or critical alternatives. |
| Learning | Behaviorism or traditional learning theory (Pavlov, Skinner, Watson)<br>Social learning or social cognitive theory (**Bandura**) | Individuals are responders; environment controls behavior.<br>People learn in social contexts, by observing or imitating. Person is an active contributor to learning. |
| Cognitive | **Piaget**'s cognitive stage theory<br>Information processing theory | Qualitative changes in cognitive processes occur between infancy and adolescence.<br>Individual are processors of symbols. |

(Continued)

TABLE 2.1  (Continued)

| PERSPECTIVE | IMPORTANT THEORIES | BASIC BELIEFS |
|---|---|---|
| Evolutionary/ Sociological | **Bowlby**'s and Ainsworth's attachment theory | Individuals have adaptive systems to survive. Crises in life are stressed. Biological and evolutionary bases for behavior and predisposition toward learning are significant. |
| Contextual | **Bronfenbrenner**'s bioeco- logical theory Vygotsky's sociocultural theory | Development occurs via interaction between a developing person and five adjacent, connecting contex- tual systems of influences, from microsystem to chronosystem. Sociocultural context is key to development. |

*(Papalia, et al., 2007).*

## Theoretical Perspectives

Early study of human growth and development was explained with theories describing this process as **stages of child development. Stage** theorists posit that child development proceeds through a sequence of general phases, with universal or common charac-teristics, skills, or expectations for each stage (Thomas, 2000). At each new phase, new, different, and more complex behaviors emerge and plateaus until the individual masters the changes and is raised to a new level of change goals.

Locke and Rousseau's simplistic philosophies of the 18th century relegated devel-opment to Locke's individual, who was born as a blank slate on which society writes, contrasted with Rousseau's individual who was born as "noble savage" to develop per his or her own natural inclinations unless corrupted by an exploitive society. Locke's perspective was the precursor of the **mechanistic model**, whereby development occurs in individuals as a reaction to environmental input. These mechanistic theorists focus on quantitative change because they believe development is continuous. Rousseau's theory was the forerunner of the **organismic model**, whereby change is internal and development occurs as the individual sets his or her own development in process. Organismic theorists focus on qualitative change because they regard development as a sequence of separate stages.

## FREUD'S PSYCHOSEXUAL DEVELOPMENTAL THEORY

In Vienna, Austria, at the end of the 19th and beginning of the 20th century, Sigmund Freud created a child development theory, retrospectively utilizing the childhood memories of adults he was treating for neurosis in his psychiatric practice. Freud's **psychosexual development theory** addressed children's means of fulfilling sexual drives from one stage of childhood to another (Murray, 1938).

Freud's five psychosexual stages were the **oral, anal, phallic, latent,** and **genital**. Each stage was associated with an erogenous zone that was a source of pleasure for the child and the amount of energy the id must produce to satisfy the part of the body. The individual's satisfying of these needs is critical to personality traits throughout life. The **libido**, or the psychosexual energy, was the driver for the behavior. Freud posited that psychosexual development in childhood occurs during these five psychosexual stages. The oral stage is the infant's first year of life, and the mouth is the source of satisfaction through eating, drinking, sucking, and babbling, which may correspond with how the individual seeks pleasure in the future (Broderick & Blewitt, 2020). During the anal stage, which is ages 1 to 3 years, the individual is learning toilet control of the bladder and bowel and seeks pleasure through satisfying the anus.

The phallic stage is from the age of 3 to 5 or 6 years, with the individual focused on the erogenous zones of the body (Papalia et al., 2004). For children, this is a time of body awareness—their own, their parent's and others' bodies—through curiosities of undressing and exploration of each other's genitals. They are able to recognize differences in boys and girls. During this stage, children experience an unconscious feeling of desire for their opposite-sex parent and jealousy and envy toward their same-sex parent (McLeod, 2018). In boys, this stage is called the Oedipus complex, and in girls it is called the Electra complex.

The envy and jealousy the young boy aims at his father owes to his becoming, unconsciously, sexually attracted to his mother. The conflict develops because the young boy wants to take the place of his father but has anxiety that he will be castrated by his father as a form of punishment. Although this anxiety and fear may be irrational, it leads to the son internalizing the characteristics, attitudes, and values of his father.

By looking to the father as a role model, the conflict is resolved and the boy acquires his superego and male sex role. He is now able to replace his desire for his mom with the desire for other women (McLeod, 2018). This same process happens for girls, who are influenced by the Electra complex.

The latency stage is age 6 to 12 years. During this time, the libido is relatively repressed and the child now begins to act on his or her impulses indirectly by focusing on activities such as school, sports, building relationships, and work (Lantz & Ray, 2020; Murray, 2000). The genital stage lasts from puberty through adulthood, and it is important that the individual uses energy for proactive social behaviors at work and develops intimate partner relationships that satisfy or replace attractions or desires for opposite-sex parents (Murray, 1938, 2000).

Freud posited that adult personality resulted from conflict of three aspects of the personality: **id**, **ego**, and **superego**. The id is the biological self, and the source of the individual's psychic energy, which everyone is born with. The id's purpose is to fulfill the individual's physical needs or instincts and is driven by the **pleasure principle**, or gratification of drives to keep the individual alive. Freud also suggested the id had innate aggressive and destructive instincts. The ego begins to develop as the individual's cognitive and physical skills increase and some psychic energy is invested in these. While the id continues to fulfill physical needs, the ego identifies rational options to meet the individual's needs. The ego operates on the **reality principle**, to protect the individual by opting for more appropriate methods of meeting needs. The superego is the constraint or the internal parent of the individual during the preschool years when the child experienced guilt for not pleasing the parent. As the individual matures, the ego must take into account the instinctual needs of the id while adhering to the external realities and constraints of the superego (Broderick & Blewitt, 2020).

According to Freud, the sexual applies to the individual's biological instincts, drives, or sensory needs. The id, ego, and superego engage in conflict as a result of experiences during the five developmental stages or psychosexual stages. He posited the changes in the id and the id's energy levels activate each new stage. The id produces energy to gratify drives in one part of the body that experienced pleasure during each stage. Freud postulated that the individual's experiences satisfying these strong needs during stage development can influence the evolution of personality characteristics throughout the individual's life (Broderick & Blewitt, 2020; Thomas, 2000).

## ERIKSON'S PERSONALITY THEORY

Erik Erikson studied psychoanalytic theory with Anna Freud, Sigmund Freud's daughter, and subsequently developed his own theory of **personality** development. Erikson departed from the Freudian "id" as the motivating influence behind all behavior and instead focused on the logical processes of the ego to explain the psychosocial characteristics of behavior, attitudes, and feelings toward the self and others.

A pioneer in the life span perspective, Erikson defined eight psychosocial stages. During each stage the individual faces a **crisis or developmental task** that must be resolved for healthy ego development (Papalia et al., 2007. These crises occur according to a developmental timetable as the individual matures and require the individual to balance the conflict or crisis that occurs in the phase, such as the negative versus the positive. A virtue or strength must also result from the experience. In infancy, the crisis is trust versus mistrust, while the virtue is hope.

TABLE 2.2    Erikson's Psychosocial Stages of Development

| STAGE OR CRISIS | AGE | SIGNIFICANT EVENT | VIRTUE DEVELOPED | NEGATIVE OUTCOME |
|---|---|---|---|---|
| Trust vs. Mistrust | Birth–1 year | Child develops a sense world is safe because of sensitive caregiving. | Hope | Fear/Mistrust |
| Autonomy vs. Shame and Doubt | 1–3 | Child develops a sense of independence tied to use of new cognitive and motor skills. | Willpower | Self-Doubt |
| Initiative vs. Guilt | 3–5 | Child tries to behave in more grown-up ways and experiments in mature roles. | Purpose | Guilt over thought/action |
| Industry vs. Inferiority | 6–12 | Child needs to learn important academic and social skills with peers. | Competence | Lack of competence |
| Identity vs. Role Confusion | 12–20 | Adolescent must move toward adulthood by making proactive choices in values and goals. | Identity and Fidelity | Inability to establish a sense of self |
| Intimacy vs. Isolation | Young Adult | Willing to share identity with others and commit to partnerships. | Love | Fear of intimacy |
| Generativity vs. Stagnation | Middle Adult | Wishes to contribute to the next generation as a mentor, community service, expert work. | Care | Self-absorption |
| Ego Integrity vs. Despair | Late Adult | Comes to terms with life's successes, failures, missed opportunities, and realizes the dignity of life. | Wisdom | Regret |

*(Broderick & Blewitt, 2020).*

## PIAGET'S COGNITIVE DEVELOPMENT THEORY

Jean Piaget was influenced by the 18th-century philosopher Jean-Jacques Rousseau, who posited that children's reasoning and comprehension develops naturally in phases and that caregivers had to allow children to learn by exploring their environment. Piaget defined stages of development of thinking logically, which he termed operational thought. His theory consisted of four stages from birth to adulthood. Each stage was named for the cognition or mental functioning that Piaget believed the child had at that age.

The **sensorimotor stage** begins with substage at birth to 1 month, in which the infant explores the environment through the inherited or unlearned reflexes (Thomas, 2000). In essence, babies come ready to operate, sucking, crying, breathing, and following other bodily functions. During the second substage (1 to 4 months), infants change sensorimotor patterns and develop **schemes** to differentiate between **assimilation** and **accommodation** in response to the environment. During this substage, the infant practices repetitive behaviors to discover skills. The third substage (4 to 8 months) begins the infant's understanding between self and outside objects, during which the infant repeats actions to connect with the environment. For example, they may hit the baby rattle with the hand by chance and hear the sound, and then hit the rattle on purpose to hear the sound. The fourth stage (8 to 12 months) shows the beginning signs of cognition when the infant looks for things out of sight. Objects and people begin to have permanence, and the infant may act intentionally to get desired results. The fifth stage (12 to 18 months) is the infant's development of tertiary circular reactions, such as experimenting with new ways to do an action or experience an object. During the sixth and final substage of **sensorimotor** (18 to 24 months), infants can begin to preplan mentally how to solve problems in their immediate space or environment.

---

### Emma, Aged 8 Months (Infant): A Running Record

In this situation, Emma had an interest in exploring her immediate environment and was able to manipulate objects using her body. She was able to move unwanted objects out of the way to gain access to those she desired and seemed to have an interest in objects that fitted together or formed a distinct set (three puzzle pieces). Emma was clearly in the sensory—motor stage of development as she explored the objects she chose with her mouth and hands, feeling the attributes of each and seeming to decide that the wooden puzzle pieces belonged together. She was able to solve problems as she encountered them by manipulating objects through maneuvering her body to move unwanted objects out of the way of the desired ones as a *natural problem solver* (Babbington, 2006).

TABLE 2.3    Piaget's Cognitive Stages of Development

| STAGE | AGE RANGE | DESCRIPTION |
|---|---|---|
| Sensorimotor | Birth to 2 years | Through six substages, the source of infants' organized actions gradually shifts. Initially, an infant's behavior is reflex, but at the end of the stage, the behavior represents thinking. |
| Preoperational | 2 to 6/7 years | Early figurative thinking is slow. Thought is focused on one thing or object or aspect of the event and is illogical. |
| Concrete operational | 7 to 11/12 years | Thinking skills improve in speed and efficiency, and the child is able to have multiple thoughts, develop logical networks in chunks of information. |
| Formal operational | 12 years to adult | Logical thinking extends now to formal or abstract information. Adolescents are able to think hypothetically. |

*(Broderick & Blewitt, 2020)*

---

**Emma, Aged 19 Months: A Narrative Account**

In another incident, Emma was able to solve her play center friend's problem of not being able to dress a doll by using the knowledge and experience of the previous day to assist her. This example of *guided participation* and construction of knowledge within a social environment showed Emma's developing skill in reflection, offering support to others and using her previously gained skills to solve a problem. A third incident showed further reflection and development of skills. Emma was able to dress her dolls and teddy with verbal guidance at first and then without guidance as she repeated the learned skill. This practice and repetition of a *scaffolded* skill shows her rapid development of problem solving to reach a desired goal (Babbington, 2006).

---

## EXPLANATION OF PIAGET'S STAGES

Piaget's **preoperational stage** was based on operations, which are the ways objects are manipulated or arranged. This can be done physically, if the objects are near at hand,

and is called concrete operations. The individual is beginning to develop mental problem solving, which is shy; this is the preoperational stage. This stage begins at about age 2 to 4, when the individual develops egocentric language. At ages 5 to 7 the child develops a greater command of speech and begins to use intuitive thinking (Thomas, 2000). Language is important for individuals for several reasons. Language facilitates the development of intelligence as the individual can communicate with others, internalize the words to form thoughts, and internalize thoughts into actions to solve problems mentally. Children at this age, however, still solve problems based on what they see or hear in their environment.

---

**Emma, Aged 2 Years: Excerpt from a Diary Account**

These anecdotal records of Emma's engagement in the problem of dressing herself, her dolls and teddy, and assisting others to dress showed a depth of engagement in problem-solving incidents. An attempt by Emma to dress herself showed her increasing need for autonomous behavior, clearly linking to development in the *preoperational* stage as she was able to reenact dressing from previous experiences (Babbington, 2006).

---

The concrete operational stage reflects the individual being able to perform problems with objects, which are perceived or thought of regarding objects in their environment (Thomas, 2000). During this stage, children begin to think rationally but not hypothetically, which can be demonstrated with solving problems with objects in their environment. Formal operational stage begins about age 12, when children can develop hypotheses or abstract reasoning to solve problems.

In Piaget's **cognitive stage theory**, the focus is on cognition, the thought processes and manifest or reveal of these processes (Papalia et al., 2007). Taking an organismic approach, Piaget viewed cognitive development as a result of the child's attempts to comprehend and act on his or her environment. Cognitive development occurs through the interworking of the processes of **organization, adaptation, and equilibrium**.

**Organization** is the individual's development of multifaceted cognitive structures called **schemes**. These schemes facilitate an individual's system of behaving and acting in different experiences and situations. **Adaptation** is how the individual manages new information based on what is already in his or her knowledge base. The two steps in adaptation are **assimilation**, which is acquisition of new knowledge and integrating it into the already existing cognitive constructs, and **accommodation**, which is actually changing the cognitive structure to include the new knowledge.

**Equilibration** is the continual trying of the cognitive structures to balance, stabilize, or obtain equilibrium as changes occur from assimilation to accommodation. Assimilation and accommodation facilitate cognitive development and work together to produce equilibrium (Papalia et al., 2007).

---

### The Case of Emma Discussion

In this observation, in which Emma was engaged in a cooking experience with her mother, many problem-solving skills were apparent. She was able to show her knowledge of her home environment by indicating the place where items for cooking were located (the kitchen pantry). She was able to move objects out of the way so that she could gain access to the desired ones, and she did this by placing the objects on the chair at her feet, clearly showing that she was able to solve this problem independently. Emma was able to place these objects on the chair by balancing them at her feet and carefully maneuvering her body to gain access to those she had been asked to retrieve. This use of prediction and thinking through a problem without the need to gain assistance shows the beginnings of the *preoperational* stage of development, whereby children are able to think in symbolic forms and perform cognitive operations. This was also evident when the butter and sugar mixture spilt onto the bench and Emma carefully collected the mixture and placed it back into the bowl as a response to her mother asking what she should do. She made the decision to do this without being told where it should go.

The *preoperational* stage of development was also evident when Emma's mother told her that the biscuit dough needed to be rolled into balls and she fetched her own red ball from her room. This symbolic understanding shows Emma's ability to make comparisons between ideas and objects and her knowledge of the spherical shape. Emma attempted to roll the biscuit dough and had difficulty doing this. When she found this was too hard for her, she asked for her mother's help. She watched her mother do this and then tried again, but her fine motor skills were not yet developed enough to manipulate the dough into balls. Her mother acknowledged and accepted her attempts as valid and seemed content with this. This acceptance of Emma's attempts to roll the dough was an important aspect of her problem-solving development as her interests in cooking and helping her mother were fostered and reinforced (Babbington, 2006).

---

## BOWLBY AND AINSWORTH ATTACHMENT THEORY

Research on the social development of children was conducted by John Bowlby. Bowlby's (Thomas, 2000) attachment theory describes the child's bonding to the primary caregiver for nurturing, care, and protection. Moreover, attachment theory emphasized that the child's main drive is to develop an attachment relationship with the caregiver for safety and care in the new environment (Whelan, 2003). Bowlby posited that attachment is innate and paramount in the child's development and social relationships throughout life. The attachment figure encourages the child to explore the environment, which is safe, secure, meets the child's immediate needs, and facilitates the skills to navigate the environment.

## BRONFENBRENNER'S BIOECOLOGICAL THEORY

Urie Bronfenbrenner was an American psychologist who posited that all biological organisms develop within the framework of environmental systems that support or stifle its growth (Thomas, 2000). Bronfenbrenner's theory has changed over time and may now be known as a **person-context-process-time** model. Initially, the bioecological theory focused on development of the individual that occurred as a continuous complex interaction with the immediate environment as the individual experienced additional environments (Papalia et al., 2007).

In the explanation of the bioecological theory, the developing person experiences various environments, which Bronfenbrenner discussed as **interconnecting systems**. The **microsystem** is the pattern of events, responsibilities, and interactions within an environment that the individual interacts with daily, such as home, school, work, or community. The microsystem is personal, bidirectional, and involves close interaction whether good or bad. The **mesosystem** is the interaction of two or more microsystems that the developing person is involved with, such as connections of child and school. The **exosystem** links multiple systems, but the developing person is not in one of the systems and is indirectly affected, such as the foster child and family court. The **macrosystem** is Bronfenbrenner's term for society's general cultural patterns. The **chronosystem** is the dimension of time and manifests the amount of change or stability in the environment of the developing person (Papalia et al., 2007; Thomas, 2000).

## VYGOTSKY'S SOCIOCULTURAL THEORY

Lev Vygotsky was a Russian psychologist who focused on the **contextual perspective** regarding children's development of their cognition. His emphasis on the child's environmental social, cultural, and historical influences was the basis of his theory. In brief, children's cognitive development is greatly affected by environmental influences (Papalia et al., 2007; Thomas, 2000). The **sociocultural theory** posited that children learn through collaborating and interacting with those in their environment. As a result, as children grow and develop, they learn from their immediate environment and assimilate the cultural, societal, and historical norms, behaviors, and cognition into their personal ways of thinking and behaving. According to Vygotsky, children must be guided and **scaffolded** by the adults in their immediate environment as they develop, which is the **zone of proximal development (ZPD)**. The adults facilitate, guide, and support the child's mastery of close skills to be accomplished by the child and gradually transition support until the child reaches autonomy and responsibility in the implementation of skills. Scaffolding is the provisional monitoring of a child by adults during skill mastery.

## BANDURA SOCIAL LEARNING THEORY

A Canadian American psychologist, Alfred Bandura, was influenced by the cognitive psychology movement and developed the basics tenets of the **social learning theory.** Bandura (2003) conducted the Bobo doll experiments in 1961 and 1963 to study patterns of aggressive behaviors, and he concluded that social learning occurs through vicarious reinforcement. He showed a group of young boys and girls a film of an individual modeling various levels of physical and aggressive behaviors on Bobo dolls in a room. After viewing the film, observers noted disparity in the children's responses during playtime in a similar room with toys and dolls. Some children imitated the negative aggressive behaviors while others did not. Bandura posited that the disparity might have resulted from extrinsic reinforcements given to the model in the video or other motivational factors.

Bandura posited that **observational learning** may occur if the individual does not imitate the observed behaviors. In the social environment, Bandura (2003) continued research of observational and vicarious learning, stating that learning may occur through either planned efforts or observation of unintentional models in the individual's environment (p. 169). Bandura further indicated that an individual's perspectives of social realities are influenced by the symbolic influences of the environment, including electronic and other forms of media. These symbolic influences may or may not have been experienced directly by the individual.

Bandura modified his theory from social learning to **social cognitive theory** (Papalia et al., 2007). Social learning theory posited that individual's cognitive reactions to experiences affect the development of the learned behavior. Hence, individuals process portions or chunks of behavioral experiences and piece them together to form new multifaceted behavior models (Papalia et al., 2007). The individual receives feedback on the behaviors, develops benchmarks to determine the effectiveness of the behavior, and selects models that meet their desired benchmarks.

# Summary

Child development theories attempt to address the growth and change processes for children. The theories focus on various aspects of development, including social, emotional, and cognitive development. Developmental theories center on how and why different facets and characteristics occur and how they affect development of the child. The stage theorists studied child development as a sequence of development, which occurs universally with children globally. Freud's psychosexual stages of development posited that child development occurs in five psychosexual stages in which sexual drives or instincts focus on a specific area of the body. Erikson's psychosocial development stage theory studied human development from birth to death. Piaget's stage theory studied children's cognitive development from simple to complex levels of thought before progressing to a new stage. Bandura posited that social learning influences development through modeling and imitating behaviors of others. Bowlby and Ainsworth studied children's development of important relationships of attachment and humans' adaptation to survive. Bronfenbrenner's bioecological theory stated an individual's development occurs through interaction with five systems. Vygotsky addressed that sociocultural context is necessary for development.

## CASE STUDY

Mark is a 7-year-old boy who was placed in state custody with his younger sister, aged 5, and a brother, aged 3 with severe birth defects. Mark has been in his foster home for about a year and is calling his caregivers Mommy and Daddy. They have adopted a 2-year-old boy and a 9-year-old girl, who are all loving and kind to Mark and his siblings. Currently, Mark is struggling in school and after repeating kindergarten is still a year behind grade-level peers in reading and math. Mark acts out in severe tantrums and cries when he cannot have his way but has a strong affection with his foster mother. Mark displays behaviors to get his caregivers' attention, such as wetting his pants, wetting the bed, screaming tantrums at night, breaking the toys, and not getting along with the rest of the family and peers at school. Mark is unkind to his siblings and foster siblings. Whether good or negative attention, Mark tries to get his caregivers' attention. The family has tried everything they can think of to address the problem. The foster mother is consulting with a psychologist to identify what his problems are and how to address them.

1.   What theory or theories might be helpful to identify Mark's issues and concerns?
2.   In what stage of development do you think Mark's needs were not met?

# Reflections and Targeted Discussion Questions

## COMPREHENSION

1. How can a child's environment influence his or her learning in positive or negative ways?
2. As you reflect on your childhood, who were the adults in your life that guided or provided scaffolding for you?
3. What are some current issues in the world that could affect development at various stages using Piaget's stages?

## CRITICAL THINKING

1. Explain how the psychosexual stages are related to personality characteristics later in life.
2. Explain the correlation of Erikson's first five stages with Freud's psychosexual stages.
3. Why is understanding human development important to your role as a counselor?

# References

Babbington, S. (2006). *Emma's story: A case study of a toddler's problem-solving development.* ACE Papers (17).

Bandura, A. (2003). Observational learning. In J. H. Byrne (Ed.), *Encyclopedia of learning and memory* (2nd ed., pp. 482–484). New York: Macmillan.

Bowlby, J. (1982). *Attachment* (2nd ed.). Attachment and loss, Vol. I. Basic Books.

Broderick, P. C., & Blewitt, P. (2020). *The life span: Human development for helping professionals* (5th ed.). Pearson Education.

Lantz, S. E., & Ray, S. (2020). Freud developmental theory. *In NCBI.* https://www.ncbi.nlm.nih.gov/books/NBK557526/

McLeod, S. A. (2018). Oedipal complex. *In Simply psychology.* https://www.simplypsychology.org/oedipal-complex.html

Murray, H. A. (1938). *Exploration in personality.* Oxford University Press.

Papalia, D. E., Olds, S. W., & Feldman, R. D. (2007). *Human development* (10th ed.). McGraw-Hill.

Smith, L. B. & Thelen, E. (2003). *Development as a dynamic system. Trends in Cognitive Sciences, 7*(8), 343–348. doi:10.1016/S1364-6613(03)00156-6

Thomas, R. M. (2000). *Comparing theories of child development* (5th ed.). Wadsworth/
    Thomson Learning.

Whelan, D. J. (2003). Using attachment theory when placing sibling in foster care.
    *Child and Adolescent Social Work Journal, 20*(1), 21–36.

# Cross-Cultural Application to Life Span Development

Kimberly N. Frazier, PhD

*Where there are experts there will be no lack of learners.*
    *—African proverb*

## Learning Objectives

After reading this chapter, you should be able to
1. Discover key concepts relevant to cross-cultural counseling.
2. Understand how cultural influences affect various stages of human development.
3. Understand how cultural influences affect client development and selection of counseling interventions.

## Introduction

Human development is a lifelong process, and to effectively treat clients we must view development using a cross-cultural lens. It is equally important to consider both the similarities and differences of the human experience to properly view how our personal experiences and our client's experiences influence the counseling process. Looking at the human condition, every counselor must remember the western societal lens focuses on gender and ethnicity, thus coloring how human development is viewed. Clients are viewed through the lens of gender and ethnicity first, shaping how the counselor conceptualizes issues and behaviors seen on the developmental spectrum. Additionally, a number of counseling models and human development models are very Eurocentric and based on a middle-class, White, western perspective. The aim of this chapter is to serve as a primer to incorporate a multicultural lens when looking at human development across the life span, accounting for intersectionality, multiple identities, and multiple group membership (Sue et al., 2019; Lee, 2013; Bond & Gorman, 2003).

## Key Concepts

- **Culture:** Includes any group of people who identify with one another based on a common purpose, need, background, or other similarities (Lee, 2013).
- **Beliefs:** Assumptions a person believes about themselves and the surrounding world. A person's beliefs are influenced by family values and personal experiences.
- **Values:** What a person considers appropriate behavioral standards that aid in decision making.
- **Ethnocentric:** The viewing of values, beliefs, concepts, and assumptions through the lens of White middle-class and western cultures (Bond & Gorman, 2003).
- **Intersectionality:** A term coined by Kimberlé Williams Crenshaw in 1989 and used to discuss the multiple identities (gender, sexual orientation, ethnicity, etc.) that encompass an individual and explore how those multiple identities influence various forms of oppression toward that individual.
- **Racial Oppression:** Defined as the unjust persecution of a group or a people based on visible phenotypical characteristics (Sue, 2003).
- **Institutional Oppression:** Defined by Sue (2003) as institutional policies and practices that prohibit or limit the rights and opportunities of people or groups of color.
- **Privilege:** Having special advantages or benefits that accrue within a system of experiences, values, perceptions, and norms based on dominate group membership and at the expense of a less dominate group.
- **Acculturation:** The process through which a minority group changes its attitudes, beliefs, values, and behaviors to mirror more closely with the dominant Eurocentric/western culture.

- **Individualistic:** Applies to cultural belief in which emphasis on an individual's goals and needs are deemed more important than the goals and needs of the group.
- **Collectivist:** The cultural belief in which the goals and needs of the group are deemed more important than an individual's goals and needs.
- **Cross-Cultural Competence:** When counselors acknowledge the multiple identities (i.e., age, values, beliefs, religion, etc.) and personal dynamics of both the client and the counselor (Lee, 2013).
- **Cross-Cultural Counseling:** Defined by Lee and Park (2013) as a working alliance between the counselor and the client that accounts for the personal dynamics of both, as well as the culture of the counselor and the client.
- **Equity:** Recognizes that disparities exist with various groups and populations by allocating needed resources and opportunities to create equality among all groups.
- **Equality:** Allocating the same resources and opportunities to all groups and populations.

## Developing a Cross-Cultural Counseling Lens

As humans, counselors inherently bring their collective worldview into the counseling relationship, and that worldview shapes their understanding, perception, and view of their clients. Counselors' worldview is the basis for their understanding and knowledge of cultures and the world around them (Frazier, 2020).

**Cross-cultural counseling** is the working alliance of the counselor and client, and the counselor's awareness of the personal dynamics and life experiences that both the counselor and client bring into the counseling relationship (Lee & Park, 2013; Sue et al., 2019). Simply put, the counselor is aware both they and the client bring into the counseling process a multitude of characteristics, including culture, beliefs, values, spirituality, education, and life experiences that have shaped them into who they are today. According to Lee and Park (2013), effective cross-cultural counseling is composed of the following six principles:

1. Culture is defined as any group of people who identify with one another based on a common purpose, need, background, or other similarities.
2. Cultural differences influence all human interactions.
3. All counseling is cross-cultural in nature.
4. Cross-cultural counseling emphasizes the diversity of all humans.

5. Counselors who are culturally competent continuously seek to develop awareness, knowledge, and skills that allow them to provide effective mental health to diverse people.

6. Cross-culturally competent counselors are also globally literate.

## MULTICULTURAL COUNSELING COMPETENCIES

### ASSOCIATION OF MULTICULTURAL COUNSELING AND DEVELOPMENT

The Association of Multicultural Counseling and Development (AMCD) introduced multicultural counseling competencies in 1992. In 2015, AMCD endorsed a revised version of the Multicultural Counseling Competencies that offered a framework for counselors to apply cultural competence to the counseling experience. The 2015 competencies provide developmental domains involving (1) counselor self-awareness; (2) client worldview; (3) the counseling relationship; and (4) counseling and advocacy interventions. These developmental domains illuminate the multiple areas in constant change that aid in multicultural and social justice competence. Additionally, the revised competencies also detail the attitudes and beliefs, knowledge, skills, and advocacy that overlap in each developmental domain (Frazier, 2020; Ratts et al., 2016).

### AMERICAN COUNSELING ASSOCIATION CODE OF ETHICS

The American Counseling Association (ACA) requires counselors and counselor trainees to have a baseline of culturally competent knowledge that should be applied each time they enter into a cross-cultural counseling encounter. To maintain and evolve the baseline skills outlined by the ACA Code of Ethics, counselors must be willing to commit to continuing education and engaging in difficult dialogues with their clients that surround topics such as race, culture, and oppression (Frazier, 2020; Jones et al., 2013).

## UNDERSTANDING MACROAGGRESSIONS AND MICROAGGRESSIONS

**Macroaggressions** are large-scale forms of discrimination and oppression reinforced through policies and laws. Macroaggressions are systemic in nature and often found in institutional policies and laws that affect access and equity of marginalized and oppressed groups. An example of a macroaggression is the racial covenants and housing policies that either prohibit or limit marginalized populations' ability to rent or own housing in certain neighborhoods. Another example is the disproportionate number of underrepresented students compared with White students who are suspended or made to endure other punitive discipline in school systems. Both examples illuminate lack of equity imposed on a large scale on marginalized populations (Donovan et al., 2013).

**Racial microaggressions** are daily verbal, behavioral, or environmental indignities that can be intentional or unintentional and racially motivated to communicate hostile insults and negative slights against people of color (Sue et al., 2007). Researchers contend most interracial encounters can turn into microaggressive interactions. Microaggressions can appear in one of three forms: microassault, microinsult, and microinvalidation. **Microassaults** are crafted to hurt the intended target by using racial epithets, avoidant behaviors, or purposeful discriminatory behavior. An example would be calling an African American person "colored." It is important to recognize that often the person perpetrating a microassault is doing it deliberately and often when they feel they are in a safe environment or have lost control in some way. A **microinsult** is an insult about a person's identity or heritage. An example could be a person of color getting a job and a White colleague stating to the person of color that they believe people should be offered jobs based on merit rather than heritage. The message communicated by the White colleague is that the person of color did not get the job based on merit, but rather was given the job based only on being a person of color. **Microinvalidation** is the act of excluding and negating the feelings and experiences of a person of color. A common microinvalidation occurs when a White person states to a person of color "I don't see color." The mere statement serves to communicate that he or she does not see the person of color and all the identities and experiences that have shaped his or her life, hence invalidating the person's identity and personal experience (Sue et al., 2007). It is important for counselors to know the types of microaggressions so that (1) they do not communicate microaggressions to their clients, and (2) they are able to put into context the information and narratives their clients discuss during their counseling sessions (Sue et al., 2007). When counselors are aware of the everyday microaggressions that occur with their clients of color, they can begin to understand their importance and effect on client wellness.

## Barriers to Cross-Cultural Competence

### COUNSELOR SELF-AWARENESS

One barrier to cross-cultural awareness is the counselor's lack of self-awareness. Some counselors can have a monolithic worldview and unable to acknowledge their own privilege that colors that worldview. Further, some counselors are unable to see how their privileged and marginalized status (i.e., socioeconomic status, cultural background, etc.) influences their perception of clients and the issues those clients bring to the counseling process. Being self-aware dictates that counselors constantly access their level of self-awareness since the various statutes that encompass privilege and marginalization can change over time. Finally, being culturally competent also requires that counselors be knowledgeable about historical events and how those events helped shape their current privileged and marginalized status (Ratts et al., 2016; Frazier, 2020).

### CLIENT WORLDVIEW

A second barrier to cross-cultural competence is a counselor's lack of understanding of the client's worldview. Being competent requires that counselors get continuous education to learn about the privilege, marginalization, and within-group differences that influence clients' worldview. Counselors lacking cultural competence are unable to see how a client's worldview also influences the professional's communication style, and the communication style and counseling theories the client responds to in the counseling process. When counselors are able to appropriately decipher the worldview of their clients, they will be better able to select interventions and serve as better advocates, communicators, and interpreters for their clients (Frazier, 2020).

### KNOWLEDGE

Another barrier to cross-cultural competence is the continuous commitment to staying abreast of knowledge that discusses how clients' own privilege, marginalization, values, and beliefs influence their worldview. Building cultural competence also requires counselors to seek out historical knowledge about events regarding oppression and racism that shape the functioning of both the client and the counselor. Finally, lack of knowledge regarding multicultural theories, models, and advocacy interventions also serves as a barrier to cultural competence (Ratts et al., 2016; Frazier, 2020).

## Cross-Cultural Considerations in Childhood and Adolescence

Major milestones in childhood include becoming more independent due to the rapid development of increased gross and fine motor skills. A child's brain is changing at a fast pace that increases the child's ability for more complex cognitive functioning. While conducting research on how young children process themes of race and ethnicity, I interviewed groups of second graders about their thoughts after reading books focused on cultural themes. The group included a mix of ethnicity and gender. When

I asked a young African American child his thoughts about the book, he told me he was not smart but that "Billy," pointing to the White boy in the group, was smart. In that moment I realized a brown boy in the second grade had already received messaging that he was incapable of being smart. This is a sobering example of how a young child processed the messaging (both *micro*aggressive and *macro*aggressive) directed to him and how that messaging influenced his perception of himself in the larger world, in this case the classroom.

It is important to be cognizant that in adolescence influence comes from both family and friends. During these stages of development, the individual is deciphering the values, beliefs, and norms passed down by their family as well as the values, beliefs, and norms that their friends bring. In addition, the desire to be more independent beyond influence of family is also present. Counselors must assess the cross-cultural impact at these stages by being aware of the various types of families that are present (i.e. blended families, multigenerational families that live together, single-parent families, etc.) as well as the roles and responsibilities that may be required of the adolescent based on cultural group membership. Considering the rapid development occurring in the areas of cognition, emotion, and skill development for children and adolescents, it is imperative that counselors consider environmental factors and continuous traumatic stress that impact proper stage development for children and adolescents from marginalized populations.

## Cross-Cultural Considerations in Adulthood

It is important for counselors to be aware of the various milestones achieved (or not achieved) in the stages that shape adulthood. Some examples include entering a career, having and raising children, and retiring. Based on access and equity, some in adulthood may be unable to create a career and instead work various jobs. Adulthood may gain a partner, but due to discriminatory policy and oppressive laws, marriage cannot be legally attained by some. Counselors must consider how traumatic events, continuous stress, and macroaggressions possibly affect an adult's ability to effectively move thorough and achieve adulthood milestones.

## Impact of Death and Dying on Development

In human development, how dying and loss of family is conceptualized at every stage needs to be explored. Dying and the grief associated with loss are influenced by culture, family, values, and beliefs. Some cultures honor those family members that have been lost through celebratory song, dance, and music. These types of celebrations have roots in African spiritual practice, and the music played is often a blend of African culture and European influences. In New Orleans, the line the follows the band and participates in the dance and celebration is commonly referred to as the "second line." The music played and dancing performed at the funeral celebration of life is ritualistic in nature and used to ensure the send-off to the next life is comparable to the life lived on earth. There are also holidays dedicated to honoring and remembering the dead that can be found in many cultures and religions. Some of these holidays include Day of the Dead, All Saints Day, and All Souls' Day.

The Day of the Dead holiday has roots in Mexican culture and focuses on family and friends gathering for prayer to remember family and friends who have died. All Saints Day is a religious holiday and used to honor all the saints, known and unknown. Depending on the country and city where All Saints Day is practiced, specific feasts and gifts (i.e. flowers, fruits, lighting candles, cakes, etc.) are given or placed on alters. It is important for counselors to inquire about each client's holidays, values, and beliefs that surround death and the loss of family. Mental health professionals must also take into account how death and loss was conceptualized for the client and their family of origin (i.e. mourning versus celebrating; marked via a holiday versus marked via the day of the loss) and how that conceptualization has shaped the client's worldview on loss and may shape their thoughts regarding their own mortality.

FIGURE 3.1    Gender Pathways

## Summary

Cross-cultural competency is important because a counselor needs to provide services to a culturally diverse population, which comes to counseling with a myriad of experiences, influences, and identities. Counselors cannot ignore the importance of the worldview, values, beliefs, and experiences influencing the counseling relationship and experience. Counselors must commit themselves to become advocates and continue to learn about diversity and inclusion to better aid their clients and the counseling profession. Counselors must also be willing to provide space and understanding for clients to reflect on how their experiences, familial influences, and multiple cultural intersections have influenced their lives. Finally, counselors must come into the helping profession knowing cultural competency is a lifelong process that requires awareness and authenticity (Malott & Schaefle, 2015; Frazier, 2020).

### CASE STUDY

Kristoff is an African American 8-year-old referred to counseling by his parents, William and Nicole. Both parents listed Kristoff's presenting issues as a lack of focus in school and home, displays of anger and agitation in school and at home, and difficulty transitioning after his parent's divorce. Both William and Nicole have observed Kristoff become agitated when asked to read before dinner or during bedtime. William states Kristoff also has meltdowns when asked to do chores or basic tasks. Nicole shares that Kristoff often becomes so frustrated he resorts to meltdowns. Both parents shared that Kristoff's teacher has noticed he is restless and unfocused during class. Kristoff's teacher also said he takes a long time to get on task to begin his work and has to be redirected to complete his work due to daydreaming.

1. When looking at this case, what are some specific developmental stage tasks that need to be considered when conceptualizing Kristoff?
2. Looking at the case through the lens of cultural competence, what specific considerations need to be looked at regarding Kristoff's meltdowns and his displays of anger and frustration?
3. How might Kristoff's struggle to transition after his parent's divorce affect some of the behaviors observed?
4. What does the counselor working with Kristoff and his parents need to be aware of culturally to ensure that cultural competence is occurring?

## Reflection and Targeted Discussion Questions

1. What incorrect assumptions do people make about the cultural group to which you ascribe? How might these incorrect assumptions affect the counselor-client relationship?

2. Using each developmental stage described in this chapter, discuss your cultural experiences at each stage. How you can use your cultural experiences at various stages to inform your cultural competency? How can your cultural experiences help you seek more knowledge regarding cultural awareness?

3. Think about the areas that you hold privilege, (i.e. identifying as cisgender or with a Caucasian American racial/ethnic identity, ascribing to the upper- or middle-class socioeconomic group, identifying your religion or spirituality as Christian, being free of intellectual, developmental, or physical disabilities, being an American citizen, etc.). How might your areas of privilege impact your ability to help clients who are part of marginalized groups in those same areas? Remember that it is possible to hold privilege and be marginalized in another area, as well as possible to have multiple areas of privilege or multiple areas of marginalization.

4. Reflecting on areas you hold privilege (as discussed in question 3), how might your areas of privilege impact your ability to effectively conceptualize your clients' issues and areas of growth when your clients hold membership in marginalized groups where you hold privilege?

5. Discuss how your privilege can exist at the expense of those who are marginalized. How can areas in which you hold membership or identify threaten to exclude others? How does this impact the counseling relationship? How might this impact the counseling experience for the client?

## References

Bond, L. A., & Gorman, K. S. (2003). Teaching developmental psychology: Celebrating the dialectics of development. In P. Bronstein & K. Quina (Eds.), *Teaching gender and multicultural awareness: Resources for the psychology classroom* (pp. 45–57). American Psychological Association.

Bronstein, P., & Quina, K. (2003). *Teaching gender and multicultural awareness: Resources for the psychology classroom.* American Psychological Association.

Donovan, R. A., Galban, D. J., Grace, R. K., Bennett, J. K., & Felicié, S. Z. (2013). Impact of racial macro- and microaggressions in Black women's lives: A preliminary analysis. *Journal of Black Psychology, 39*(2), 185–196.

Frazier, K. N. (2020). Preparing counselors across cultures. In A. Adekson (Ed.), *Handbook of counseling and counselor education* (pp. 143–152). Routledge.

Jones, J., Sander, J., & Booker, K. (2013). Multicultural competency building: Practical solutions for training and evaluating student progress. *Training and Education in Professional Psychology, 7*(1), 12–22.

Lee, C. C. (2013). The cross-cultural encounter: Meeting the challenge of culturally competent counseling. In C. C. Lee (Ed.), *Multicultural issues in counseling: New approach to diversity* (4th ed., pp. 3–12). American Counseling Association.

Lee, C. C., & Park, D. (2013). A conceptual framework for counseling across cultures. In C. C. Lee. (Ed.), *Multicultural issues in counseling: New approach to diversity* (4th ed., pp. 13–19). American Counseling Association.

Malott, K. M., & Schaefle, S. (2015). Addressing clients' experiences of racism: A model for clinical practice. *Journal of Counseling and Development. 93*, 361–369.

Ratts, M. J., Singh, A. A., Nassar-McMillian, S., Butler, S. K., & McCullough, J. R. (2016). *Multicultural and social justice counseling competencies.* American Counseling Association.

Sue, D. W. (2003). *Overcoming our racism: The journey to liberation.* Jossey-Bass.

Sue, D. W., Capodilupo, C. M., Torino, G. C., Bucceri, J. M., Holder, A. M. B., Nadal, K. L., & Esquilin, M. (2007). Racial microaggressions in everyday life: Implications for clinical practice. *American Psychologist, 62*(4), 271–286. https://doi.org/10.1037/0003-066X.62.4.271

Sue, D. W., Sue, D., Neville, H. A., & Smith, L. (2019). *Counseling the culturally diverse: Theory and practice* (8th ed.). Wiley.

## Credit

# LGBTQ+ and Human Development

Stacy Speedlin Gonzalez, PhD; Chelsea Barron Davila Conaway, MS; and Aneesa Anderson, MS

*We should indeed keep calm in the face of difference, and live our lives in a state of inclusion and wonder at the diversity of humanity.*

—George Takei

## Learning Objectives

After reading this chapter, you should be able to:

1. Define key concepts relevant to the developmental processes of identity with LGBTQ persons.
2. Describe human growth and development from a bioecological and psychosocial developmental lens.
3. Illuminate inclusive practices and social justice-oriented actions for working with this population in clinical and school settings.

# Introduction

The emphasis on social justice and multicultural counseling continues to expand within counselor educational settings (Toporek et al., 2009). Counselors who work with LGBTQ persons, groups, and communities should seek competency to promote more inclusive and affirmative practices. Therefore, understanding LGBTQ persons from a developmental lens should also include multicultural awareness and practices. In this chapter, we focus on counseling LGBTQ persons across the life span from a bioecological and psychosocial perspective. Further, we discuss the appropriate use of pronouns. Finally, we illuminate how the misuse of pronouns are experienced as microaggressions.

# Key Concepts

Key concepts in this section are divided into the following three subsections: 1) affectional/sexual orientation; 2) gender expansive (used to describe gender identity); and 3) LGBTQ identity. These terms have been separated to help the reader understand the difference between identity related to *gender* and *affectional/sexuality* because the developmental and growth needs of these groups vary significantly. This section will not include all terms, as these terms are still being developed and constructed. The terms included, however, should provide context to assist the reader in understanding a basis of nonbinary language. The *LGBTQ identity* section includes key terms related to *sexual orientation and gender identity prejudice (SOGIP), heterosexism,* and *cisgender privilege.*

- **Affectional/Sexual Orientation:** Defined as "each person's capacity for profound emotional, affectional and sexual attraction to, and intimate and sexual relations with, individuals of a different gender or the same gender or more than one gender" (O'Flaherty & Fisher, 2008, p. 207). Examples of affectional/sexual orientation labels include lesbian, gay, bisexual, pansexual, asexual, queer, questioning, and heterosexual.
- **Gender Expansive:** This term is utilized by the Association of Lesbian, Gay, Bisexual, and Transgender Issues in Counseling (ALGBTIC) task force (2017) to recognize the increasing awareness of the different categories of gender identities and variations. "Gender expansive is an umbrella term, used by organizations ranging from Gender Spectrum to the Human Rights Campaign, that describes individuals that

broaden commonly held definitions of gender, including its expression, associated identities, and/or other perceived gender norms in one or more aspects of their life" (Goodrich et al., 2017, p. 204). Examples of gender include, but are not limited to, transgender, two-spirited, gender nonconforming, gender queer, gender fluid, cisgender, agender, androgynous, nonbinary, nongender, bi-gender, etc. Research describes the role of genes, heredity, and variation (genotype and phenotype) and makes some recommendations for how gender assignment can be appropriated by physicians (Shabir et al., 2015).

- **LGBTQ Identity Development:** LGBTQ identity is an imperative concept to working affirmatively with this population. Identity development in this chapter refers to an active process of exploring and assessing aspects of one's identity and to establishing a commitment to identity while embracing aspects of others (Bosma & Kunnen, 2001). As with other populations, identity is more effectively conceptualized in stage models; however, processes of sexual/affectional/gender self-definition, self-confidence, and self-acceptance are independent yet intersecting dimensions. Hence, the importance for counselors and clinicians to familiarize themselves with the terminology, culture, effect of oppression, and historical framework.

- **Sexual Orientation and Gender Identity Prejudice:** Cramwinckel et al. (2018) define this term (or acronym SOGIP) as "negative attitudes about certain behaviors, individuals or groups based on—or related to—their sexual orientation, gender identity, gender role or gender expression" (p.185). Such worldviews, along with social and political biases, complicate the identity process for LGBTQ persons.

- **Heterosexism:** Defined as "an ideology that not only privileges heterosexuality but also actively degrades and punishes any alternative, nonheterosexual constellations of relationships, identities, and behaviors" (Nunn & Bolt, 2015, p. 278).

- **Cisgender Privilege:** In 2010, Walls and Costello termed the phrase cisgender privilege as "the set of unearned advantages that individuals who identify as the gender they were assigned at birth accrue solely due to having a cisgender identity" (p. 83). Essentially, they posit that identity congruent with the born or assigned gender comes with opportunities transgender or gender nonconforming are not given.

## The Human Developing Process

### ERIKSON'S EIGHT STAGES OF PSYCHOSOCIAL DEVELOPMENT

Erikson's model provides a psycho-developmental overview as a context for understanding client developmental processes and how this translates into the therapeutic relationship (Knight, 2017). Erikson's model examines various life stages from a binary health perspective. For example, adolescent stage is conceptualized through the lens of identity cohesion versus role confusion. Further, the young adult stage is viewed from a perspective of intimacy versus isolation—a pertinent context for understanding young adult experience (Table 4.1). Psychosocial development occurs as an individual navigates his or her own internal processes within social, familial, and communal influences.

LGBTQ persons' experience can also be conceptualized using Erikson's model. LGBTQ identity is a developmental process that often occurs in early life stages and can be mediated by external sources of pressure and/or support. Unlike developmental stages that explain cognitive or growth milestones, Erikson's eight-stage model examines identification and relational growth. Self-identity and self-acceptance can be better understood through the view of adolescent stage (identity cohesion versus role confusion). Beyond the self-identity and "coming out" experiences, LGBTQ persons must navigate mental health and wellness along with healthy relational strategies. The intimacy versus isolation stage can serve as a lens for navigating such adjustments.

**TABLE 4.1**    Erikson's Psychosocial Development Model (1950)

| STAGES | STAGE DESCRIPTION (SYNTONIC TENDENCY—DYSTONIC TENDENCY) | ADAPTIVE STRENGTH/ VIRTUE | MALDEVELOPMENT (MALADAPTIVE TENDENCY—MALIGNANT TENDENCY) |
| --- | --- | --- | --- |
| Infancy | Basic Trust vs. Mistrust | Hope | Sensory Maladjustment–Withdrawal |
| Early Childhood | Autonomy vs. Shame and Doubt | Will | Shameless Willfulness–Compulsion |
| Play Age | Initiative vs. Guilt | Purpose | Ruthlessness–Inhibition |
| School Age | Industriousness vs. Inferiority | Competence | Narrow Virtuosity–Inertia |

(Continued)

TABLE 4.1   (Continued)

| STAGES | STAGE DESCRIPTION (SYNTONIC TENDENCY– DYSTONIC TENDENCY) | ADAPTIVE STRENGTH/ VIRTUE | MALDEVELOPMENT (MALADAPTIVE TENDENCY— MALIGNANT TENDENCY) |
|---|---|---|---|
| Adolescence | Identity Cohesion vs. Role Confusion | Fidelity | Fanaticism–Repudiation |
| Young Adulthood | Intimacy vs. Isolation | Love | Promiscuity–Exclusivity |
| Adulthood | Generativity vs. Stagnation/Self-Absorption | Care | Overextension–Rejectivity |
| Old Age | Integrity vs. Despair | Wisdom | Presumption–Disdain |

## BRONFENBRENNER'S ECOLOGICAL STAGE MODEL

To better understand the influence of external systems, Bronfenbrenner (1994) developed the ecological stage model to explain how environmental experiences affect an individual's growth and development. Different aspects or levels of the environment that influence development were labeled to better conceptualize the effects, including the macrosystem, microsystem, mesosystem, and exosystem (Bronfenbrenner, 1994). This theory can examine LGBTQ persons' experiences within their own various systems. Macrosystems include systems such as political and societal. Counselors or clinicians can understand how laws, politics, and policies can influence LGBTQ persons. Microsystems involve familial systems, whether they are nuclear or extended. Family acceptance or rejection can be viewed and taken into consideration as a significant client experience. Mesosystems and exosystems can involve communities and culture (Figure 4.1).

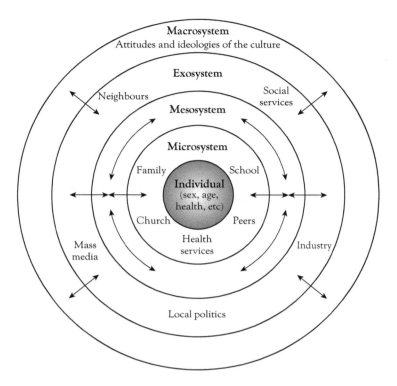

**FIGURE 4.1**

## PHYSICAL AND COGNITIVE

Multiple developmental models demonstrate how individuals grow through milestones. Pertaining to physical growth and cognitive development, LGBTQ persons do not differ from their heterosexual and cisgendered counterparts.

## SOCIAL AND EMOTIONAL

Multiple developmental models demonstrate how individuals grow through milestones. Pertaining to social and emotional development, LGBTQ persons do not differ from their heterosexual and cisgendered counterparts. However, social and emotional development can be impacted by experiences of microaggressions, microinsults, and microinvalidations at the macro-, meso-, and micro-levels. For example, LGBTQ persons must navigate familial issues, religious disenfranchisement, lack of political support systems, and significant health and mental health disparities. Further, LGBTQ persons with intersecting identities—such as ethnic minorities or those with physical challenges or low SES, etc.—deal with double-bind marginalization, which can further affect their social and emotional wellness. Therefore, counselors who work with this population should remain aware of these impediments to their growth and assist clients with developing their own healthy social/emotional microcosms.

## Scientific Contributions

Historically, the scientific and research community has viewed LGBTQ persons from a pathological perspective (ALGBTIC LGBTQQIA Competencies Task Force, 2013). Prior to 1973, the term "homosexual" was termed as a mental disorder under the umbrella of personality disorders in the *Diagnostic and Statistical Manual* (DSM-II, 1968). Later versions of DSM were to include *"transsexual"* and *"gender identity disorder"* in DSM III and DSM IV (Oberheim et al., 2017). Gender identity disorder is found in DSM 5 for the purposes of accessing medicalized diagnosis and treatments for persons identifying as transgender; however, there still exists some concern about continued practice that enforces stigma within the counseling, psychology, and medical communities. Internalized beliefs derived from dominant heterosexist/cisgender discourses translate into direct practice (Schope & Eliason, 2000; Saltzburg, 2015). LGBT clients are at risk of having their lives evaluated and prescribed using such norms. This lack of clinician understanding creates barriers to providing culturally responsive and effective services.

The current body of literature acknowledges the health disparities related to discrimination, stigma, and general lack of understanding that results in poor wellness outcomes for LGBTQ persons (U.S. Department of Health and Human Services, 2017; Blosnich et al., 2014; Sexton et al., 2018). Further, counseling research has illuminated similar reports of stigma and discrimination experiences toward LGBTQ persons. Recent literature also acknowledges a need to incorporate the strengths and resiliencies of LGBTQ individuals, groups, and communities into counseling efforts. This would require acknowledgment of historical, political, and social traumas while examining how LGBTQ experiences strengthen the individual and prepare them for life's obstacles.

Deconstructing binary language and heteronormative/heterosexist influences on research, literature, and scholarly work has been a gradual and unfinished process. A need for more LGBT-affirming language is imperative. Therefore, counselors and counselor educators should incorporate awareness of this language and the effects into their professional lexicon (Smith et al., 2012). Also, since research outcomes dictate the current knowledge body of this population, LGBTQ-competent measures and instruments are necessary for research. Counselors, school counselors, and clinicians who work with this population should be aware that social, economic, political, and systemic issues still arise for their clients, and, therefore, they need to become more aware of how to advocate for their clients beyond the office or school setting. Further, counselors and counselor educators need to take a role in developing allies and teaching ally development.

## Theoretical Considerations

The intrinsic and extrinsic factors described in this chapter have a significant effect on LGBTQ persons' development across the life span. Professionals working with this population can aid in the progression of healthy development at all stages by acknowledging the effects of these processes on development. Moreover, it is critical for these professionals to conceptualize LGBTQ individuals' experiences and development within the context of their diverse intersections. To achieve these goals, the authors position this chapter within the framework of Erikson's (1950) psychosocial theory of human development and Bronfenbrenner's (1994) ecological stage theory. In doing so, the authors examine both internal psychosocial processes and external environmental factors that affect LGBTQ persons' development across the life span.

## Strengths and Challenges from the "ISMs" Perspectives

SOGIP is deeply rooted in heterosexist and transphobic attitudes and beliefs within the chronosystem and macrosystem. For LGBTQ individuals, these attitudes and beliefs can have a significant effect on development throughout the life span, and these experiences may be complicated by multiple marginalizations for persons who identify with additional marginalized identities. The following sections will explore the effects of various ISMs on LGBTQ development across the life span within the context of bioecological and psychosocial development.

### MULTICULTURAL

Racialized LGBTQ persons develop within the context of the double marginalization of racism and SOGIP. Racism manifests in the form of race-based biases, prejudice, and discrimination at the primary contextual level. Many LGBTQ persons of color report enduring both racism and SOGIP from members of dominant groups, engendering feelings of isolation and rejection (Anzaldúa, 2012). Despite the pervasiveness of SOGIP, the LGBTQ community is not immune to within-group marginalization. Racialized individuals also report experiences of racism within the LGBTQ community (Han, 2017; Hunter, 2010). These experiences can compound the effect of double marginalization and increase both depression and anxiety for LGBTQ persons of color (Sutter & Perrin, 2016).

Despite a history of racism within the LGBTQ community, contemporary social justice leaders have argued for the necessity of addressing the intersection of racial and LGBTQ identity and cultivating an inclusive, anti-racist LGBTQ movement (Carruthers, 2019; Green, 2019). Recent anti-racist movements such as Black Lives Matter have sought to build solidarity between LGBTQ and racialized communities, giving voice to historically silenced and marginalized LGBTQ persons of color (Green, 2019). It remains essential for professionals working with this population, however, to acknowledge the effect of double marginalization in the context of racial and LGBTQ identity. Processing these experiences may enhance resilience and support positive development (Godsay, 2018).

FIGURE 4.2    Be You, Love You

## DIVERSITY

As indicated in previous chapters, diversity at the primary contextual level can strengthen development across the life span. Similarly, positive representation at all ecological levels can foster a sense of validation, empowerment, and solidarity (Caswell et al., 2017). Historically, LGBTQ representation in popular media was minimal. LGBTQ media representation was often limited to harmful stereotypes and negative tropes (Dhoest & Simons, 2012; McInroy & Craig, 2017). Moreover, expressions of

LGBTQ identity in public spaces were sparse due to the prejudice and discrimination associated with being "out" (Murphy & Bjorngaard, 2019).

Representation of LGBTQ individuals, however, is on the rise. Trailblazers such as Laverne Cox have advocated for the inclusion of queer and gender expansive individuals in popular media. Additionally, organizations such as Southern Poverty Law Center have fought for LGBTQ diversity and inclusion in the workplace (Supreme Court of the U.S., 2019). The increase of diversity and representation at the primary contextual level can strengthen bioecological and psychosocial development throughout the life span as LGBTQ individuals develop a sense of acceptance and belonging. It is important to note that LGBTQ individuals living or working in non-inclusive spaces can experience negative mental health outcomes, such as anxiety, depression, and suicidal ideation (Sutter & Perrin, 2016). Discussing experiences of diversity and inclusion with LGBTQ persons will enable counselors and educators to gain an enhanced understanding of the effect these factors have on psychosocial development.

## GENDER

Contemporary scholarship suggests that gender exists on a spectrum and encompasses a wide range of expressions and ideas about the self (Coleman et al., 2011; Yarbrough, 2018). Traditional patriarchal values and beliefs resist this perspective as it undermines the gender binary, which is essential to the perpetuation of patriarchal power systems (Ward, 2016). Hence, gender expansive individuals across the gender spectrum experience a wide variety of prejudice and discrimination, ranging from non-affirming messages and a lack of access to resources to aggression and violence.

These experiences can have a profound effect on development across the life span. Harmful interactions with others and internalized negative beliefs can impede gender expansive individuals' ability to successfully navigate psychosocial crises at each developmental stage. Moreover, prejudice and discrimination can limit this population's willingness to seek support at various contextual levels. It is imperative that counselors and educators serving gender-expansive clients work from a gender-affirming perspective and remain knowledgeable about best practices in working with this population.

## SEXUAL ORIENTATION

Heterosexism is a system of attitudes and beliefs that maintains power for heterosexual individuals through the subjugation of nonheterosexual persons (Nunn & Bolt, 2015). For LGBTQ individuals, heterosexism manifests at the primary contextual level in the form of biases, prejudice, and discrimination. These experiences can include microaggressions, aggression, threats, and physical violence (Vacarro & Koob, 2019). Despite a long history of systematic prejudice and discrimination, the LGBTQ community has made significant strides toward equality (Murphy & Bjorngaard, 2019); however, many LGBTQ individuals still encounter heterosexist biases, prejudice, and discrimination at the primary contextual level. These experiences can have a negative effect across the life span as individuals confront psychosocial crises within the context of SOGIP. Prejudice and discrimination within individuals' extrinsic environment may hinder their ability to successfully resolve these crises at each stage of development.

Although many LGBTQ persons experience hostility and rejection from friends and family (Klein et al., 2015), marginalization can also occur within the LGBTQ community itself (Schimanski & Treharne, 2019). For example, biphobia, or prejudice and discrimination against bisexual individuals, has persisted in the gay community for several years (Obradors-Campos, 2011). This within-group marginalization can have a profound effect on the development of marginalized subgroups and contribute to feelings of isolation, powerlessness, and alienation (Obradors-Campos, 2011).

Despite experiences of prejudice and discrimination, LGBTQ persons may develop a significant sense of connection as they cultivate supportive relationships within the LGBTQ community (Klein et al., 2015).

FIGURE 4.3    The Best Place to Be Is Together

## ABLEISM

Ableism refers to values, attitudes, and beliefs that privilege the experiences and narratives of able-bodied individuals while disempowering and marginalizing persons with disabilities (Smith et al., 2008). Ableism can hinder disabled individuals' ability to access physical and social spaces. For LGBTQ persons with disabilities, these barriers can complicate the experiences of SOGIP (described in previous sections) and contribute to a sense of double marginalization. Moreover, persons with disabilities are often infantilized and desexualized (Block et al., 2012; Hirschmann, 2013). LGBTQ persons with disabilities may conceptualize infantilization and desexualization as invalidation of their LGBTQ identity. Moreover, LGBTQ young adults with disabilities may find building romantic relationships challenging as they navigate the double marginalization of SOGIP and desexualization. Despite these challenges, LGBTQ persons with disabilities may be motivated to seek out supportive individuals and draw from their varying intersections as a source of strength.

## AGEISM

Ageism within the LGBTQ community emphasizes the needs and experiences of the young and minimizes those of older LGBTQ adults. Representation of LGBTQ persons in popular media tends to focus on young adults, and LGBTQ-friendly spaces often cater to the interests of young adults. This lack of representation coupled with the perpetuation of SOGIP and ageist attitudes and beliefs can present challenges for LGBTQ individuals navigating the psychosocial challenges of adulthood and old age.

Despite this double marginalization, older LGBTQ persons have a unique ability to build supportive connections at the primary contextual level. LGBTQ community centers may offer spaces or events specifically catering to older community members. Connecting with other older LGBTQ adults and engaging in the community can foster a sense of connection and purpose that may act as a protective factor to healthy development during the final two psychosocial stages. Moreover, this population has the ability to connect with and mentor younger LGBTQ individuals, which may also contribute to a sense of purpose and belonging.

FIGURE 4.4    Love and Happiness at Any Age

## MORTALITY AWARENESS

Mortality awareness and fear of death are universal human experiences (Yalom, 2009). Individuals across all intersections will very likely experience varying levels of mortality awareness and death anxiety across the life span. As indicated in previous chapters, the intensity of mortality awareness varies across developmental stages. Mortality awareness tends to be highest in middle age and decrease during late adulthood and old age (Cicirelli, 2006). There is no evidence to suggest that experiences of mortality awareness and death anxiety differ for LGBTQ individuals. This population will most likely experience the same mortality awareness curve described previously. (See other chapters for detailed information concerning mortality awareness across the life span.)

## Summary

Counseling and educating LGBTQ persons requires knowledge beyond traditional counseling and teaching practices. When working with this population, counselors and educators should work to better understand the needs of this group through a developmental, multicultural, and social justice lens. The authors believe

Bronfenbrenner's ecological theory infused with Erikson's stage of development model provide a unique lens for conceptualizing development. Further, counselors and educators can benefit from examining how intersectionalities of race, gender, citizen status, and sexual/affectional orientation affect the experiences of LGBTQ persons.

---

### CASE STUDY

Michi is a 23-year-old Mexican American who identifies as gender fluid. Michi prefers pronouns such as "they/them/their." Michi's family of origin migrated to the United States when Michi was 3 years old. Michi's mother is accepting of Michi's orientation, but their father and siblings are not accepting. Michi is unsure who they are attracted to; they have had romantic feelings toward men but are not sure they are sexually attracted to anyone. Further, Michi has no desire to take hormones or undergo any surgical processes, and Michi prefers to dress fluidly and express gender in a nonbinary fashion.

Michi's family is experiencing increased stress due to Michi's father not being an American citizen. Following threats in the community of ICE deporting individuals, Michi's father has quit his job and is staying home. This has resulted in elevated stress for Michi because their father wants Michi to "stop drawing attention" and is asking Michi to "be the boy that I raised you to be. You don't want me to be deported because of your nonsense, do you?" Michi honors their father's wish but grows increasingly depressed and stops associating with friends and members of the LGBTQ community.

Michi attempts to talk to their brother and sister about feeling sad. The brother tells Michi to "get over himself. Can't you see that there are bigger problems in our family than you?" Michi's sister states, "Really, you should not be doing this. We need to support Dad. What will Mom do if Dad gets deported? We will all be lost." Michi follows the siblings' recommendations but grows increasingly depressed. Michi's friends also became upset after an incident in which one of their friends was killed and Michi did not show up to the eulogy. Michi begins to feel alone and think that they do not fit anywhere.

Michi goes to the local community center to seek counseling. Upon arriving, Michi is given intake paperwork that asks to identify gender. Michi notices there are two boxes to check: *male* or *female*. Further, Michi looks around the counseling center and does not see anyone of color or anyone who appears to be a safe space. Michi does not see any rainbow flags, trans ally flags, or safe zone stickers. Michi's counselor calls their name, and Michi goes into the office and sits, begrudgingly. The counselor asks Michi, "Why are you dressed like a girl?" Michi looks down, unsure how to respond. The counselor proceeds, "Ok. I am going to ask you some questions, sort of an assessment. I need you to answer honestly. That is the only way I can help you. First question: Tell me about your childhood …" Michi stands immediately, then states, "I don't think I can do this" and walks out of the counseling center. After Michi left, the neighboring counselor asks, "What happened?" Michi's counselor states, "Oh, you know, Mexican clients are so resistant to counseling."

## Reflections and Targeted Discussion Questions

1. After reviewing the case study, how would you conceptualize Michi's identity from a multicultural lens? How does intersectionality of various nondominant constructs (race, gender, citizen status, sexual/affectional orientation) play a role in Michi's identity and, therefore, counseling needs?

2. If Michi were your client coming into a first session, how would you work with Michi? (Please take into account both developmental models. Include needs based on macro, meso, and micro levels.)

## References

ALGBTIC LGBTQQIA Competencies Task Force. Harper, A., Finnerty, P., Martinez, M., Brace, A., Crethar, H. C., Loos, B., Harper, B., Graham, S., Singh, A., Kocet, M., Travis, L., Lambert, S., Burnes, T., Dickey, L. M., & Hammer, T. R. (2013). Association for Lesbian, Gay, Bisexual, and Transgender Issues. In Counseling competencies for counseling with lesbian, gay, bisexual, queer: Questioning, intersex, and ally individuals. *Journal of LGBT Issues in Counseling, 7*(1), 2–43. doi: 10.1080/15538605.2013.755444

American Psychiatric Association. (1968). DSM-II. *Diagnostic and statistical manual of mental disorders, 2.*

Anzaldúa, G. (2012). *Borderlands/La Frontera* (4th ed.). Aunt Lute Books.

Block, P., Shuttleworth, R., Pratt, J., Block, H., & Rammler, L. (2012). Disability, sexuality, and intimacy. In N. Pollard & D. Sakellariou (Eds.), *Politics of occupation-centered practice* (pp. 162–179). John Wiley & Sons.

Blosnich, J. R., Farmer, G. W., Lee, J. G., Silenzio, V. M., & Bowen, D. J. (2014). Health inequalities among sexual minority adults: Evidence from ten US states, 2010. *American Journal of Preventive Medicine, 46*(4), 337– 349.

Bosma, H. A., & Kunnen, E. S. (2001). Determinants and mechanisms in ego identity development: A review and synthesis. *Developmental Review, 21*(1), 39–66.

Bronfenbrenner, U. (1994). Ecological models of human development. *Readings on the Development of Children, 2*(1), 37–43.

Carruthers, C. A. (2019). *Unapologetic.* Beacon Press.

Caswell, M., Migoni, A. A., Geraci, N., & Cifor, M. (2017). *"To be able to imagine otherwise": Community archives and the importance of representation.* Archives and Records (38, 5–26). doi:10.1080/23257962.2016.1260445

Cicirelli, V. G. (2006). Fear of death in mid-old age. *Journal of Gerontology, 61B,* 75–81. doi:10.1093/geronb/61.2.p75

Coleman, E., Bockting, W., Botzer, M., Cohen-Kettenis, P., DeCuypere, G., Feldman, J., Fraser , L., Green, J., Knudson, G., Meyer, W. J., Monstrey , S., Adler, R. K., Brown, G. R., Devor, A. H., Ehrbar, R., Ettner, R., Eyler, E., Garofalo, R., Karasic, D. H., Lev, A. I., … Zucker, K. (2011). Standards of care for the health of transsexual, transgender, and gender-nonconforming people (Version 7). *International Journal of Transgenderism.* doi:10.1080/15532739.2011.700873

Cramwinckel, F. M., Scheepers, D. T., & van der Toorn, J. M. (2018). Interventions to reduce blatant and subtle sexual orientation and gender identity prejudice (SOGIP): Current knowledge and future directions. *Social Issues and Policy Review, 12,* 183–217. doi:10.1111/sipr.12044

Dhoest, A., & Simons, N. (2012). Questioning queer audiences: Exploring diversity in lesbian and gay men's media uses and readings. In K. Ross (Ed.), *The handbook of gender, sex, and media* (pp. 260–276). John Wiley & Sons.

Godsay, S. (2018). Resilience and empowerment in the face of racism: From "resisting the stereotype" to "maintaining a movement" (Doctoral dissertation). ProQuest (No. 10746074).

Goodrich, K. M., Farmer, L. B., Watson, J. C., Davis, R. J., Luke, M. Dispenza, F., Akers, W., & Griffith, C. (2017). Standards of care in assessment of lesbian, gay, bisexual, transgender, gender expansive, and queer: Questioning (LGBTGEQ+) persons. *Journal of LGBT Issues in Counseling, 11*(4), 203–211. doi: 10.1080/15538605.2017.1380548

Green, D. B., Jr. (2019). Hearing the queer roots of Black Lives Matter. https://medium.com/national-center-for-institutional-diversity/hearing-the-queer-roots-of-black-lives-matter-2e69834a65cd

Han, W. C. (2017). The deliberate racism making #gaymediasowhite. *Contexts, 16,* 70–71. doi:10.1177/1536504217742397

Hirschmann, N. J. (2013). Queer/fear: Disability, sexuality and the other. *Journal of Medical Humanities, 34,* 139–147. doi:10.1007/s10912-013-9208-x

Hunter, M. A. (2010). All the gays are White and all the Blacks are straight: Black gay men, identity, and community. *Sexual Research and Social Policy, 7,* 81–92. doi:10.1007/s13178-010-0011-4

Klein, K., Holtby, A., Cook, K., & Travers, R. (2015). Complicating the coming out narrative: Becoming oneself in a heterosexist and cissexist world. *Journal of Homosexuality, 62,* 297–326. doi:10.1080/00918369.2014.970829

Knight, Z. G. (2017). A proposed model of psychodynamic psychotherapy linked to Erik Erikson's eight stages of psychosocial development. *Clinical psychology & psychotherapy, 24*(5), 1047–1058.

McInroy, L. B., & Craig, S. L. (2017). Perspectives of LGBTQ emerging adults on the depiction and impact of LGBTQ media representation. *Journal of Youth Studies, 20*, 32–46. doi:10.1080/13676261.2016.1184243

Murphy, M. J., & Bjorngaard, B. (2019). *Living out loud: An introduction to LGBTQ history, society, and culture.* Routledge.

Nunn, L. M., & Bolt, S. C. (2015). Wearing a rainbow bumper sticker: Experiential learning on homophobia, heteronormativity, and heterosexual privilege. *Journal of LGBT Youth, 12*(3), 276–301.

Oberheim, S., Swank, J., & DePue, M. (2017). Building culturally sensitive assessments for transgender clients: Best practices for instrument development and the adaptation process. *Journal of LGBT Issues in Counseling, 11*(4), 259–270. doi: 10.1080/15538605.2017.1380554

Obradors-Campos, M. (2011). Deconstructing biphobia. *Journal of Bisexuality, 11*, 207–226. doi:10.1080/15299716.2011.571986

O'Flaherty, M., & Fisher, J. (2008). Sexual orientation, gender identity and international human rights law: Contextualising the Yogyakarta principles. *Human Rights Law Review, 8*(2), 207–248.

Saltzburg, S. (2015). Pedagogy for unpacking heterosexist and cisgender bias in social work education in the United States. In *Lesbian, gay, bisexual and trans health inequalities* (pp. 205–222).

Schimanski, I. D., & Treharne, G. J. (2019). Extra marginalisation within the community: Queer individuals' perspectives on suicidality, discrimination and gay pride events. *Psychology & Sexuality, 10*, 31–44. doi: 10.1080/19419899.2018.1524394

Schope, R., & Eliason, M. (2000). Thinking versus acting: Assessing the relationship between heterosexual attitudes and behaviors toward homosexuals. *Journal of Gay and Lesbian Social Services, 11*(4), 69–92.

Sexton, P, Flores, D., & Bauermeister, J. (2018). Young sexual minority women's definition of community: Toward addressing health disparities in the LGBTQQ community. *Journal of Community Psychology, 46*, 133–145.

Shabir, I., Khurana, M. L., Joseph, A. A., Eunice, M., Mehta, M., & Ammini, A. C. (2015). Phenotype, genotype and gender identity in a large cohort of patients from India with 5α-reductase 2 deficiency. *Andrology, 3*(6), 1132–1139.

Smith, L., Foley, P. F., & Chaney, M. P. (2008). Addressing classism, ableism, and heterosexism in counselor education. *Journal of Counseling & Development, 83*, 303–309. doi:10.1002/j.1556-6678.2008.tb00513.x

Smith, L. C., Shin, R. Q., & Officer, L. M. (2012). Moving counseling forward on LGB and transgender issues: Speaking queerly on discourses and microaggressions. *The Counseling Psychologist, 40*(3), 385–408. https://doi.org/10.1177/0011000011403165

Supreme Court of the United States. (2019). Brief of the Southern Poverty Law Center, Children's Defense Fund, Dēmos, Economic Policy Institute, National Association of Social Workers, National Center for Law and Economic Justice, Poverty & Race Research Action Council, and 9to5, National Association of Working Women, as amici curiae in support of the employees (PDF file). https://www.splcenter.org/sites/default/files/2019-07-02_amicus.pdf

Sutter, M., & Perrin, P. B. (2016). Discrimination, mental health, and suicidal ideation among LGBTQ people of color. *Journal of Counseling Psychology, 63,* 98–105. doi:10.1037/cou0000126

Toporek, R. L., Lewis, J. A., & Crethar, H. C. (2009). Promoting systemic change through ACA advocacy competencies. *Journal of Counseling and Development, 87,* 260–268.

U.S. Department of Health and Human Services, Office of Disease Prevention and Health Promotion. (2017). *Healthy People 2020.*

Vacarro, A., & Koob, R. M. (2019). A critical and intersectional model of LGBTQ microaggressions: Toward a more comprehensive understanding. *Journal of Homosexuality, 66,* 1217–1344. doi:10.1080/00918369.018.1539583

Walls, N. E., & Costello, K. (2010). "Head ladies center for teacup chain." Exploring cisgender privilege in a (predominantly) gay male context. In *Explorations in diversity: Examining privilege and oppression in a multicultural society* (pp. 81–93).

Ward, J. (2016). It's not about the gender binary, it's about the gender hierarchy: A reply to "Letting go of the gender binary." *International Review of the Red Cross, 98,* 275–298. doi:10.1017/S1816383117000121

Yalom, I. (2009). *Staring at the sun: Overcoming the terror of death.* Jossey-Bass.

Yarbrough, E. (2018). *Transgender mental health.* American Psychiatric Association Publishing.

## Credits

# Birth and Infancy

Zdravko Rozic, MS

*Love and trust, in the space between what's said and what's heard in
our life, can make all the difference in the world.* —*Fred Rogers*

## Learning Objectives

After reading this chapter, you should be able to
1. Understand physical and cognitive development in newborns and infants.
2. Understand social and emotional development of newborns and infants.
3. Learn how we as counselors can effectively support the development of newborns
   and infants.

## Introduction

As a new parent I was very interested in learning about the development of newborns
and infants. While the reading has given me a good basis of knowledge of what to
expect, it is difficult to put into words the journey new parents undergo while watching

their children grow, develop, and learn new skills. From a counseling perspective, there is not a lot we can directly do with a 4-month-old child. We can determine whether the child is on track in their development, but our work, for the most part, will be in an educational and support role with the caregiver(s). To be able to help caregivers offer a positive environment and stimulation for the child's growth, we must first understand the enormous amount of growth and development that children undergo in their first year of life.

## Key Concepts

- **Developmental Milestones:** Skills that a child develops at a particular age.
- **Sensorimotor Stage:** Piaget's first stage of development from birth to age 2, with four substages.
- **Reflex:** Substage in which a newborn reacts purely involuntarily to external stimuli.
- **Primary Circular Reactions:** Substage in which reflexive behaviors become slowly more voluntary and some behaviors are reproduced.
- **Secondary Circular Reactions:** Substage in which the child's repetition of actions leads to an early understanding of cause and effect.
- **Coordination of Secondary Circular Reactions:** Substage in which the previously learned reactions gain more clarity and the child acts with more intent.
- **Tertiary circular reaction:** Substage in which a child gains object permanence.
- **Symbolic thought:** Substage in which a child engages in symbolic thought, develops problem-solving skills, and engages in imaginative play.
- **Zone of Proximal Development (ZPD):** The space between a child's ability to perform a task with help and the ability to perform it independently.
- **Scaffolding:** A method of teaching a child new skills while offering only as much assistance as necessary.
- **Trust versus Mistrust:** Ericson's first stage of development.
- **Attachment:** Connection between a child and a caregiver.
- **Insecure-Avoidant:** Attachment style in which a child has little reaction toward the caregiver.
- **Secure:** Attachment style in which a child has confidence in the caregiver to provide appropriate nurture and comfort.
- **Ambivalent-Resistant:** Attachment style in which the child exhibits attention-seeking behavior but refuses the caregiver's attempts to comfort.

- **Goodness-of-Fit:** Model that focuses on the fit between a parenting style and the child's disposition.
- **The Easy Child:** Generally shows regular patterns of eating, sleeping, etc. Child adapts easily to new circumstances and has a generally stable mood.
- **The Difficult Child:** Has irregular patterns and reacts negatively to new situations, crying frequently.
- **The Slow-to-Warm-Up Child:** Can have some negative reactions to new situations, but can accept them through repeated exposure. Generally exhibits regular patterns.
- **Child-Centered Play Therapy (CCPT):** A humanist therapeutic approach developed by Virginia Axline.
- **Filial Therapy:** A therapeutic approach in which parents are taught to utilize CCPT principles with their children.

## The Human Developing Process

In the first 2 years of life, children go from being completely helpless and interacting with the environment purely through reflex to being able to walk unassisted and expressing themselves in much more complex ways, including talking. The development that takes place in the first 2 years prepares the child for the next stage of early and middle childhood. One of the main ways we see the child's development is through the use of **developmental milestones**, skills that children develop at different ages. While the age at which children reach milestones can be indicative of future development (Ghassabian et al., 2016; Heineman et al., 2018), it is important to note that the milestones vary both within and between cultures. According to Super and Harkness (2015), the Kipsig people in western Kenya did not teach their babies to crawl because it was perceived as being more dangerous. Thus, crawling, which is considered one of the milestones in the western world, was a rare occurrence among children in this area. So it stands that parental/caretaker involvement and support of child development is instrumental in the child reaching not only the milestones but also their own potential. This shows us, however, that children are much more likely to reach appropriate milestones when they receive support and encouragement from parents/caretakers. Since children spend most of their time with parents/caretakers, our responsibility is to share with caregivers knowledge and skills and support them in taking care of their children to the best of their ability.

As counselors, we must stay cognizant of the fact that parenting is difficult. On average, one in nine women experience postpartum depression (Ko et al., 2017). Parents affected by postpartum depression and/or high levels of stress that are associated with raising a child, in addition to all the other responsibilities of being an adult, may have a difficult time being effective parents. Therefore, it is important to support them in order to help the child thrive. Strategies such as mindfulness, individual and family counseling, support groups, and activities that do not include the child can be very useful. Of course, we always must consider the parents' situation. A single parent without family support might not be able to secure appropriate care for the child to get away for an evening. In such a situation, we should make sure the parent is connected with suitable resources (e.g., local agencies that provide parental support). Assisting them in finding social support through people and/or communities around them can also be extremely helpful. And let us not forget to provide referrals to medical professionals if we believe that they are suffering from depression or other untreated mental health issues.

We can support parents through providing education about how to minimize some of the dangers to the child. Approximately 3,600 children under 1 year of age die suddenly without an obvious cause (Centers for Disease Control and Prevention [CDC], 2020). These deaths are grouped under the term sudden unexpected infant deaths (SUID). There are three types of SUID: sudden infant death syndrome (SIDS), unknown cause, and accidental suffocation and strangulation in bed (ASSB). Rates of SUID dropped most significantly during the 1990s when the American Academy of Pediatrics issued safe sleep recommendations and the Back to Sleep (now Safe to Sleep) campaign was initiated. It is important to acknowledge that there are still stark differences in SUID rates based on race. Native American/Alaska Native and non-Hispanic Black populations have the highest rates of SUID, while Non-Hispanic White, Hispanic, and Asian/Pacific Islander populations have significantly lower numbers. While the causes of SUID are mostly unknown, the CDC has issued some guidelines to help parents and caregivers reduce the risk. The guidelines include the following:

- Placing the baby on their back for all sleep times—naps and at night.
- Using a firm, flat sleep surface, such as a mattress in a safety-approved crib, covered by a fitted sheet.
- Keeping the baby's sleep area (for example, a crib or bassinet) in the same room where parents sleep until the baby is at least 6 months old, or ideally, until the baby is 1 year old.
- Keeping soft bedding such as blankets, pillows, bumper pads, and soft toys out of the baby's sleep area.

- Not covering the baby's head or allowing the baby to get too hot. Signs of the baby getting too hot include their body sweating or their chest feeling hot.

Another opportunity for support occurs even before the child is born. The CDC notes that Fetal alcohol spectrum disorders (FASD) are not a diagnosis in themselves, but a group of conditions that can occur when a mother has been drinking alcohol during pregnancy. The diagnoses which make up FASD are fetal alcohol syndrome (FAS), alcohol-related neurodevelopmental disorder (ARND), alcohol-related birth defects (ARBD), and neurobehavioral disorder associated with prenatal alcohol exposure (ND-PAE). While different FASDs vary in symptoms, some of the possible effects include

- Low body weight
- Poor coordination
- Hyperactive behavior
- Difficulty with attention
- Poor memory
- Difficulty in school (especially with math)
- Learning disabilities
- Speech and language delays
- Intellectual disability or low IQ
- Poor reasoning and judgment skills
- Sleep and sucking problems as a baby
- Vision or hearing problems
- Problems with the heart, kidneys, or bones
- Shorter-than-average height
- Small head size
- Abnormal facial features, such as a smooth ridge between the nose and upper lip (this ridge is called the philtrum)

*(CDC, "Basics about FASDs", Signs and Symptoms)*

FAS is one of the more involved diagnoses, including several physical and developmental factors. The prevalence of FAS in infants measured from medical and other records is somewhere between 2% and 15% for live births (CDC, 2002). Another study, using in-person assessments of school-aged children estimates the number at 6% to 9% (May et al., 2009; May et al., 2014). Since there is no treatment for FASDs and any amount of alcohol can cause a variety of issues, a key part of the intervention is prevention. This involves screening for alcohol use among women who are pregnant (or may become pregnant) and using interventions like motivational interviewing to reduce the risk of FASD.

### PHYSICAL AND COGNITIVE

There are a number of physical and cognitive milestones a child reaches in the first 2 years. According to Piaget (1971), the child during this period is in the first half of the **sensorimotor** stage of development, which is further broken up into four substages. In the first month, the child only acts on **reflex**. Between 1 and 4 months, in the **primary circular reactions** substage, those reflexive behaviors become slowly more voluntary, and some behaviors are reproduced. The **secondary circular reactions** substage develops during the subsequent four months when the child's repetition of actions leads to an early understanding of cause and effect. Between 8 and 12 months, the child experiences the **coordination of secondary circular reactions** substage in which the previously learned reactions gain more clarity and the child acts with more intent. This is also the stage where object permanence is acquired. **Tertiary circular reactions** occur between the ages of 12-18 months and consist of novel ways of interacting with objects. One marker is that a child is able to look for a hidden object in multiple locations. Between the age of 18 months and 2 years, children enter the **symbolic thought** stage in which they become capable of symbolic thought, resulting in the ability to solve problems and engage in make-believe play. Piaget's work has come under scrutiny, in part due to the independence of the child in learning and progressing through the stages. Nevertheless, the stages in the first year seem to correspond to infants' general development.

Vygotsky (1978), on the other hand, focused on the value of learning through interaction with others. He posited the **zone of proximal development (ZPD)**, which can be defined as the space between a child's ability to perform a task with help and the ability to perform it independently. According to Vygotsky, this is the area in which most of the learning occurs, but it is very dependent on social interaction. **Scaffolding** is the tool

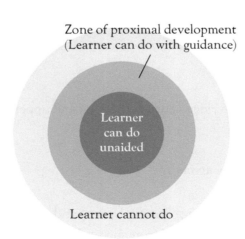

Zone of proximal development
(Learner can do with guidance)

Learner
can do
unaided

Learner cannot do

**FIGURE 5.1**  Vygotsky's Zone of Proximal Development

used to help a child move through the ZPD. Scaffolding is done by offering just enough help to children while still allowing them to push themselves and learn a new skill in the process.

Ultimately, we must stay vigilant about how much importance we place on the child meeting milestones. Not only will the times for reaching them vary throughout cultures, but even within a culture children are all unique and may reach the milestones at their own pace. Some may even skip certain milestones (e.g., a child who never crawls but learns to walk at about the milestone age). That said, missed milestones should prompt us to investigate further and consult to determine whether the child has any medical or developmental issues. When working with parents, it would be useful to share the variability of development. We also must take particular care when working with populations outside of the White, western-dominant culture, as most of the measurement criteria is determined by it. Whether we are working with people of color, immigrants, or any other group outside the dominant culture sphere, we must consider, as noted earlier in the example by Super and Harkness (2015), that different cultures may place value on different milestones. As counselors, we should learn about our clients and from them, how to better serve the population.

One important aspect of physical development is the development of vision. The milestones are integrated in the following list, but since a child cannot express having problems with their vision, difficulties may be harder to recognize. The American Optometric Association (AOA) notes the following signs that may indicate a problem:

- Red or encrusted eyelids could be a sign of an eye infection.
- Constant eye turning may signal a problem with eye muscle control.
- Extreme sensitivity to light may indicate an elevated pressure in the eye.

   *(AOA, n.d., "Infant Vision: Birth to 24 Months of Age," Signs of eye and vision problems)*

Aside from monitoring for the signs, parents can support their child's vision development by adopting a number of strategies that the AOA recommends.

**Birth to 8 months**
- Keep reach-and-touch toys within the baby's focus, about eight to 12 inches.
- Talk to the baby while walking around the room.

- Hang a mobile, crib gym, or various objects across the crib for the baby to grab, pull, and kick.
- Give the baby plenty of time to play and explore on the floor.

**9 months to 2 years**
- Name objects when talking, to encourage the baby's word association and vocabulary development skills.
- Encourage crawling and creeping.
- Roll a ball back and forth to help the child track objects with the eyes visually.

*(AOA, n.d., "Infant Vision: Birth to 24 Months of Age," What parents can do to help with visual development)*

According to the CDC, what follows are the expected milestones for children of various age ranges. As you will note, there is some arbitrariness to how the milestones are grouped and some overlap because certain milestones are harder to categorize then others.

- 2 Months, Physical Milestones
  - Can hold themselves up and begins to push when lying on tummy.
  - Makes smoother movements with arms and legs.
- 2 Months, Cognitive Milestones
  - Pays attention to faces.
  - Follows things with eyes and recognizes people at a distance.
  - Gets bored (cries, fussy) if activities do not change.
- 4 Months, Physical Milestones
  - Holds head steady, unsupported.
  - Pushes down on legs when feet are on a hard surface.
  - May be able to roll over from tummy to back.
  - Can hold a toy, shake it, and swing at dangling toys.
  - Brings hands to mouth.
  - When lying on stomach, pushes up to elbows.
- 4 Months, Cognitive Milestones
  - Demonstrates if happy or sad.
  - Responds to affection.
  - Reaches for toy with one hand.
  - Uses hands and eyes together, such as seeing a toy and reaching for it.
  - Follows moving things with eyes from side to side.

CDC, Milestone Moments, https://www.cdc.gov/ncbddd/actearly/pdf/parents_pdfs/milestonemomentseng508.pdf.

- Watches faces closely.
- Recognizes familiar people and things at a distance.
- 6 Months, Physical Milestones
    - Rolls over in both directions (front to back, back to front).
    - Begins to sit without support.
    - When standing, supports weight on legs and might bounce.
    - Rocks back and forth, sometimes crawling backward before moving forward.
- 6 Months, Cognitive Milestones
    - Looks around at things nearby.
    - Brings things to mouth.
    - Shows curiosity about things and tries to get things that are out of reach.
    - Begins to pass things from one hand to the other.
- 9 Months, Physical Milestones
    - Stands, holding on.
    - Can get into sitting position.
    - Sits without support.
    - Pulls to stand.
    - Crawls.
- 9 Months, Cognitive Milestones
    - Watches the path of something as it falls.
    - Looks for things they see you hide.
    - Plays peek-a-boo.
    - Puts things in their mouth.
    - Moves things smoothly from one hand to the other.
    - Picks up things such as cereal between thumb and index finger (pincer grip).
- 1 Year, Physical Milestones
    - Gets to a sitting position without help.
    - Pulls up to stand, and walks holding on to furniture ("cruising").
    - May take a few steps without holding on.
    - May stand alone.
- 1 Year, Cognitive Milestones
    - Explores things in different ways, such as shaking, banging, throwing.
    - Finds hidden things easily.
    - Looks at the right picture or thing when it's named.
    - Copies gestures.

- Starts to use things correctly; for example, drinks from a cup or brushes hair.
- Bangs two things together.
- Puts things in a container, takes things out of a container.
- Lets things go without help.
- Pokes with index (pointer) finger.
- Follows simple directions such as "pick up the toy."
- 18 Months, Physical Milestones
  - Walks alone.
  - May walk up steps and run.
  - Pulls toys while walking.
  - Can help undress themselves.
  - Drinks from a cup.
  - Eats with a spoon.
- 18 Months, Cognitive Milestones
  - Knows what ordinary things are (e.g., telephone, brush, and spoon).
  - Points to get attention of others.
  - Shows interest in a doll or a stuffed animal by pretending to feed.
  - Points to one body part.
  - Scribbles on their own.
  - Can follow one-step verbal commands without any gestures (e.g., sits when you say "sit down").
- 2 Years, Physical Milestones
  - Stands on tiptoe.
  - Kicks a ball.
  - Begins to run.
  - Climbs onto and down from furniture without help.
  - Walks up and down stairs holding on.
  - Throws ball overhand.
  - Makes or copies straight lines and circles.
- 2 Years, Cognitive Milestones
  - Finds things even when hidden under two or three covers.
  - Begins to sort shapes and colors.
  - Completes sentences and rhymes in familiar books.
  - Plays simple make-believe games.
  - Builds towers of four or more blocks.
  - Might use one hand more than the other.

- Follows two-step instructions like "Pick up your shoes, and put them in the closet."
- Names items in a picture book such as cat, bird, or dog.

*(CDC, "Important Milestones," Milestone Moments.)*

## SOCIAL AND EMOTIONAL

As noted earlier, the distinction between the types of milestones is somewhat arbitrary, but it helps us contextualize different aspects of development in a more manageable way. As with meeting physical and cognitive milestones, the interaction through play and verbal stimulation with parents/caregivers is key to developing healthy social and emotional skills (Mendelsohn et al., 2018; Page et al., 2010). According to Erikson, the first stage during infancy is **trust versus mistrust**. Here the child learns whether the world around the individual is safe and whether it will meet their needs. If the needs are met, the child develops a basic sense of trust in both the world and also in the surrounding caregivers. Bowlby (1952), who noted that the children he observed generally had a primary attachment figure, described attachment between a child and caregivers. Ainsworth constructed a test for attachment called the "strange situation" and was able to identify the following three main **attachment styles** associated with the interaction style between the child and caregiver(s) (Ainsworth & Bell, 1970).

- **Insecure-Avoidant:** Grows out of rejection of the child by the primary caregiver. This is associated with social and emotional behavior problems as children develop.
- **Secure Attachment:** When the child feels confident, the caregiver will provide help and nurturance when needed.
- **Ambivalent-Resistant:** When a child exhibits attention-seeking behaviors but rejects the caretaker when they try to interact.

The CDC has language/communication milestones as a separate list. Here we have combined it with social and emotional milestones; however, it could just as easily be considered part of cognitive development or even a separate track of its own. One major consideration in language development is that for children growing up in households where two or more languages are spoken, speaking may be slightly delayed as they process understanding multiple languages. It should still occur within normal age range (Bahtia & Ritchie, 2013). If the speech is significantly delayed, proper steps should be taken to determine the cause. Due to an expectation of delayed language acquisition, bilingual children are often tested in a simplified manner that places them in danger of having an undiagnosed language disorder (Nayeb et al., 2015). Generally, bilingual infants experience broad cognitive benefits (Singh et al., 2015).

- 2 Months, Social and Emotional Milestones
  - Begins to smile at people.
  - Can briefly calm self (may bring hands to mouth and suck on hand).
  - Tries to look at parent.
  - Coos, makes gurgling sounds.
  - Turns head toward sounds.
- 4 Months, Social and Emotional Milestones
  - Smiles spontaneously, especially at people.
  - Likes to play with people and might cry when playing stops.
  - Copies some movements and facial expressions, such as smiling or frowning.
  - Begins to babble.
  - Babbles with expression and copies sounds heard.
  - Cries in different ways to show hunger, pain, or being tired.
- 6 Months, Social and Emotional Milestones
  - Knows familiar faces and begins to know if someone is a stranger.
  - Likes to play with others, especially parents.
  - Responds to other people's emotions and often seems happy.
  - Likes to look at self in a mirror.
  - Responds to sounds by making sounds.
  - Strings vowels together when babbling ("ah," "eh," "oh") and likes taking turns with parent while making sounds.
  - Responds to own name.
  - Makes sounds to show joy and displeasure.
  - Begins to say consonant sounds (jabbering with "m," "b").
- 9 Months, Social and Emotional Milestones
  - May be afraid of strangers.
  - May be clingy with familiar adults.
  - Has favorite toys.
  - Understands "no."
  - Makes a lot of different sounds such as "mamamama" and "babababababa."
  - Copies sounds and gestures of others.
  - Uses fingers to point at things.

- 1 Year, Social and Emotional Milestones
  - Is shy or nervous with strangers.
  - Cries when mom or dad leaves.
  - Has favorite things and people.
  - Shows fear in some situations.
  - Hands you a book when wanting to hear a story.
  - Repeats sounds or actions to get attention.
  - Puts out an arm or leg to help with dressing.
  - Plays games such as peekaboo and pat-a-cake.
  - Responds to simple spoken requests.
  - Uses simple gestures, such as shaking head no or waving bye-bye.
  - Makes sounds with changes in tone (sounds more like speech).
  - Says "mama" and "dada" and exclamations such as "uh-oh!"
  - Tries to say words you say.
- 18 Months, Social and Emotional Milestones
  - Likes to hand things to others as play.
  - May have temper tantrums.
  - May be afraid of strangers.
  - Shows affection to familiar people.
  - Plays simple pretend such as feeding a doll.
  - May cling to caregivers in new situations.
  - Points to show others something interesting.
  - Explores alone but with parent close by.
  - Says several single words.
  - Says and shakes head no
  - Points to show wants.
- 2 Years, Social and Emotional Milestones
  - Copies others, especially adults and older children.
  - Gets excited when with other children.
  - Shows more and more independence.
  - Shows defiant behavior (doing what they were told not to).
  - Plays mainly beside other children, but is beginning to include other children, such as in chase games.
  - Points to things or pictures when named.
  - Knows names of familiar people and body parts.
  - Says sentences with two to four words.
  - Follows simple instructions.

- Repeats words overheard in conversation.
- Points to things in a book.

## Theoretical Considerations

There are a number of theories that attempt to explain and describe the development of a child in all the various areas. Here we will cover a few of the most well-known theories. Erikson's stages of development, Piaget's theory of cognitive development, Vygotsky's social cultural theory, Bowlby's attachment theory, Thomas and Chess's goodness-of-fit model, and filial therapy. This is only a small sampling of a variety of theories that have helped grow the understanding of child therapy. Therapists working with infants are generally specialists and will find evidence-based theoretical approaches that are appropriate for the population.

### ERIKSON

Erikson's stages of psychosocial development (Erikson et al., 1959) state that the first stage in a child's development is trust versus mistrust. During the first 2 years of life, the child determines whether the surrounding world is a safe place and whether their needs are being met. If the stage is resolved positively, the child develops trust in the world; if not, the child sees the world as an insecure place.

### PIAGET

Piaget's theory is based on stages of development. Children move sequentially through four universal stages.

1. **Sensorimotor:** Birth to 2 years
2. **Preoperational:** 2–7 years
3. **Concrete Operational:** 7–12 years
4. **Formal Operational:** 12+ years

The sensorimotor stage is further broken down into six substages.

1. **Reflexes (0–1 month):** Child mostly interacts with the world through reflexive behaviors.
2. **Primary Circular Reactions (1–4 months):** Child sheds purely reflexive action and starts to repeat some pleasurable behaviors.

3.  **Secondary Circular Reactions (4–8 months):** Child becomes more aware of the surrounding world and starts to act with intent.

4.  **Coordination of Reactions (8–12 months):** Child acts with intent and starts combining schemas to achieve goals. The child also starts imitating observed behaviors and recognizing objects for their qualities.

5.  **Tertiary circular reaction (12–18 months):** Child gains object permanence, imitates behaviors of others, and understands properties of objects.

6.  **Symbolic thought (18–24 months):** Child engages in symbolic thought, develops problem-solving skills, and engages in imaginative play.

## VYGOTSKY

Vygotsky's (1978) CHAT theory was very broad, but some of the more salient aspects for child development focused on the importance of social interactions to learning and development. The **zone of proximal development (ZPD)** is the space between what the child can do for oneself and what can be accomplished with assistance. The caregivers use **scaffolding** to help the child bridge this gap. In scaffolding, the caregiver provides only enough assistance to help the child accomplish the task, while allowing the child to still build new skills in the process.

## ATTACHMENT

Bowlby's theory of attachment (1952) was tested by Ainsworth and Bell (1970) using the strange situation experiment. They identified three attachment styles:

*   **Insecure-avoidant** (Type A) grows out of rejection of the child by the primary caregiver. This is associated with social and emotional behavior problems as children develop.
*   **Secure** (Type B) attachment occurs when the child feels confident the caregiver will provide help and nurturance when needed.
*   **Ambivalent-resistant** (Type C) is when a child exhibits attention-seeking behaviors but rejects the caretaker when he or she tries to interact.

## GOODNESS-OF-FIT MODEL

This model was developed by Thomas and Chess (1977). Through a large number of assessments, they posited that children fall into the following three categories:

*   **The easy child** generally shows regular patterns of eating, sleeping, etc. The child adapts easily to new circumstances and has a generally stable mood.

- **The difficult child** has irregular patterns and reacts negatively to new situations, crying frequently.
- **The slow-to-warm-up child** can have negative reactions to new situations but can accept them through repeated exposure. The child has generally regular patterns.

The core of the model argues that the key to the child's development is the fit between the parenting style and the child's disposition. The therapist's goal is to help parents determine the right parenting approach for their child.

## FILIAL THERAPY

Filial therapy is based on child-centered play therapy (CCPT) developed by Virginia Axline (1947, 1969). Axline noted eight key principles of CCPT:

1. The therapist must develop a warm, friendly relationship with the child to establish rapport.
2. The therapist accepts the child exactly as he or she is.
3. The therapist establishes an atmosphere of acceptance so that the child feels free to express personal feelings completely.
4. The therapist recognizes the feelings the child is expressing and reflects them back to the child to communicate understanding.
5. The therapist maintains a deep respect for the child's ability to solve their problems if given an opportunity to do so.
6. The child "leads the way." The therapist does not attempt to direct the child's actions or conversation in any manner.
7. The therapist recognizes that play therapy is a gradual process and does not attempt to hurry the child.
8. The therapist establishes only those limitations necessary to anchor the therapy to the world of reality and to make the child aware of their responsibility in the relationship.

The main aspect of filial therapy is that instead of directly working with the child, the therapist teaches parents how to conduct child-centered play sessions with their child. The idea is that the parents have a much stronger effect on the child than the therapist. It also serves to change the interactional patterns between the child and parents. While the child becomes more confident and responsible, parents become more open to the child's motivations and independence (Ginsberg, 2012). As lined out by Ginsberg (2012), the basic phases of filial therapy are

- Thorough understanding of the presenting issue relevant to the child's development and family dynamics. This will typically include a family play observation.
- Parents are informed of the principles and methods of filial therapy, gain an understanding and confidence in this approach and how it meets their needs and interests, and form a collaborative relationship with the whole family.
- Play-session demonstration (therapist holds child-centered play sessions with each child while parents observe).
- Training (therapist can use mock play sessions with prompting, modeling, reinforcement, and shaping to improve parents' comfort and skill).
- Supervised parent–child play sessions, followed by therapist's feedback and discussion with parents.
- Discussion of play themes, parent reactions, family dynamics, and problem solving with parents.
- Home play sessions, with parents reporting the results regularly to the therapist.
- Generalization of skills.
- Maintenance of play sessions and skills over time
- Therapist shifts to a consulting relationship with the family.

While filial therapy is generally employed with older children, it can also be used with children in the first year of life.

## Strengths and Challenges from the "ISMs" Perspectives

There are a lot of things to consider when working with infants and their caregivers. One of the major concerns would be evaluating the child's development through a cultural lens. We must consider the culturally appropriate development milestones and understand that they may be different than the milestones we generally look for. At the same time, we should be careful not to dismiss an issue simply because we believe it is within norm. The best way to help the child grow is to help the parents through interventions such as referrals to counseling or agencies that help parents deal with the stress of raising a child. Classes can teach parents what their child is doing and why, and help them be more effective in their parenting styles. Approaches such as filial therapy may be most effective because they change the interaction between parents and children; however, we also must stay mindful that they may not be appropriate in all circumstances. Some cultures may not welcome the child-led play interactions that are the core of CCPT and filial therapy. Some parents may want a more practical and straightforward approach to solving their problems. It is up to us to learn about, and from, our clients and figure out how to best help them in the manner they want us to help. In some situations we may have to refer out and accept that we are not best suited to help a particular client.

The research on child development is always growing and becoming more diverse. The bulk of it, however, is still based on the middle-class, White majority population. We must consider this when working with underrepresented populations. This includes underrepresented groups based not only on race, but also considering economic, gender, sexual orientation, ability, age, etc. All these conditions present unique challenges for parents and children in the first year of life and beyond. In some instances we may act more as a caseworker, connecting the client with resources and orchestrating care. Other times we may take a more psychoeducational role. Some clients may need emotional support to get through the difficult task of raising a child and dealing with the loss of their old life. In all situations, our main goal is the well-being of those who entrust themselves and their loved ones into our care.

## Summary

In the first 2 years of life, children grow and develop at an incredible pace. This break-neck pace of development can overwhelm parents as new skills seemingly develop daily and a child's needs are constantly changing. The milestones are still the best gauge of whether the child is developing properly or whether extra support and care is needed. We must, however, stay vigilant of over-interpreting small deviations and maintain awareness of different cultural expectations. During this time the child develops both a view of the world as safe or unsafe and also an attachment style toward the primary caregiver(s). The attachment styles can have consequences for the child's future functioning and development. Often, we will have to work through parents to help the child. This may include offering psychoeducation, referrals, and emotional support, and approaches such as filial therapy to engage the parents in the child's treatment. Any intervention we utilize should consider the family's unique situation and cultural beliefs to effectively help them.

## CASE #1

Billy is a 9-month-old White boy who was placed with a foster family after being severely neglected by his biological parents. Billy's biological parents would leave him alone in his crib for long stretches of time while they used heroin. After a report to CPS, Billy was found malnourished and dirty in his crib. Billy was 7 months old at that time. Since being placed with a foster family, Billy has gained weight and is receiving proper care. Billy barely makes any sounds, and he mostly sits and plays alone with the toys around him; he rarely interacts with his foster parents or anyone else. He rarely cries, and when he does, it is very hard to determine the cause. Any attempts by the foster parents to comfort him fail, and he eventually stops crying by himself. The foster parents are having a hard time dealing with Billy and have expressed that they believe he is being difficult on purpose.

1.  What are some theories that might be useful in understanding Billy's development and possible issues?
2.  How would you approach working with Billy?
    a.  Would you work with him one-on-one or involve the foster parents?
    b.  Are there any particular theoretical approaches you would implement or specific strategies you would attempt?
3.  How can you advocate for Billy?

## CASE #2

Maria is an 11-month-old girl. Her father is White, and her mother Latina. Maria lives with her parents and maternal grandmother, who cares for Maria while the parents are at work. The grandmother speaks only Spanish, but the parents speak mostly English with each other and to Maria when at home. Maria is developmentally on track, except for her vocal expression. At her last doctor's visit, a 10-month wellness check, it was noted that she rarely babbles and still only makes vowel sounds. The parents were reassured that because Maria is hearing and learning multiple languages, the speech will probably be delayed, and they were encouraged to give her more time. According to the pediatrician, Maria will eventually catch up and be fine. The doctor did not see any reason for further concern and or additional testing.

1.  What, if any, are the main concerns when looking at Maria's development?
2.  How would you approach Maria's treatment?
3.  What are some opportunities for advocacy on Maria's behalf?

## Reflections and Targeted Discussion Questions

1.  How would you approach working with parents who are asking for help dealing with a newborn?
2.  A parent of a 6-month-old claims the child does things on purpose to annoy him. How do you intervene to help the parent and the child?
3.  A parent expresses concern that her 4-month-old child is still not able to roll over. How do you address her concerns? Are there any specific actions you should take?
4.  A 9-month-old is brought in by the parents who are concerned that he started crying and was scared of his grandfather. The grandfather does not live locally and has visited infrequently. How do you address the parents' concerns?
5.  The parents of an 8-month-old are concerned the child is taking too long to learn things. They take the approach that the child should just figure things out for herself but are concerned she is learning too slowly. What are some possible ways you can help them support the child's learning?
6.  The mother of a 10-month-old child states that she is having a difficult time interacting with her son. According to the mother, all the interactions center around correcting behaviors and frustrating attempts to feed, change, or put her son to sleep. What are your considerations in working with this client?
7.  In your first session with an 11-month-old, the child immediately approaches you, climbs in your lap, and cuddles up to you. What would your next considerations be in assessing this child?
8.  The parent of a 4-month-old notes that she has been feeling a bit down since she had the baby. She is worried she is not being a good mom because she doesn't really know what she's doing. She's also concerned because she doesn't think that she feels about the baby the way she's supposed to. She just sees the baby as something that requires care and doesn't feel the love everyone expects her to feel. Occasionally, she gets angry and is worried she may cause harm to the baby. She's also been crying a lot when alone. What are your initial thoughts? What are some steps you can take?

## References

Ainsworth, M. D. S., & Bell, S. M. (1970). Attachment, exploration, and separation: Illustrated by the behavior of one-year-olds in a strange situation. *Child Development, 41(1)*, 49–67. https://doi-org.jpllnet.sfsu.edu/10.2307/1127388

American Optometric Association. (n.d.). *Infant Vision: Birth to 24 Months of Age.* https://www.aoa.org/healthy-eyes/eye-health-for-life/infant-vision?sso=y

Axline, V. (1947). *Play therapy.* Houghton Mifflin.

Axline, V. (1969). *Play therapy* (rev. ed.). Ballantine Books.

Bahtia, T. K., & Ritchie, W. C. (2013). *The Handbook of bilingualism and multilingualism.* Blackwell Publishing.

Bowlby, J. (1952). *Maternal care and mental health.* Shocken.

Centers for Disease Control and Prevention (CDC). (2002). Fetal alcohol syndrome—Alaska, Arizona, Colorado, and New York, 1995-1997. *Morbidity and Mortality Weekly Report: MMWR, 51*(20), 433–435.

Centers for Disease Control and Prevention. (2020, April 29). About SUID and SIDS. https://www.cdc.gov/sids/about/index.htm?CDC_AA_refVal=https%3A%2F%2Fwww.cdc.gov%2Fsids%2FAboutSUIDandSIDS.htm

Center for Disease Control and Prevention. (2021, March 31). Important milestones: milestone Moments. https://www.cdc.gov/ncbddd/actearly/milestones/milestones-2yr.html

Erikson, E. H., Paul, I. H., Heider, F., & Gardner, R. W. (1959). *Psychological issues.* International Universities Press.

Ghassabian, A., Sundaram, R., Bell, E., Bello, S., Kus, C., & Yeung, E. (2016). Gross motor milestones and subsequent development. *Pediatrics, 138*(1). e20154372; https://doi.org/10.1542/peds.2015-4372

Ginsberg, B. G. (2012). Filial therapy: An attachment based, emotion focused, and skill training approach. *VISTAS Online.* https://www.counseling.org/docs/default-source/vistas/filial-therapy-an-attachment-based-emotion-focused-and-skill.pdf?sfvrsn=dedfaa57_12

Heineman, K. R., Schendelaar, P., Van den Heuvel, E. R., & Hadders-Algra, M. (2018). Motor development in infancy is related to cognitive function at 4 years of age. *Developmental Medicine & Child Neurology, 60*(11), 1149–1155. doi:10.1111/dmcn.13761

Ko, J. Y., Rockhill, K. M., Tong, V. T., Morrow B., & Farr S. L. (2017). Trends in postpartum depressive symptoms—27 states, 2004, 2008, and 2012. *Morbidity and Mortality Weekly Report, 66,* 153–158. http://dx.doi.org/10.15585/mmwr.mm6606a1

May, P. A., Baete, A., Russo, J., Elliott, A. J., Blankenship, J., Kalberg, W. O., Buckley, D., Brooks, M., Hasken, J., Abdul-Rahman, O., Adam, M. P., Robinson, L. K., Manning, M., & Hoyme, H. E. (2014). Prevalence and characteristics of fetal alcohol spectrum disorders. *Pediatrics, 134*(5), 855–866. https://doi.org/10.1542/peds.2013-331

May, Philip A, Gossage, J Phillip, Kalberg, Wendy O, Robinson, Luther K, Buckley, David, Manning, Melanie, & Hoyme, H Eugene. (2009). Prevalence and epidemiologic characteristics of FASD from various research methods with an emphasis on recent in-school studies. *Developmental Disabilities Research Reviews., 15*(3), 176–192. https://doi.org/10.1002/ddrr.68

Mendelsohn, A. L., Brockmeyer Cates, C., Weisleader, A., Berkule Johnson, S., Seery, A. M., Canfield, C. F., Huberman, H. S., & Dreyer, B. P. (2018). Reading aloud, play, and social-emotional development. *Pediatrics, 141*(5), e20173393. https://doi.org/10.1542/peds.2017-3393

Nayeb, L., Wallby, T., Westerlund, M., Salameh, E.-K., & Sarkadi, A. (2015). Child healthcare nurses believe that bilingual children show slower language development, simplify screening procedures and delay referrals. *Acta Paediatrica, 104*(2), 198–205. https://doi-org.jpllnet.sfsu.edu/10.1111/apa.12834

Page, M., Wilhelm, M. S., Gamble, W. C., & Card, N. A. (2010). A comparison of maternal sensitivity and verbal stimulation as unique predictors of infant social–emotional and cognitive development. *Infant Behavior and Development, 33*(1), 101–110. https://doi.org/10.1016/j.infbeh.2009.12.001

Piaget, J. (1971). *Mental imagery in the child: A study of the development of imaginal representation.* Routledge and Kegan Paul.

Singh, L., Fu, C. S. L., Rahman, A. A., Hameed, W. B., Sanmugam, S., Agarwal, P., Jiang, B., Chong, Y. S., Meaney, M. J., & Rifkin-Graboi, A. (2015). Back to basics: A bilingual advantage in infant visual habituation. *Child Development, 86*(1), 294–302. doi:10.1111/cdev.12271

Super, C. M., & Harkness, S. (2015). Charting infant development: Milestones along the way. In L. A. Jensen (Ed.), *The Oxford handbook of human development and culture: An interdisciplinary perspective.* Oxford University Press. doi:10.1093/oxfordhb/9780199948550.013.6

Thomas, A., & Chess, S. (1977). *Temperament and development.* Brunner/Mazel.

Vygotsky, L. S., Cole, M., John-Steiner, V., Scribner, S., & Souberman, E. (1978). *Mind in society: The development of higher psychological processes.* Harvard University Press.

## Credit

# Early Childhood Development

Dianne Parr, PhD, and Noréal F. Armstrong, PhD

*Children are not things to be molded, but are people to be unfolded.*
    —*Jess Lair*

## Learning Objectives

After reading this chapter, you should be able to

1. Explain developmental expected performances for each age range based on milestones that are identified for physical and cognitive development.
2. Identify distinguishing levels of performance and capabilities for each age range.
3. Demonstrate an understanding of various factors that affect early childhood development.

## Introduction

Humans are a unique species, and understanding the developing process can be complex and may be addressed in several ways. The human developing process can be explained from a plethora of perspectives, depending on theory or combination of theories being applied. Some theorists may propose the developing process in terms of direction, from birth to death or reaching milestones. Others focus on the processes of growth. And still other theorists chart the course of development as a hierarchy of stages. This chapter will address the human developing processes from a variety of perspectives. The simplest form of studying life-span development is classifying children's development by age group; therefore, the focus of this chapter is early childhood, beginning at age 2 and continuing to age 5.

## Key Concepts

- **Milestone:** Defined as a significant point in progress or development. In addition, the chapter will include a discussion on nature, hereditary versus nurture, and environmental influences.
- **Attention:** Defined as cognition and sensory assessments that conjunctively process information of our environment.
- **Attention Network Approach:** Consists of three distinct networks—alerting, orienting, and executive attention.
- **Encoding:** Changing sensory input information into a form that the system can cope with for storage.
- **Storage:** The process of where, how long, how much, and what kind of information is kept for later retrieval.
- **Retrieval:** The process of getting information out of storage.
- **Generic Memory:** Includes helping the child recall routines that occur.
- **Episodic Memory:** Unique or specific major experiences or events that the child can recall on his or her own at some point in the future.

## The Human Developing Process: Ages 2 to 4

### PHYSICAL MILESTONES

Every child is different, but as a developmental group, young children are often normed as toddlers to address the skills expected to develop. The toddler is a child between age 2 and 4. Milestones begin to develop in 2-year-old children and are generally completed by the end of their third year. Gross motor skills describe development of big muscles, while fine motor skills involve development of small muscle movements. In summary, the average child grows and develops quickly from birth to age 4 years.

As children develop **gross motor skills,** they may be able to

- Walk, run, and learn to jump with both feet.
- Pull or carry toys while walking.
- Throw and kick a ball and try to catch with both hands.
- Climb on furniture and playground equipment.
- Ascend stairs while holding the railing, and may alternate feet.
- Stand on tiptoes and balance one foot.

As children develop **fine motor skills,** they may be able to

- Pull pants up and down.
- Build a block tower of at least four blocks.
- Hold utensils and crayons with fingers instead of a fist, though the grasp may not be quite right.
- Start practicing with snaps and zippers.
- Turn the water faucet to wash hands.

## COGNITIVE MILESTONES

Children may begin to start thinking in new ways and learning skills and techniques to solve problems. This may include pretending or playing with items that are not traditional toys, such empty boxes, pots and pans, or other items within their reach in the home environment.

Other cognitive milestones may include

- Solving three- to four-piece puzzles.
- Grouping toys by size, color, or type.
- Reciting favorite phrases from books or nursery rhymes, or singing simple songs with the parent or childcare provider.
- Following simple two-step directions.

## LANGUAGE MILESTONES

At the end of the third year, most children have increased vocabulary and understand much of what is said to them but are not always able to follow directions. Regarding communication skills, understanding language is more important for the young child than speaking it. When children understand, children will communicate. The toddler's first communication is usually labels for names of people, animals, or things that are important to the child. Young children usually understand, then they communicate; however, they will imitate what they hear, learn new words daily, begin making sentences with the words they know, and be willing to communicate with the language skills they have.

FIGURE 6.1    Example of children learning language and mimicking communication styles.

At this age, most children can

- Understand the words for familiar people, everyday objects, and body parts.
- Recognize their name and refer to self by name.
- Understand and use the word no.
- Ask for drinks or snacks.
- Understand simple questions and commands.
- Name pictures and actions.
- Use a variety of single words by 18 months, speak in sentences of two to four words by age 2 years, and have a 200-plus-word vocabulary by 3 years.
- Repeat words they hear.
- Have a two- to three-sentence conversation with self, toys, and people.
- Begin to ask "what's that?" and "why?" to get more information.
- Begin to use plurals and basic pronouns (me, you), but grammar may not be correct.
- Tell their name, the name of one friend, and the names of some common objects.

# Children 4 Years of Age

Children in the 4-year-old age group may show physical, cognitive, and language differences when compared with younger children. Physical milestones include growing taller and gaining about 5 pounds.

## PHYSICAL DEVELOPMENT

Gross motor skills include

- Controlling movement more easily; start, stop, turn, and go around obstacles while running.
- Doing various movements, such as a log roll, somersaults, and trot.
- Throwing and bouncing a ball.
- Jumping over objects and climbing ladders.
- Peddling and steering a tricycle or bike.
- Dressing themselves with minimal help (zippers, snaps, and buttons may still be hard for them).

Fine motor skills may include

- Drawing or copying basic shapes and crosses (milestones known as "crossing the midline").
- Writing some letters.
- Stacking a tower at least 10 blocks high.
- Stringing beads or O-shaped cereal to make necklaces.
- Pinching or shaping clay or playdough into recognizable objects.

## COGNITIVE MILESTONES

During this year, children begin to think and learn beyond the basics of their immediate environment. At 4 years children begin to think and understand things they cannot see or touch and express their own ideas.

Cognitive milestones include

- Understanding the difference between real and make-believe.
- Understanding that pictures and symbols stand for real things.
- Exploring relationships between ideas, using "if" and "when" to express them.
- Starting to think in logical steps, seeing how to do things and consequences.
- Beginning to understand abstract ideas such as size and time, including bigger, more, less, later, and soon.
- Putting things in order, such as biggest to smallest or shortest to longest.
- Sticking with an activity for 10 to 15 minutes.

## LANGUAGE MILESTONES

Language development increases exponentially during this year, which may include increasing vocabulary. At age 4, children may have a vocabulary of 1,000 words and use complex sentences that combine more than one thought. Children at this age begin to ask questions, using who, what, when, where, and why, and may be able to answer some of these questions as well.

A 4-year-old's milestones include

- Singing silly songs, making up goofy words, and practicing rhyming.
- Following simple, unrelated directions.
- Changing speech patterns depending on who the child is conversing with, which may include using short sentences with younger siblings while using longer sentences with adults.
- Asking for a definition of unfamiliar words.
- Making up stories about their thoughts.
- Arguing, even when the argument may not be logical.

## SPEECH DEVELOPMENT

The development of speech in the toddler has a broad range of variance from birth to age 6. Speech intelligibility guidelines are general and change based on numerous factors. Speech and sound development guidelines are used to determine a child's readiness to produce the required sounds, based on norms of children in the same age group (Hanks, 2010).

General guidelines for understanding speech are

- Child's speech is normally 25% intelligible by 18 months.
- Child's speech is normally 50% to 75% intelligible by 24 months.
- Child's speech is normally 75% to 100% intelligible by 36 months.

# Children 5 Years or Kindergarten Age

At 5 years old children must master many milestones to be ready for school at the kindergarten level. As kindergartners, children begin to understand many things about the world in which they live and show these understandings in their normal activities.

## PHYSICAL DEVELOPMENT

Gross motor skills include

- Catching a ball the size of a softball.
- Moving actively without tripping over their own feet.
- Being active as kindergartners—usually hop, skip, jump, and dance.
- Walking on tiptoes and heel-to-toe such as on a balance beam.
- Beginning to move in different ways at the same time to do things such as dribbling a ball, dancing, or swimming.

Fine motor skills include

- Using one hand more than the other or developing hand dominance.
- Holding a pencil using a tripod grip or two fingers and a thumb.
- Cutting out basic shapes with scissors; may be able to cut in a straight line.
- Using a fork, spoon, and a knife easily.
- Being able to wipe and wash after using the bathroom.

## COGNITIVE MILESTONES

- Recognizing names of colors and basic shapes.
- Knowing the letters of the alphabet and the letter sounds.
- Reciting their name, address, and phone number.
- Understanding the basic concepts about print on a page, such as the direction of the pages and how words are read from left to right and top to bottom.
- Knowing that stories have a beginning, middle, and end.
- Counting groups of objects up to 10 and reciting numbers up to 20.
- Retaining focus on an activity for 15 minutes and completing a short project.
- Making plans about how to play, what to build, or what to draw.

## LANGUAGE MILESTONES

- Understanding and using thousands of words in sentences that are five to eight words long.
- Using words to argue, trying to reason with people, and tending to use the word "because" often.
- Using most plurals, pronouns, and tenses correctly.
- Understanding simple puns; can tell stories, jokes, and riddles.
- Using language to talk about opposites and making comparisons with simple things.
- Following simple multistep directions.

- Recognizing common words and may begin reading three-letter words.
- Talking about experiences that occurred and those that are going to occur.

### SPEECH MILESTONES

- Speaking clearly enough so that most people understand.
- Answering simple questions, which include yes and no questions and questions about their daily activities.
- Showing interest and starting conversations.
- Taking turns talking and keeping a conversation going.

## Social and Emotional

Understanding children's social and emotional development facilitates information on each individual's ability to address change and stability. Moreover, the beginnings of emotions, personality, and social relationships occur during the early developmental years and continue to influence the individual's self-esteem, social fit, cognitive functioning, and physical capabilities (Papalia et al., 2007; Olds, Feldman, & Gross, 2007). Emotional well-being and social competence are foundations for emerging cognitive skills and necessities for success in school and later in life (Center on the Developing Child, 2007). Development is an integrated process that helps us understand the person as a whole.

Social and emotional development for 2-year-old children may depend on many factors and include many of the following behaviors. When children reach the toddler stage, they usually become more independent and show an interest in other children. Child development is different for each child; therefore, 2-year-old children may not have mastered enough language to express themselves and may tend to be irritated or upset by this inability. Children at this age may exhibit some of the following behaviors (Papalia et al., 2007):

- Mimicking other children or adult behaviors, speech, and inflection.
- Being happy to play near, if not with, other children.
- Beginning to realize they can do things without help.
- Disobeying directions more than previously, which includes doing things they are told not to do to test the boundaries and see what might happen.
- Having tantrums when frustrated.
- Possibly showing separation anxiety, but by the end of age 2 becoming more independent and aware of self.

Children between the ages of 3 and 4 years continue to develop social and emotional behaviors. The social and emotional behaviors common for this age group include

- Starting to show and communicate a wider range of emotions.
- Beginning to play with other children.
- Enjoying pretend play but often confusing real and make-believe.
- Still displaying tantrums because of changes in routine or not getting what they want.
- Showing spontaneous kindness and caring traits.

Children between the ages of 5 and 6 experience a wide range of social and emotional development. The social and emotional behaviors common for this age group include

- Being aware of their gender; may choose to play with same-sex peers.
- Enjoying playing with peers and being more conversational and independent.
- Testing boundaries while being eager to please and help others.
- Beginning to understand what it means to be embarrassed.

## Scientific Contributions

Scientific contributions to the study of life-span development often begin with researching early child development. Neuroscience research on the brain has indicated that early experiences do influence how well the individual's mental faculties' function in learning, health, and behaviors (Center on the Developing Child, 2007). This early neurodevelopment can be stable or fragile, which has major implications for the individual throughout the life span. Some of the scientific contributions will be discussed in this section of the chapter.

### LEARNING WITH OPERANT AND CLASSICAL CONDITIONING

How children learn is another facet of early childhood development. Major scientific contributions for learning were the result of classical and operant conditioning research. In research of dogs' digestive processes in response to various incentives, a Russian physiologist, Ivan Pavlov, accidentally developed what is known as the **classical conditioning theory**. Pavlov experimented with dogs, whom he trained to salivate at the sound of a bell. At the dog's feeding time, Pavlov rang a bell and fed the dog. After repeated pairings of the bell (controlled stimulus) and food (stimulus), the dog began to salivate (respond) at the sound of the bell. Classical conditioning is learning based on pairing a stimulus or an incentive that does not usually produce a response with another stimulus/incentive that does produce the response (Papalia et al., 2007). Learning happens over time as gradual exposures with the neutral stimulus occur. The stimulus used is the conditioned stimulus and the response or learned behavior is the conditioned response (Juneja, 2015). John Watson, an America behaviorist, studied classical conditioning, or the stimulus response theory, with children (Papalia et al., 2007). Watson trained an 11-month-old infant boy, Little Albert, to be afraid of "furry white objects." Little Albert was exposed to a loud noise that made him cry just before being allowed to touch the furry white rat. After repeated loud noise pairings with the white rat, Little Albert cried in fear at the sight of the rat. The classical conditioning theory led to further studies on the impact of conditioning on learning behaviors.

**Operant conditioning** is learning based on reinforcement or punishment (Juneja, 2015). B. F. Skinner, considered the Father of Operant Conditioning, experimented with connecting the causes of behaviors with the consequence of the behavior. **Reinforcement** strengthens acceptable behaviors to increase their occurrence, while **punishment** weakens the unwanted or undesired behavior. The reinforcement schedule can be manipulated in varying intervals or fixed intervals to enhance or decrease the occurrence of the behaviors. Initially, Skinner worked with rats and pigeons, but conducted research with humans to support his theory. Rooted in the simplistic classical conditioning, Skinner's research focused on the complex observable behaviors of humans, rather than internal mental events and involuntary behavior. Skinner posited that reinforcement could be positive or negative. **Negative reinforcement** is taking away unwanted, aversive, or disliked things or experiences to encourage repeating the preferred behavior. Negative reinforcement may be confused with punishment. Punishment suppresses behaviors by using aversive experience to decrease repeating the non-preferred behavior. If behaviors are not reinforced, the behavior will eventually **extinguish** or not occur. Skinner was a front-runner in the study of operant conditioning and its impact on learning behaviors (Papalia et al., 2007).

American psychologist, Albert Bandura, developed social learning or social cognitive theory. Bandura theorized that development is intrinsic and comes from learning by observation (Broderick & Blewitt, 2020). Observational learning or modeling occurs when the individual watches another person's behavior and learns to duplicate the observed behavior. Bandura performed the Bobo doll experiment as he was formulating his social learning theory. The Bobo doll experiment placed preschool children in a room where they watched an adult model aggressive behaviors toward an inflatable Bobo doll. A control group saw nonaggressive behaviors. Then, all the children were placed in the room with a variety of toys and the Bobo doll to observe their reactions. Among the study's results were the findings that children who witnessed the adult's aggressive behavior were more likely to engage in similar aggressive behaviors. In 1989, Bandura updated his theory to the social cognitive theory that increased emphasis on cognitive processing. Cognitive processing includes people observing models and learning and processing new portions of behavior to create complex, newly developed behavioral patterns. Children develop self-efficacy as they receive constructive feedback on their behaviors (Papalia et al., 2007).

## ATTENTION: DEFINITION AND FACTORS FOR EARLY CHILD DEVELOPMENT

**Attention** is defined as cognition and sensory assessments that conjunctively process information of our environment (Juneja, 2015). The process of attention begins at birth. Research on attention in preschool children is somewhat limited and has been focused on pairing the attention span with the activity of the child (Bestor, 1934; Broderick & Blewitt, 2020). Researchers have documented attention-getting activities in the early child's life. As children grow and experience additional environments, however, researchers identify that attention is important to all mental processes, including thinking, imagining, and showing interest, which are all relevant to learning (Juneja). School environments present many challenges to educators and administrators. When providing instruction, educators have to engage the child's attention, create an environment focused on learning—an environment free from distractions—motivate learners to attend, and use supplemental audiovisual artifacts to support learning. Moreover, involving learners in the lesson promotes attending and retention of the information (Juneja).

Children's attention practices, however, vary due to numerous factors. Federico et al. (2017) studied attention in children and suggested that attention is better achieved by studying the **attention network approach**, which consists of three distinct networks: alerting, orienting, and executive attention. Each has a different function and neuroanatomical network. Moreover, attention is purposeful and selective, focusing on specific stimuli (Thomas, 2000). The alerting network is the person's capability to attend to inbound information, while the orienting network handles the capacity to choose and focus on the stimuli needing attention, and the executive control network monitors the person's behavior to complete goals and settle struggles with optional responses (Federico et al., 2017). The child's age and other factors determine the level of each network's functioning.

Discussions on attention typically include attention-deficit/hyperactivity disorder (ADHD). The National Institute of Mental Health (NIMH) reports attention-deficit is not just a childhood disorder but may also occur in adolescents and adults. However, ADHD is a disorder that may go undiagnosed in children, who often display a series of unidentifiable symptoms and, as such, it is challenging for these children to focus attention on sustaining involvement in activities. Research data indicate attention-deficit disorder can have genetic or environmental origins. Nongenetic origins may include prenatal drug or alcohol abuse, low birth weight, environmental toxins such as high lead levels, or brain injuries. Indicators of the disorder include inattention, hyperactivity, and extreme acting out or impulsivity, which makes it socially, cognitively, and behaviorally difficult for individuals in structured environments to engage with others. Individuals make careless errors or misunderstand tasks and have difficulty sustaining focus with listening, following directions, completing tasks, sequencing, organizing, and using executive functioning. Attention-deficit disorder (ADD) occurs with some individuals who exhibit similar issues minus the hyperactivity. It should be noted that these behaviors may indicate other disorders, such as anxiety, depression, or learning disabilities.

## MEMORY

Albert Bandura, who postulated that information is maintained in memory, studied children's learning of new behaviors—the knowledge structures of images and verbal symbols (Thomas, 2000). Rakowsky (2011)—posited that preschool children do not retain much in the short- or long-term memory beyond a week or two, until they reach school age. Although individuals do not remember infancy to 4 years of age, research on preschool memories may indicate that these early memories influence the development of individuals as adults (Cathey, 2020). Cathey posited that infants' and toddlers' memories are still in developing stages, but short-term memory may last a few minutes and long-term memory may endure for weeks or months. Memory is the mind's filing system, which consists of three processes: encoding, storage, and retrieval (Papalia et al., 2007). **Encoding** is changing sensory input information into a form that the system can cope with for storage. There are three ways information can be encoded: (1) visual (picture), (2) acoustic (sound), and (3) semantic (meaning). **Storage** is the process determining where, how long, how much, and what kind of information is kept for later retrieval. Information held within short-term memory is for a brief duration, whereas storage within long-term memory is unlimited. **Retrieval** is the process of getting information out of storage. Short-term memory is stored and retrieved sequentially while long-term memory is stored and retrieved by association. Association is why you can remember what you were looking for if you return to the room where you first thought about it (McLeod, 2007).

Although memory in early childhood is minimal and limited, parents or caregivers facilitate the child's memory by filling in the details, termed **generic memory**, which includes helping the child recall routines that occur. **Episodic memory** involves unique or specific major experiences or events that the child can recall on their own at some point in the future. These episodic memories may be sensory related and deeply encoded in "memory storage," becoming part of the child's autobiography and recalled when associated with experiences later in life.

## PRIVATE SPEECH

Young children sometimes speak aloud to themselves with no intent to communicate with others. Normally children aged 2 to 10 years practice private speech as an expression of their world. Toddlers from 2 to 3 years of age tend to babble while enjoying using their voice and speech to experiment with sounds. At ages 4 and 5, children use their private speech to express make-believe and imaginary friends and feelings (Papalia et al., 2007). Children 5 to 10 years old use private speech by talking under their breath and mumbling thoughts. Hence, private speech is a normal experience for children in growth and development.

## LISTENING WELL

Communication involves speaking and listening. The development of listening skills, however, is paramount to children's progress in all environments. Listening well is key to communication, as children understand what others say, comprehend the spoken language to complete tasks, follow oral directions, and interact with others in their environment (Goodson & Layzer, 2009). When children listen well, they may enjoy listening to stories, books, or music. Moreover, listening involves both talking and listening in social or public settings, and by participating in the social rules of conversation, taking turns while listening to other speakers. When asking questions, good listeners follow the flow of the communication to interject queries related to the topic or current discussion. In addition, listening is crucial to learning and acquiring necessary information (Goodson & Layzer).

## PLAY

Play is the work of children, a means to explore their world, and a channel for learning. Preschool children learn foundational skills for successful educational progress through playing (Broderick & Blewitt, 2020). Children learn imagination, imitation, cooperation, flexibility, and other foundational skills through playing with peers and adults. Play facilitates children's fine and gross motor skills and involves all sensory organs. In addition, play enhances children's cognition, physical and social development, and problem-solving skills.

Children's play varies, depending on the age of the child. Pretend play is make-believe people, situations, or objects (Broderick & Blewitt, 2020). Pretend play can include drama, fantasy, or other ways children express their emotions, ideas, and experiences. Functional play, which begins in infancy, is active, repetitious, and uses gross motor skills. Preschoolers enjoy constructive play, such as manipulating blocks and objects to build structures and even to color and draw pictures. Parallel play occurs when children play independent of another child and focus on their own activities, while social and cooperative play occurs when children play a game, play with other toys together, and role-play in make-believe activities. Solitary play is a child playing alone in a nonsocial manner, and it is intrinsic for the child. Boys and girls play differently. Boys tend to be more active, physical, and competitive in play, while girls may be quieter, more cooperative, and more willing to share than boys.

## Theoretical Considerations

Several major theorists and psychologists studied early childhood development. Prominent theorists in this discipline were Freud, Erikson, and Piaget. Freud's psychoanalytic theory stated that the psyche is structured in three parts: the **id, ego, and superego,** and develops in stages (McLeod, 2007). The id focuses on the child's need to satisfy biological impulses or drives (Broderick & Blewitt, 2020). In Freud's psychosexual stages of psychological development, the oral, anal, and phallic stages influence early childhood development. The oral stage involves oral behaviors while the anal stage is focused on withholding and learning toileting behaviors. Freud posited that conflict in these drives results from a child's experiences during the five developmental stages because the energy level of the id instigated each stage change.

Although not connected to sexual senses, the id's energy focus is on drive satisfaction for one part of the body. In the infancy stage, the mouth provides babies with the most pleasure. The infant's experiences with feeding and parental nurturing may affect the individual's efforts to satisfy this drive in the future. The phallic stage is from 3 to 6 years of age, and the source of the id's pleasure is the genitals. The child feels "attracted emotionally" to the opposite-sex parent, which makes the same-sex parent the rival. The child is in competition with the same-sex parent, or rival, for love and affection from the opposite-sex parent. Satisfying the id in each stage is necessary prior to moving to the next stage of development (Broderick & Blewitt, 2020).

## Freud's Five Psychosexual Stages of Development

| Oral Stage | Anal Stage | Phallic Stage | Latency Stage | Genital Stage |
|---|---|---|---|---|
| Birth to 12 months | 1 to 3 years | 3 to 6 years | 7 to 11 years | Puberty onwards |
| Infant's pleasure centers on mouth 'suckling' | Child's pleasure focuses on anus and from climination<br><br>Toilet Training<br>Relationship between parents | Child's pleasure focuses on **Genitals**<br><br>Oedipus (boys) Electra (girls)<br><br>*Penis envy* | Child represses sexual interest and develops social and Intellectual skills<br><br>An interlude | A time of sexual reawakening: source of sexual pleasure becomes someone outside of the family<br><br>continues |

**FIGURE 6.2** Freud's Psychosexual Stages

Erikson's psychosocial stages differ from others because the stages continue through adult life. During early childhood, children experience three major stages, which appear as crises involving two conflicting traits that must be resolved before moving to the next stage. From infancy to 18 months, trust versus mistrust crises must be resolved so the child knows who can be depended on for nurturing, providing protection, and supplying basic needs. If the trust crisis is unresolved, the damage may be lifelong, though other adults may support the child and trust needs may be partly resolved (Thomas, 2000). Autonomy versus shame or doubt is the psychosocial crisis to overcome between ages two and three. The goal of this stage is to attain the virtue of *will*. If supported by caregivers, children will become self-reliant, self-disciplined, responsible, and capable of sound judgment (Psychology Notes, 2019). Children from ages 3 to 5 must battle between initiative versus guilt (Thomas). "These children like to act out various family scenes and roles, such as teachers, police officers, doctors, as they see on TV. They make up stories with toys to demonstrate what they believe is the adult world. They also begin to explore their environment and ask a lot of 'why' questions" (Psychology Notes, 2019). If successful, a child will attain the virtue of *purpose*, which is demonstrated by how the child makes decisions, plays with others, and develops new ideas.

Piaget's psychosocial development focused on the early child's cognition from infancy to about age 7 years. During this time, the child is learning to understand and act in their environment (Papalia et al., 2007). At each stage, the child has to cognitively develop a new way of operating. From birth to 2 years of age, Piaget posited that infants are in the sensorimotor stage and able to manage activities in their environment through sensory and motor activities. The **preoperational stage** is from age 2 to 7 years, as the child transitions from using symbols and figures to represent people, places, and experiences. The child transitions from early childhood to middle childhood at about age 6 to 7.

Knowing key elements and stage progression of children during the early years of life provides a foundation for counselors to assess how best to support the needs of children. Cognitive behavioral therapy, play therapy, and theraplay have been successful for working with children at this stage of development. The commonality between these theories focuses on the parent and child interaction, to reduce or eliminate unwanted behaviors and replace them with positive, strength-based behaviors. There is scant information about specific theories that support specific child mental health disorders (CDC).

## Strengths and Challenges from the "ISMs" Perspectives

### DIVERSITY

Since we are connected globally, understanding the cultural differences in emotional expression, recognizing emotions, and playing with young children are important to our knowledge of this age group. Cultures vary in the way emotions are expressed and recognized. Huang (2018) posited that children's development is established by the interactive processes of their cultural environment; hence, children growing up in other cultures obtain different beliefs, behaviors, and values.

Communication within different cultures influences development of the child. In infancy, maternal caregivers interact and talk with their babies relative to the culture. German mothers focus on the baby's needs and wants while African tribal group Nso mothers emphasize the family interactions, context, and constructs of the culture. In Asian, African, and South American cultures, children are trained to adhere to social roles and their relation to the adults, such as "I am my mother's son." When preschoolers were asked about their feelings or choices, Chinese and Korean children were guarded in their brief responses, passive in interactions, and respectful toward elders and authority. Thus, children in different cultures are raised to think of themselves and relate to others in their culture. Parents within different cultures shape and mold their children's behaviors and thinking, their development of sociocultural rules, and their expectations and taboos (Huang). Knowledge of other cultures facilitates understanding the growth and development of their children.

FIGURE 6.3    Play and Quality Time Is Important Across Cultures

FIGURE 6.4    Growth Through Play

Play in different cultures parallels the practices and traditions in that culture that reflect adult role models, attitudes, and behaviors. Some examples are in South America Indian communities, where boys might play with bow and arrows, and children of various ages dive and swim in rivers or play tag in the village community. Preschool children use natural objects from the environment in pretend in imaginary play, such as sand, stone, water, plants, tree limbs, etc. At about age 3, play may become gender specific.

## GENDER

Gender identity occurs at birth and internally with the child at about age 2 years (Rafferty, 2018). Moreover, young children are aware of physical differences between boys and girls by the age of two, and by age three children may be able to state whether they are a boy or girl. By the age of four, children can distinguish gender role behaviors. Some stereotype roles include what girls do, such as playing with dolls, cooking, and homemaking, and what boys do, such as playing sports, building, and playing with trucks. These interests are traditional stereotypes and learned from the performance of adults, parents, schools, and society who expose children to gender-specific toys, media, and recreational activities. Times have changed, and children are now encouraged to play and learn activities that do not limit their enjoyment to previous gender-specific roles (Rafferty).

## ABLEISM

Some children in early childhood have illnesses and diagnoses that may affect their development and functionality in life. Preschool children aged 2 through 5 may be eligible for Early Childhood Special Education Services provided by their local school districts per the Individuals with Disabilities Education Act (IDEA). IDEA is a federal law that ensures states provide early interventions to eligible individuals.

Autism is a developmental disorder of the brain in which the child's functioning in social interactions, communications, imagination, and gross motor skills may be impaired across a broad range (Papalia et al., 2007). A child with autism in early childhood may refuse to notice others' emotions, cuddle, make eye contact, or other antisocial behaviors. Autisim spectrum disorder ranges from mild to severe (Papalia et al., 2007).

An infant with Down syndrome—a chromosomal disorder—may experience moderate to severe below-development mental intelligence and have some physical signs as well. These chromosomal disorders may develop from genetic or prenatal causes and occur more often with older birth parents. With early intervention, these children improve in their academic and developmental skills.

Chronic illness is a physical health condition that is lengthy, challenging to treat, and may affect the child and family. In early childhood, chronic illness may affect the child's developmental progress negatively and have major implications for the future (Bell et al., 2016). Chronic illness in early childhood may be detrimental to school readiness for the child and result in lower achievement. Early interventions for children with extensive medical conditions are paramount for the children to achieve both academically and socially.

Early childhood mental health concerns may have genetic or hereditary origins. Schizophrenia, alcoholism, and depression are disorders that have been identified in family history but may also be induced by environmental factors.

### MORTALITY AWARENESS

Children in this age range may experience adverse causes of death. The number one cause of death for children is motor vehicle accidents, either as passengers, pedestrians, or cycling (Papalia et al., 2007). Some vehicle accident deaths involve an operator under the influence of alcohol or other substances. Some additional contributing causes of death include ingesting toxins, medications, or other unhealthy substances found in children's systems postmortem. In other developing countries, infant mortality is higher primarily due to health-care system functionality. Some primary causes for death are neonatal encephalopathy or brain dysfunction due to lack of oxygen at birth. Other deaths may be attributed to infections, prenatal complications, lower respiratory infections, and diarrheal diseases.

## Summary

Early childhood development includes a multitude of physical, cognitive, social, and emotional changes, and theorists have presented growth and development in a variety of theories to address these changes. Milestones are used to assess children's development at different age levels. Children during this stage of development begin to master moving better, have increased gross and fine motor skills, and learn to listen and socialize with others. Cognitively, children see increases in attention, focus, and memory. Socially and emotionally, children engage in more play, mimic speech and action, show a range of emotions, and participate in make-believe play. Cultural differences, disabilities, and gender identity develop as children grow and can affect development.

Rebecca is a 28-year-old school counselor at a predominately White school in upstate New York. Rebecca was called into an emergency meeting with the principal and Mr. Deville, a kindergarten teacher. Mr. Deville was appalled by the behavior of two of his students in class but did not know what else to do so he reached out to the principal and Rebecca. In the meeting, Mr. Deville shared what happened: "The kids were at recess and when I looked up, Blake, who is 5 years old, was down on the ground with his hands behind his back and Hunter, who just turned 6, was kneeling on his neck and shouting, 'Stop moving, nigger!' I ran over as fast as I could, pulled them apart, and sent them to the principal's office. I don't know why they would do such a thing." The three of them sat quietly, until the principal broke the silence and said, "We need to have a serious discussion with Blake and Hunter and possibly the entire kindergarten class. Rebecca, what plans do you have?" Rebecca took a deep breath and shared that they needed to carefully address the situation because Blake, Hunter, and the other kindergartners are at a formation stage of development. Mr. Deville exhaled, and said, "Well, how did they know to even do that? Where did they learn that? I teach tolerance in my class."

1. How would you help Mr. Deville understand what is happening with Blake and Hunter?
2. What lessons or activities would you develop to help the students and faculty increase their cultural awareness?
3. Thinking of Erikson's stages, what could Blake and Hunter's pretend play symbolize?

## Reflections and Targeted Discussion Questions

### COMPREHENSION

1. What are several changes in growth and development for a child at 2, 3, and 4 years old?
2. How does knowing the various age milestones help you counsel children and their families? Provide a specific example.

### CRITICAL THINKING

1. How might early childhood trauma affect attention, memory, and how information is encoded for storage?
2. What are two or three social, cultural, and environmental events that could arrest early childhood milestone development? How would you adapt your counseling approach to help the child reach his or her milestone goal?

# References

Bell, M. F., Bayliss, D. M., Glauert, R., Harrison, A., & Ohan, J. L. (2016). Chronic illness and developmental vulnerability at school entry. *Pediatrics*, *137*(5). DOI:https://doi.org/10.1542/peds.2015-2475

Bestor, M. F. (1934). A study of attention in young children. *Child Development*, *5*(4), 368. https://doi.org/10.2307/1125852

Broderick, P. C., & Blewitt, P. (2020). *The life span: Human development for helping professionals* (5th ed.). Pearson Education.

Cathey, K. (2020). Early childhood memories and psychological development of a child. https://intelligentmother.com/childhood-memories

Center on the Developing Child. (2007). *The science of early childhood development* (in brief). www.developingchild.harvard.edu

Federico, F., Marotta, A., Martella, D., & Casagrande, M. (2017). Development in attention functions and social processing: Evidence from the Attention Network Test. *British Journal of Developmental Psychology*, *35*(2), 169–185. https://doi.org/10.1111/bjdp.12154

Goodson, B., & Layzer, C. (2009). *Learning to talk and listen: Developing early literacy.* Report of the National Early Literacy Panel. National Institute for Literacy.

Hanks, H. (2010). *When are speech sounds developed?* www.Mommyspeechtherapy.com

Huang, C. (2018). *How culture influences children's development.* Lecturer in psychology, Bournemouth University. https://theconversation.com/how-culture-influences-childrens-development-99791

Juneja, P. (2015). Learning theories: Classical conditioning, operant conditioning, and learning by observation. https://managementstudyguide.com/introduction-to-psychology.html

McLeod, S. A. (2007). Stages of memory—Encoding storage and retrieval. www.simplypsychology.org/memory.html

McLeod, S. (2019). Freud's psychosexual stages of development. *Simply Psychology.* https://www.simplypsychology.org/psychosexual.html#:~:text=Freud%20proposed%20that%20psychological%20development,different%20area%20of%20the%20body

National Institute for Mental Health. Attention-deficit/hyperactivity disorder. https://www.nimh.nih.gov/health/topics/attention-deficit-hyperactivity-disorder-adhd/

New York Times (1976). *The wild boy of Aveyron.* See the article in original context from May 16, 1976, p. 214. https://www.nytimes.com/1976/05/16/archives/the-wild-boy-of-aveyron.html?auth=link-dismiss-google1tap

Papalia, D. E., Olds, S. W., Feldman, R. D. (2007). *Human development* (10th ed.). McGraw-Hill.

*Psychology Notes*. (2019). Erik Erikson's theory of psychosocial development. https://www.psychologynoteshq.com/erikson-stages/

Rafferty, J. (2018). Gender identity development in children. American Academy of Pediatrics. https://www.healthychildren.org/English/ages-stages/gradeschool/Pages/Gender-Identity-and Gender-Confusion-In-Children.aspx

Rakowsky, J. (2011). A child's memory in military time: Guidance for families preparing for deployments, homecomings. *The Harvard Gazette*. https://news.harvard.edu/gazette/story/2011/10/a-childs-memory-in-military-time/

Thomas, R. M. (2000). *Comparing theories of child development* (5th ed.). Wadsworth/Thomas Learning.

## Credits

# Middle Childhood Development

Dianne Parr, PhD, and Noréal F. Armstrong, PhD

*Logic will get you from A to B. Imagination will take you everywhere.*
    —*Albert Einstein*

## Learning Objectives

After reading this chapter, you should be able to
1. Understand physical and cognitive development in middle childhood.
2. Understand social and emotional development during middle childhood.
3. Learn how we as counselors can effectively support the development during middle childhood.

## Introduction

In this chapter, children have transitioned from the "terrible twos" and "quizzical threes" to a point in the middle of their development process. Middle childhood is a major change in children's growth, cognition, performance, and development during the elementary years. This chapter will explore the physical and cognitive development of children at this age and provide information to help you understand the social, emotional, and environmental factors that influence development at this stage of life.

## Key Concepts

- **Family Systems Theory:** A method to comprehend human operation that focuses on relationships between people in a family, between the family and the framework in which the family is entrenched (Watson, 2012).
- **Warmth Dimension:** Parenting style based on the warmth response of the parent or the emotional climate or level of positivity.
- **Control Dimension:** A parenting style involving the parent's level of demands or power over child's behaviors.
- **Modeling or Observational Learning:** Begins with infants shortly after birth and persists throughout the parent–child relationship.
- **Heredity:** The genetic blueprint the child inherits from the biological parents.
- **Environment:** The world the child is exposed to and learns to navigate through.
- **Reinforcement:** An incentive or consequence that increases the likelihood for the recurrence of the behavior.
- **Punishment:** The stimulus or consequence that discourages repetition of the behavior.
- **Negative Reinforcement Trap:** Occurs when parents may end up unwittingly reinforcing the behavior they wish to discourage.

## The Human Developing Process

Middle childhood, sometimes known as the school years, is approximately ages 6 through 11 years (Papalia et al., 2007). But since there is such a disparity of developmental skills in this group, some researchers divide the middle childhood into two groups: **early middle childhood** begins at about age 6 through 8 years of age, and **late middle childhood** starts about age 9 through 11 years (Morin & Garbi, 2020). School environment enhances skills and is important for the child's physical, cognitive, and psychosocial growth and development. Children experience numerous physical, cognitive, and social changes during this time. Their unique qualities and talents begin to surface as well as special needs, due to the proficiencies necessary for school success. Talents and proficiencies also affect self-esteem and social skill development with peers (Papalia et al., 2007). Middle childhood is a very important stage in preparation for the turbulence that may be experienced in adolescence.

# Development in Early Childhood

Children's growth and development during this stage slows and varies for each child. Children are grouped in classroom grade levels by age, which generally correlates with their physical, cognitive, and psychosocial development. Children grow taller, stronger, heavier, and they develop motor skills while interacting with their peers in games and organized sports activities. While memory, thinking, and moral judgment advance during this age range as well, children's individuality becomes more apparent and important to their cognitive and psychosocial development (Papalia et al., 2004).

## MILESTONES IN 6- AND 7-YEAR-OLD CHILDREN

General milestones for children aged 6 and 7 years are on a continuum. Children grow and develop at various rates in this age range, and size, weight, height, and performance can vary depending on a number of factors. Children in this age group grow about 2.5 inches in a year and gain 4 to 7 pounds yearly. At 6 and 7 years, children began to develop a body image (Papalia et al., 2007).

- Physical development shows as
  - Steady growth at this age; children become more slender and proportioned like adults.
  - Handedness appears, and fine and gross motor skills and strength improve.
  - Children begin to lose their baby teeth, which are replaced by permanent adult teeth.
- Language development depends on numerous factors, but in general children are able to
  - Speak in simple and complete five- to seven-word sentences.
  - Follow a series of three commands in a row.
  - Begin to know that some words have multiple meanings. This facilitates understanding humor and beginning to use humor in jokes.
- Cognitive development in children appears as they
  - Begin to show growth in mental ability.
  - Begin to read and understand developmental and age-appropriate books.
  - Sound out or decode unfamiliar words.
  - Focus on a task in school for 15 minutes.

- Understand the concept of numbers.
- Know day from night and left from right.
- Be able to repeat three numbers backward.

## PHYSICAL AND GROWTH DEVELOPMENT FOR 8-YEAR-OLD CHILDREN

At 8 years, children continue to grow and develop at a fast pace, varying in size, weight, and physical development and performance.

- Children are more coordinated physically, jumping, skipping, and chasing.
- Can dress and groom themselves independently.
- Lose about four baby teeth each year.
- May have arms and legs that seem too long for their bodies.
- Make complaints about their health; tummy, leg pains, etc.

## COGNITIVE AND LANGUAGE DEVELOPMENT

- These children are typically in the third grade.
- Continue to develop complex language skills.
- Improve in focus and attention span.
- Improve in pronunciation and are able to follow more commands in a row.
- Improve in reading comprehension skills.
- Understand words have multiple meanings and can participate in jokes and humor.
- Can count backwards, know the date, days of week, month, and year.
- Enjoy collecting things, such as toys, action figures, etc.

## SOCIAL AND EMOTIONAL DEVELOPMENT

Middle childhood development is fluid, and children's social and emotional behaviors may cover a broad range of behaviors because maturation may occur at different rates. Beginning at age 6 or early middle childhood, children become more aware of their own and others' feelings and emotions as they are grouped together academically with same-age peers beginning in kindergarten or even in preschool settings. Same-gender friendships, usually peers or classmates, become important during this time. Based on commonalities, these comrades enjoy sharing such social activities as skating, bike riding, playing games, attending parties, and other experiences.

Children in early middle childhood begin to display gifts and talents, develop better self-control, and maintain emotional stability at about age 7 or 8. As this group matures, children develop a sense of self, enjoy spending solo time doing hobbies or interests, care about the thoughts and feelings of others, and experience peer pressure.

An 8-year-old can appear more advanced, share multifaceted feelings, and mask communicating thoughts and emotions depending on the situation. Supportive family and friends facilitate the older middle child's development of interests, talents, and self-identity (Morin & Garbi, 2020; Papalia et al., 2007). Prosocial skills are a sign of emotional and social security.

Between the ages 6, 7, and 8, children continue to develop more social and emotional skills and behaviors. Children's emotional and social development may include

- Becoming more aware of the perceptions of others.
- Complaining about their friendships and other children's reactions.
- Wanting to have good behavior but not attending to following directions.
- Trying to express feelings with words but possibly opting for aggressive behaviors when upset.

## Late Middle Childhood Development

Children ages 9 to 11 are in late middle childhood. The physical, emotional, and cognitive development varies based on numerous factors in the child's life (Broderick & Blewitt, 2020). Physical growth slows, yet children are all shapes and sizes during this age range (Papalia et al., 2007). Cognitive skills begin to become more complex as the child ascends to the upper elementary years. The brain is built over time, beginning before birth and continuing into adulthood (Center on the Developing Child, 2007). Moreover, children during middle childhood experience changes in their ability to use executive functioning (Broderick & Blewitt, 2020). The brain's growth and organization during middle childhood is part of the learning process that children encounter as they interact with the environment and begin to associate more with peers. Meanwhile, children's experiences with the onset of puberty may be influenced by genetics and gender. Children in the late middle years change at diverse developmental rates, while still transitioning on a continuum that includes future developmental challenges (Broderick & Blewitt, 2020).

### PHYSICAL DEVELOPMENT

Physical growth development for 9-year-old children varies (Broderick & Blewitt, 2020; Morin & Garbi, 2020; Papalia et al., 2007).

- May become stronger and have more muscle control.
- Are able to extend physical limits and interests in sports.
- May get taller, ganglier, and heavier in weight.
- Different parts of the body grow and change at different times.

- May experience puberty early, and gender may be a factor.
- Girls may start development around age 8 to 9.

Physical growth development for 10-year-olds is at a slower pace. The child's growth may be affected by genetic, environmental, or other factors; however, this is still a time of transition for the child (Broderick & Blewitt, 2020; Morin, 2019).

- Start to experience growth spurts.
- May perform better in agility, speed, and balance.
- May increase in small muscle coordination.
- Girls may grow faster and taller than boys their age.
- Boys may begin to show development of puberty.

At 11, children's physical growth and development may bring major changes. These changes are different based on gender and possibly genetic factors (Broderick & Blewitt, 2020; Morin & Garbi, 2020).

- May have already started puberty, but it may occur later.
- May begin to grow into their bodies, which might be confusing and awkward.
- Sweat glands may become more active.
- May need more sleep and food.
- Girls' physical changes may include body fat, breast development, underarm and pubic hair growth, widening hips, onset of first menstrual cycle.
- Boys' physical changes may include larger muscles, voice changes, beginning of hair growth on underarms, face, and pubic area, and darkening of male pubic area.

## COGNITIVE DEVELOPMENT OF 9-YEAR-OLDS

Children in this age group begin to develop higher-level thinking skills. As fourth-graders, they begin to construct thoughts when given evidence or facts to solve problems or projects. Facing more challenging academics, these children enjoy working on skills until they gain mastery of the problem or topic. Math is more complicated, requiring beginning skills in analysis and logical thinking. Language skills include more reading fiction and nonfiction and writing complex sentences and various types of literature projects (Morin & Garbi, 2020).

## COGNITIVE DEVELOPMENT OF 10-YEAR-OLDS

Children at age 10 show many signs of cognitive development through their mastery of thinking and communication skills. These children can discuss their thoughts on topics of interest or information obtained in the academic system (Morin, 2019).

Generally, they are fifth-graders preparing for middle school by learning complex math, reading, and content subjects. Logic, deductive thinking, and abstract thinking make academics more challenging. They begin to use the library and computers to research information for reports and presentations. They look forward to the middle school experience.

**FIGURE 7.1**    During Middle Childhood, Children Increase Their Interest in Self-Learning

### COGNITIVE DEVELOPMENT OF 11-YEAR-OLDS

Children at this age are learning to analyze information, situations, and circumstances in various ways (Morin, 2019). They are beginning sixth grade or middle school, depending on the structure of the school system, and they employ higher-level thinking skills to solve academic issues and complete projects. Their interest may remain focused or change quickly.

## Social and Emotional Development

Children in this age range continue to grow and acquire more skills physically, socially, and cognitively (Broderick & Blewitt, 2020; Morin & Garbi, 2020). Thinking and problem-solving skills improve as children attend school to address their learning needs, while interacting with grade-level peers. Family is still important, but socializing with new friends and peers begins to take precedence. Middle childhood is a complicated experience for children and their families and, again, can be divided into the early middle childhood, ages 6 through 8 years, and the late middle childhood, ages 9 through 11 (Morin & Garbi, 2020).

## SOCIAL AND EMOTIONAL DEVELOPMENT OF LATE MIDDLE CHILDHOOD

As children mature into late middle childhood, they become more empathic and able to display pro-social behaviors in a variety of environments and circumstances (Broderick & Blewitt, 2020; Morin & Garbi, 2020; Papalia et al., 2007). Although still influenced by parents, peer influence plays a major role on the late middle child's social and emotional skill development. These children enjoy being part of groups and want to participate in the social order of school or sports organizations. At home and school, the late middle child may desire autonomy and make mistakes, yet will listen to reason and apologize when wrong. As they mature through late childhood, the child may have better control over feelings and be able to negotiate conflicts with peers. Girls may have more mood swings and have concerns about image and relationships, but males may exhibit moody behaviors due to changes in the body. Most of all, these children imitate peers they admire, begin to question authority, and may begin risky behaviors as they model group identity and cliques form. Complex friendships become dominant and more important with less interest in family.

In the late middle childhood stage, between ages 9, 10, and 11 years, children begin the preteen or tween stage. Changes in their social and emotional development include the following:

- Starting to share secrets and jokes with a smaller select group of close friends.
- Responding to peers' "group think," which is accepting peer thinking and being more like peers.
- Exhibiting social emotional characteristics may range from affectionate, silly, and curious to selfish, rude, and argumentative.
- Starting to develop their own identity and may not spend as much time with family.
- Showing physical changes in their bodies, as puberty may begin, which also affects their social and emotional behaviors.

## FAMILY SYSTEMS

Traditionally, the system for bearing and raising children is in a family. **Family systems theory** is based on systems theories, focused on the complicated interconnected underlying processes in development (Broderick & Blewitt, 2020). The systems vary and are based on the interactions of community, culture, institutions, and other factors. Based on systems theories, family systems theory is a method to comprehend human operation that focuses on relationships between people in a family, between the family, and the framework in which the family is entrenched (Watson, 2012). The family framework consists of emotions, behaviors, communications, boundaries, values, and many other factors that children learn and emulate as they develop.

## PARENTING STYLES

Parenting styles influence the behaviors that distinguish the value of parenting to the child (Broderick & Blewitt, 2020). Parenting style has two dimensions: warmth and control. The **warmth dimension** is based on the warmth response of the parent or the emotional climate or level of positivity; the **control dimension** is the parent's level of demands or power over the child's behaviors. The parenting styles are based on research by Diana Baumrind (1989). Able to control but increase expectations of responsible behavior as the child matures, the **authoritative** parental style is accepting, responsive, and child-centered. The **authoritarian** parental style demands behaviors from the child to fit specific criteria, but has negative dimensions, is unresponsive, and parent-centered. The **permissive** parental style does not control the child and has minimal behavioral expectations, so the child is in control of behaviors. **Neglectful** parental style is uninvolved and centered on meeting the parent's own needs while making few behavioral demands and being unresponsive to the child's needs (Baumrind, 1989). Parenting styles correlate with the child's behavioral outcomes and choices (Broderick & Blewitt, 2020).

|  | **Supportive** <br> Parent is accepting and child-centered | **Unsupportive** <br> Parent is rejecting and parent-centered |
|---|---|---|
| **Demanding** <br> Parent expects much of child | **Authoritative Parenting** <br><br> Relationship is reciprocal, responsive; high in bidirectional communication | **Authoritarian Parenting** <br><br> Relationship is controlling, power-assertive; high in unidirectional communication |
| **Undemanding** <br> Parent expects little of child | **Permissive Parenting** <br><br> Relationship is indulgent; low in control attempts | **Rejecting-Neglecting Parenting** <br><br> Relationship is rejecting or neglecting; uninvolved |

FIGURE 7.2    Study Flashcard of the Four Types of Parenting Styles

Parental behavior research revealed an association between parenting style and the child's behavioral results (Broderick & Blewitt, 2020). Children of authoritative parents tend to have positive behaviors, such as pro-social skills with all ages and situations, proactive self-development, and ability to self-regulate behaviors. Authoritarian parents' offspring tend to be ambivalent about their feelings of anxiety and anger, insecure with social settings, and often exhibit lack of self-control. Children of permissive parents may display impulsive, uncontrollable, and aggressive social behaviors. Offspring of neglectful and uninvolved parents show impulsivity, aggressiveness, and blaming others or self for problems in the family. Truly, parenting styles make a difference in children's behavioral outcomes.

Parents are the child's first teachers, and modeling appropriate behaviors in relationships is an important role for parents. **Modeling** or **observational learning** begins with infants shortly after birth and persists throughout the parent–child relationship (Broderick & Blewitt, 2020). Parents play an important role in modeling appropriate social skills and interactions with the child and in the presence of the child. Bandura (2003) termed this **social learning theory**, modeling, or observational learning.

Another important role for parents is providing feedback for the child's behaviors or performance. **Feedback** is positive or negative reinforcement or punishment to influence a particular behavior to occur or stop (Papalia et al., 2007). Based on Skinner's research, **operant conditioning** is learning through positive or negative reinforcement. **Reinforcement** is an incentive or consequence (Kail & Cavanaugh, 2016) that increases the recurrence of the behavior. **Punishment** is the stimulus or consequence that discourages repetition of the behavior. **Negative reinforcement trap** occurs when children negotiate with parents to avoid the punishment or consequence for inappropriate behaviors; parents may end up unwittingly reinforcing the behavior they wish to discourage (Kail & Cavanaugh, 2016).

## CULTURE AND SOCIOECONOMIC STATUS

Culture and socioeconomic factors may play a role in child development, although research on the effect on families is challenging. **Socioeconomic status** is defined as the class or social level or power of the adults in the family and it includes education, income, and occupational backgrounds (Broderick & Blewitt, 2020). Socioeconomic status limits the choice of where and how families live and how the child develops (Papalia et al., 2007). **Culture** is a community's common foods, industry, values, rituals, psychological processes, norms, language, traditions, tools, artifacts, and practices (Broderick & Blewitt, 2020; Papalia et al., 2007). Culture is the group's way of life and is shared in the family system.

## CHILD TEMPERAMENT

Child **temperament** and personality may exist on a spectrum and vary within the same family. Temperament is the difference in the innate characteristics of a child that are displayed early in life and influence relationships with the caregivers, others in the family, and other environments (Keogh, 2009). Seen in infants, a baby with a negative temperament may be extremely fussy, sensitive to noises, upset, and eating and sleeping irregularly. Individual differences in temperament may also affect the child's learning or attention problems.

## SIBLINGS AND BIRTH ORDER

Siblings share many experiences in families. Birth order, however, provides advantages and preferences for the child's position in the family (Thomas, 2000). The firstborn child has a privileged position in the family, which includes the undivided attention and resources of parents and extended family. Additional siblings may burden the family's resources. When later-born siblings arrive, firstborn children will strive to maintain their privileges, especially the attention of parents, and only share what they have to share, which might be resources they do not control. Siblings will try to individualize their position with behaviors that demand attention and make them special. This may be the source of sibling rivalry as children grow up. Other factors may override birth order differentiation, such as gender, parents' situations and relationship changes, temperament, and personality patterns in the family.

**FIGURE 7.3**   Sibling Rivalry

## FAMILY STRUCTURE

**Family structure** is the makeup of the family and has changed markedly from previous generations. In past generations, children grew up in traditional families. Biological or adoptive parents were married and heterosexual. Often, the mother did not work and was the homemaker and caregiver for the children (Papalia et al., 2004). Family structure changed as parents' relationships changed. Divorce, single parents, blended families, gay/lesbian parents, and grandparents are some of the families that currently provide homes for children (Papalia et al., 2007). Although some may suggest that children function better in a traditional home, a positive authoritative environment improves the child's adjustment more than the adults' marital or relationship status.

Adoptions have occurred throughout history. In the United States, however, adoption may be by kinship or family relationship. **Adoption** is a legal process in which adults may become a parent via application to public or private institutions. Currently, single adults, same-sex couples, and multiracial adults are adopting children in the United States, Africa, Asia, and South America to provide nurturing homes for children. Challenges affecting adoptive families include integrating the child into the family, explaining what it adoption means when a child can process the information, and even helping the child find their biological parents later in life if they so desire. All of these factors aid the child in developing a healthy sense of self and adjusting to the transitions that occur during and after the process. In the past, confidential adoption was the rule. Today some families agree and manage open adoptions for the benefit of the child, which means maintaining contact with biological parents within legal restrictions.

Divorce can be a challenging experience for a child or family, depending on numerous variables. The parent's or caregiver's relationship with each child before, during, and after the divorce is paramount to the child's adjustment throughout the transition (Broderick & Blewitt, 2020; Papalia et al., 2007). Cooperative parenting and communicating with the child may provide the necessary support for the child's adjustment. Factors that may affect the child's adjustment are social, emotional, and relationship concerns; conduct problems; academic issues; self-blame; internal fears and anxieties; and many more. Maintaining the support of both parents is the best option, with shared custody and frequent contact with each parent. If parents remarry or engage in a new relationship, it is important that the child is included in developing changes in the family and is supported through adjustments to stepparents and stepsiblings.

## RELATIONSHIPS IN MIDDLE CHILDHOOD

Friendships in early childhood are different than those of middle childhood and are important for the emotional and social development of children. Although children spend time with their peer groups, friendship is limited to one or two people. Children seek friends who share some commonalities, such as same age, sex, ethnicity or interests. A friend is a person the child feels comfortable with, feels affection toward, likes to be with, shares secrets and feelings with, and knows well. Friends trust each other, are committed to each other, and treat each other as equals. Friendship is an important relationship as it facilitates children learning to communicate, cooperate, and compromise to resolve conflict that occurs in relationship. Friendship helps children learn to understand the perspective of another person's needs as well as their own. Children need to have stability in order to make friends.

Children who live in the same community forms groups based on commonalities (Papalia et al., 2007). Some commonalities occur from being in the same school, classroom, or recreational group. Peer groups tend to be gender specific and begin to form in schools, sports programs, clubs, troops, or other recreational groups or organizations. Peer groups positively and negatively influence children's character development, sometimes known as **peer pressure**. Positive peer groups facilitate development of gender- and age-appropriate decisions that children can make outside of family relationships. These influences include gauging abilities against those of peers, developing proactive relationships, and developing positive self-efficacy. Negative peer pressure may influence children toward inappropriate or antisocial choices, biases, or behaviors such as substance abuse. Peer pressure may negatively coerce the child to participate in behaviors that are against the upbringing and moral character of the parents or caregivers.

Participation with certain peer groups may affect the child's popularity or rejection by peers. Popular children are usually esteemed by peers, adept in many different social environments, and display positive character traits (Papalia et al., 2007). These children have many friends. An example of this is that sometimes in late middle childhood aggressive behaviors in boys make them popular, while lack of outgoing demeanor and aggression in boys may be rejected by peers. For girls the opposite can be true; aggressive behavior is often rejected. Parents can facilitate proactive behaviors in their children by identifying how they interact with friends and peers.

Bullying peaks for boys and girls during middle childhood. **Bullying** (Peters, 2012) involves aggressive and threatening behaviors of a child toward another child, with the victim perceived to be weak, anxious, and different from peers. Bullying is group behavior led by one aggressive child who leads others to watch or participate as bystanders and to not tell others or report the incident. Victims have few friends and are intimidated not to tell. Encouraging bystanders and victims to tell trusted adults helps to extinguish the behaviors.

The middle child has been exposed since preschool to communication through technology (Broderick & Blewitt, 2020; Papalia et al., 2007). As infants, children were exposed to visual media programming developed just for that age group, and this continued throughout their growth and development. Middle childhood students are familiar with using technology to do research, both at home and at school. Academic classes have scheduled computer time for collecting information, completing assessments, and practicing in a variety of content disciplines. The average middle child also enjoys playing video games on specialized equipment, which may or may not involve violence or other inappropriate activities. The research on whether these programs negatively influence children's behavior is not yet conclusive.

## Theoretical Considerations

Children's brains change in size and organization in middle childhood (Broderick & Blewitt, 2020). Genetics correlated with experience facilitate changes in the brain. By studying the changes in the brain's cognition, Piaget posited that the major stages in middle childhood were completing the **preoperational stage,** ages 2 to 7, completing the **concrete operational stage**, ages 7 to 11, and beginning the **formal operations stage** at age 11+ (Thomas, 2000; Papalia et al., 2007; Broderick and Blewitt, 2020).

The **preoperational stage** for the early middle child is done during kindergarten and first grade of elementary school. Children increase their understanding of space, causality, identities, categorization, and number sense, which may have been initiated in early childhood but achieved in middle childhood. The **concrete operational stage** is developed in early middle childhood as children's cognition gradually becomes faster, more accurate, and able to multitask or decenter, which is having more than one thought at a time. Children develop the ability to logically link relationships and information; however, information still must be represented in the real world or material format for children to better understand it. As the child transitions in the school system to upper elementary and late middle childhood, the child is able to link experience with information that is not concrete, which is the beginning of the **formal operational stage** for children. Experience and knowledge facilitate children in understanding and making sense of more advanced information and cognitive processing. The information processing approach addresses the differences in child perception, learning, memory, and problem solving. This approach focuses on detailing how learning occurs, how problems are solved, and how the child remembers the information.

During middle childhood, memory improves. Short-term memory is related to the individual's senses, or sensory memory, as the senses access the environment, providing brief retention of the experience (Broderick & Blewitt, 2020). Memory is categorized by length of retention time and capacity for storage. Short term, working memory characteristics include limited information that is temporarily stored and organized for a short time and retrieved for immediate use. Working memory has a limited capacity for new information and stores it for short-term retrieval to solve problems or complete projects. Long-term memory requires rehearsal or repeating the information until it is easily recalled and ruminating on it. In middle childhood, rehearsing and thinking about information expands the individual's working memory. As children grow during late middle childhood, they process information faster and increase knowledge about many things to add to their working memory.

## THEORIES OF INTELLIGENCE AND INTELLIGENCE TESTING

Intelligence has been researched since the beginning of psychology. Forsythe (2020) discussed several intelligence theories from different research perspectives. The fluid and crystallized intelligence theory was developed by Cattell. **Fluid intelligence** is inductive and deductive reasoning to understand inferences and connections between stimuli, which are basic skills for learning. **Crystallized intelligence** refers to increasing vocabulary and cultural knowledge, learned in formal educational settings and through life experiences. Cattell's theory used psychometric measures to assess qualitative differences and abilities. Cognitive-contextual is Piaget's explanation of the four stages of intellectual development, and Piaget posited that children integrate information from one experience or environment by applying different ways of thinking about the world. As the child gathers information from various experiences, the child generates new and improved ways of thinking about the information.

Psychometric testing for intelligence can be done at all ages to quantitatively measure the individual's intelligence quotient, or IQ (Papalia et al., 2007; Broderick & Blewitt, 2020). The IQ tests assess the individual's performance in comprehension, reasoning, and other factors to predict future academic performance by comparing each individual's results to other normed test-takers. The Wechsler Intelligence Scale for Children (WISC) is used to assess verbal and performance abilities of middle childhood. Middle childhood students may also take group tests to assess abilities, such as the Otis-Lennon School Ability Test that has levels from kindergarten through the 12th grade.

Individuals' ability to be sensitive to self and others is emotional intelligence. The Emotional intelligence theory was created by psychologists, Peter Salovey and John Mayer. Important for success in life, Daniel Goleman added other qualities to the construct of emotional intelligence, including optimism, conscientiousness, motivation, empathy, and social competence. Emotional intelligence is an important trait for individuals on teams, in professional relationships, in leadership positions, and in social relationships. Individuals with emotional intelligence must be self-aware, self-managed, socially aware, and able to apply relationship management skills (Papalia et al., 2007).

## Strengths and Challenges from the "ISMs" Perspectives

Children are different in a plethora of ways—culture, language, abilities, socioeconomic status, developmental levels, and many other factors. Diversity can be viewed as a strength if children are encouraged to embrace their gifts, talents, and differences as their voice in their world.

### MULTICULTURAL

#### FACTORS ON INTELLIGENCE TESTING

Children's heredity and environment influence their lives academically and socially. **Heredity** is the genetic blueprint that the child inherits from his or her biological parents. **Environment** is the world the child is exposed to and learns to navigate through. Researchers have studied the connection of heredity and environment on intelligence and posited that there is a connection, but they have not answered the question regarding the level that each contributes to intelligence.

The intelligence test has led to questions regarding bias and unfairness for ethnic and socioeconomic status groups. Questioning the norms, validity, and reliability of these standardized assessments raises concerns that the test underestimates the abilities of certain ethnicities, low socioeconomic groups, and those who do not perform well on such tests (Papalia et al., 2007). The tests are timed, identify information some children know already, and are based on educational exposure or culture that may vary depending on the test-takers' experiences. The tests are focused on the experiences of the White or privileged society. Intelligence test scores among ethnic groups have a broad range, giving credence to the belief that the tests are unfair or include **cultural bias.** Cultural bias may explain the below average scores of low socioeconomic status groups that may lack resources and have academic curriculum deficiencies.

## DIVERSITY

Some children enter the school system from other regions or countries and may not speak or read the curriculum as developed for other learners. **English as a Second Language Learners (ELL)** are students in the U.S. school systems who may speak dialectically about 350 languages (Broderick & Blewitt, 2020). Their parents have migrated from other regions or countries, with the children enrolled in schools where the parents may be employed. These children represent a diverse community and culture. As such, they may need a variety of interventions to navigate the school system and improve academically.

Sometimes, underrepresented groups and immigrant children experience prejudice and racism in the school system. Discrimination is maltreatment, such as bullying or isolation, by peers due to membership in a group. Teachers and staff members may expect poor performance, grade unfairly, ignore them, or label them with behavioral issues. Encouraging immigrant students to speak bilingually would facilitate maintaining their ethnic identity while learning English (Broderick & Blewitt, 2020).

Social skills develop in different cultures for this age group. Immigrant children are encouraged by the family system to follow the social skills established in their community (Broderick and Blewitt, 2020). In general, children are respectful, cooperative, and responsible to adults and peers as these character traits are values established in the family. When these children attend schools, they may interact with same-age peers and associate with others from their community or they may remain in isolation. They may be limited by learning differences in language, understanding how to interact with host country peers, and navigating other socially appropriate behaviors they have not been exposed to for this age group. Counselors can assist these children by engaging in support interventions to facilitate adjustment.

## GENDER

Children experience physical changes in the body during middle childhood. **Gender identity** is the individual's awareness of their gender role and understanding what it means, which occurs in the early childhood years (Broderick and Blewitt, 2020). **Gender stability** is the child's realization that the gender identified remains the same. Although gender identity and stability develop during the early childhood years, as the child transitions into puberty and experiences physical changes in the body, gender identity becomes important again. In middle childhood, children begin to understand their sexual characteristics as their bodies change (Papalia et al., 2007). **Primary sex characteristics** are the organs needed for reproduction. In females, the reproductive organs are the ovaries, fallopian tubes, uterus, and vagina. In males, the reproductive organs are the testes, scrotum, penis, seminal vesicles, and the prostate gland.

**Secondary sex characteristics** are physical changes in the body evidencing sexual maturation. Girls experience breast growth, pubic hair, body growth, and **menarche**, or menstruation. Boys experience growth of the scrotum and testes, the voice deepens, and pubic hair develops. Girls may experience secondary sex characteristics at a younger age than boys, yet the experience is based on heredity and other factors (Papalia et al., 2007). Gender differences in motor skills and physical fitness and participating in sports has changed. Boys and girls are encouraged to participate in a wide range of physical activities and are no longer limited to gender-specific sports or games (Broderick & Blewitt, 2020). Girls in middle childhood begin to experience the changes in their emotional and physical development, which influences the types of activities they select. Schools require physical education and provide a variety of sports and physical activities, including track and field, softball, basketball, and gymnastics during school and after school. Boys during middle childhood are active, play roughly, and identify specific sports they enjoy. Boys strive toward mastery and competition in team sports such as basketball, baseball, and football both with peers and in extracurricular activities, clubs, or teams. In recent times, boys have shown more interest in video games and less with outdoor physical skills. (Broderick & Blewitt, 2020).

Children's gender roles may vary in different cultures and be influenced by religions or traditions to shelter the development. Female roles are limited to strict customs and geared toward homemaking and adapting traditional appropriate activities (Broderick & Blewitt, 2020; Thomas, 2000). In some cultures, females who are promised during the middle years for marriage or mating with older males are kept in same-gender relationships until the marriage occurs. This may include minimal education and socializing outside of the female gender. Conversely, males are privileged and control every aspect of the community (McKay & McKay, 2010). Males gain rites of passage, which include economic, political, educational, social, and financial privileges that are not generally available to females. This privilege is acknowledged in countries and cultures based on a history of male dominance in the family, which is determined by religion and tradition.

## ABLEISM

### GIFTED CHILDREN

Educational systems identify a student's abilities by a number of standardized, quantitative psychometric assessments (Papalia et al., 2007), but giftedness is challenging to measure and identify. Traditionally, children are **gifted** if their intelligence quotient (IQ) is about 130 or above the national average in the 98th percentile, which may exclude or limit the creativeness of other children due to a test score. Recently, in addition to IQ, educators have included multiple criteria for identifying giftedness in students, such as academic achievement, other measures of performance, creativity, and parent and educator referrals. These students have characteristics of high motivation, passion for learning, and a drive to excel. Socially, these students associate with peers who are outstanding in academic performance yet still need parent and educator support.

### LEARNING AND INTELLECTUAL DISABILITY

Middle childhood is a major milestone for children. Educational and social issues should be addressed as early as possible in preschool, early childhood, or early elementary middle childhood (Papalia et al., 2007). Children with learning and intellectual disabilities have to meet criteria established by the federal and state government agencies under the Individual with Disabilities Education Act (IDEA), which requires educators to provide services in an Individual Education Program (IEP). The IEP's purpose is to scaffold the student's academic, emotional, social, and learning needs by meeting the criteria of goals and objectives set to identify mastery and following the student's progress in the school environment. If children require services, parents and teachers can request an evaluation at any point in the child's educational experience.

## MALTREATMENT

### ABUSE AND NEGLECT

The child's home environment is important at all ages. Some believe parents are the child's first teachers. Research has indicated maltreatment, abuse, and neglect produces major consequences for children of all ages, particularly in middle childhood or the learning years (Papalia et al., 2007). These children become aggressive and withdrawn in every environment. Physical abuse causes children to gravitate toward aggressive and emotionally or socially inappropriate behaviors at home, school, and in other settings. They are withdrawn with peers due to rejection from the negative interaction. Children who are neglected tend to have medical or developmental growth issues, academic delays, and social malfunctioning with peers. They may turn to delinquent behaviors to meet their lack of resources during neglected periods. Sexual abuse is traumatic for any child and has long-range effects. If unaddressed and prolonged, these conditions have grave implications and outcomes for children and families.

## TRAUMA IN MIDDLE CHILDHOOD

Often, children are confronted with traumatizing experiences at a young age. By the time the child reaches middle childhood, the child may reexperience trauma through memories, relationships, environments, or similar experiences of additional traumas that induce anxiety (Broderick & Blewitt, 2020). The experiences may include child abuse and neglect, sexual molestation, reactive attachment, and exposure to violence. Helping victims of trauma includes dispelling fears, identifying benefits of recovery, and learning acceptance to transition past trauma. Counselors can do this by providing a safe place, encouraging use of mindfulness and relaxing coping interventions, and increasing victim efficacy, which is the ability to control the anxiety associated with the trauma while supporting resilience and prevention of recurrence and despair.

## MORTALITY AWARENESS

Children's understanding of mortality is connected to cognitive development (Papalia et al., 2007). Although the early child attaches illness and mortality to his or her personal behaviors of being bad, children in the middle childhood age group understand that being healthy is a choice. Main causes of death at this age are accidents and firearms. In the past decade, middle age children's deaths occurred due to accidents on bicycles, snowmobiles, trampolines, and other physical activities in which safety measures were in question. Introduction of negative influences and peer pressure may also influence the middle child's choices and experiences. Peer pressure to experiment with **gateway drugs**, such as tobacco, alcohol, and marijuana, is challenging for middle childhood individuals who want to fit in with the group (Papalia et al., 2007). The gateway drugs impair the middle child's functioning socially, academically, and behaviorally, and their use may lead to using more harmful illegal substances.

## Summary

Middle childhood is an important time for children's growth and development. This time of the child's life is often called the "learning years." Children are in school most of the day, 9 months of the year, and practice honing social and behavioral skills learned in early childhood. They transition from early middle childhood in kindergarten through third grade to late middle childhood in fourth through fifth grades. Cognitive skills are addressed and gradually improve. Parents, educators, and significant adults must scaffold, support, and provide a proactive home environment for their child as well as intervene when milestones are unmet or the child displays present-level needs and concerns.

Tiana is an 11-year-old Black girl from New Orleans. She has an older sister, Nyla, who recently turned 13. Tiana and Nyla relate well most days, but sometimes their arguments sound like a WWE wrestling match. Tiana is constantly being compared to Nyla by her teachers and her gymnastics coach. Tiana is popular, earns good grades, and is liked by many of her teachers. However, Nyla was more popular (especially with boys), made better grades, and became the favorite of all the teachers. Tiana did not know what she could do to be outshined Nyla in those areas, but for a while, gymnastics was her domain. She was the best at tumbling, vaulting, and the beam. Then, out of nowhere, Nyla decided she wanted to learn gymnastics to add to her cheering abilities.

After a few weeks of being on the same all-star team, Nyla was being recognized more than Tiana and given all the attention by the coaches. Days were soon filled with nonsensical arguments over minor things, silent treatments at the dinner table, and destruction of each other's belongings.

One night after an intense gymnastics practice, the girls shouted at each other the entire trip home and throughout dinner. Tiana had taken Nyla's wrist tape out of her bag and would not let Nyla use hers. The girls' parents were frustrated and told Tiana that if she did one more thing to Nyla she would not be allowed to go to gymnastics for three weeks. Suddenly, they heard Nyla shout, "Why, Tiana, why would you throw that sweater at me while I was trying to do homework? You knocked my soda over, and my computer is all wet!" Tiana, with a tinge of sarcasm in her voice, replied, "Well, you said I better give you your sweater back, and I thought now was the best time." Their dad decreed, "Go to your room. That's it, no gymnastics for three weeks." As she walked across the hall, Tiana's cold scowl transformed into a Cheshire grin, knowing her plan to skip gymnastics was a success.

1. How does the slight difference in age affect the way Tiana and Nyla relate to each other?
2. From Tiana's actions, what is she struggling with? As her counselor, how would you help her navigate what she is feeling?
3. What were Tiana's parents trying to do, and what did they fall victim to?
4. How would you work with the family to resolve the different issues that are occurring?

## Reflections and Targeted Discussion Questions

1. When children do not master physical milestones in early middle childhood development, will this affect congruent stages of development in late middle childhood development? How? Why?
2. Why is understanding all the cognitive processing of middle childhood development important for working with children?
3. How can children's growth and development be influenced by parenting style and temperament?

# References

Bandura, A. (2003). On the psychosocial impact and mechanisms of spiritual modeling. *The International Journal for the Psychology of Religion, 13*(3), 167–173.

Baumrind, D. (1989). Rearing competent children. In W. Damon (Ed.), *Child development today and tomorrow* (pp. 349–378). Jossey-Bass.

Broderick, P. C., & Blewitt, P. (2020). *The life span: Human development for helping professionals* (5th ed.). Pearson Education.

Center on the Developing Child. (2007). *The science of early childhood development* (in brief). www.developingchild.harvard.edu

Forsythe, F. (2020). Four most interesting theories of intelligence in psychology. *Learning Mind.* https://www.learning-mind.com/theories-of-intelligence-in-psychology/#:~:text=%20Theories%20of%20Intelligence%20in%20Psychology%20%201,Development.%20This%20theory%20of%20intelligence%20is...%20More%20

Kail, R. V., & Cavanaugh, J. C. (2016). *Human development: A life-span view* (7th ed.). Cengage Learning.

Keogh, B. (2009). *How temperament affects parents, children, and family life.* https://www.greatschools.org/gk/articles/temperament-affects-parents-children-family/

McKay, B., & Mckay, K. (2010). 8 Interesting (and Insane) Male Rites of Passage. In *A man's life: On manhood, rites of passage.* https://www.artofmanliness.com/articles/male-rites-of-passage-from-around-the-world/

Morin, A. (2019). Through the years: Child development milestones. *Verywell Family.* https://www.verywellfamily.com/10-year-old-developmental-milestones-620710#cognitive-development

Morin, A., & Garbi, L. (2020). Through the years: Child development milestones. *Verywell Family.* https://www.verywellfamily.com/9-year-old-developmental-milestones-620731

New York Times. (1976). *The wild boy of Aveyron.* See the article in original context from May 16, 1976, p. 214. https://www.nytimes.com/1976/05/16/archives/the-wild-boy-of-aveyron.html?auth=link-dismiss-google1tap

Papalia, D. E., Olds, S. W., & Feldman, R. D. (2007). *Human development* (10th ed.). McGraw-Hill.

Peters, D. K. (2012). *Covert bullying: When do teachers recognize it?* (Order No. 3490611, Texas A&M University–Commerce). *ProQuest Dissertations and Theses, 67.* http://search.proquest.com/docview/916916694?accountid=458. (916916694)

Thomas, R. M. (2000). *Comparing theories of child development* (5th ed.). Wadsworth/Thomas Learning.

Watson, W. H. (2012). Family systems. *Encyclopedia of Human Behavior.* https://www.sciencedirect.com/topics/medicine-and-dentistry/family-systems-theory

## Credits

# Adolescent Development

Noréal F. Armstrong, PhD

*Childhood tends to life, Adolescence tries life, and an old age regrets about it.* —Pierre Bolste

## Learning Objectives

After reading this chapter, you should be able to
1. Define key concepts relevant to adolescent development.
2. Explain how physical, cognitive, social, cultural, and environmental factors intersect and affect adolescent development.
3. Develop a theoretical foundation for working with adolescents.

## Introduction

Adolescence is the period of development when a child transitions from childhood to adulthood (Berk, 2014). The beginning of the transitional time often marks puberty and is the catalyst for young children to begin mastering complex tasks. Those tasks include navigating biological, environmental, cognitive, emotional, and social changes; learning about sexuality, health issues, identity development, and how to cope with peer pressure, relationship, substance use, and other factors related to becoming an adult. Adolescence is a period of time that requires rapid growth in many areas of development at the same time and over a short period. This chapter will address the different growth areas, what is occurring during each, and how knowing this information will be of use in the therapeutic setting. Furthermore, this chapter will highlight how mental health disorders may connect with issues during adolescent development. Lastly, this chapter will challenge the reader to assess how current social, cultural, and environmental changes affect adolescent development, engagement from a systemic perspective, and counseling adolescents.

## Key Concepts

- **Ego Identity:** The conscious sense of self we gain from social interaction.
- **Fidelity:** The psychological virtue characterized by an individual's ability to relate to others and form genuine connections.
- **Differentiation**: To become different in the process of growth and to be aware of what makes someone different.
- **Hypo-Deductive Reasoning:** The ability to think scientifically through generating predictions, or hypotheses, and answering questions.
- **Acculturation:** Changes in behavior, cognition, values, language cultural activities, personal relationship styles, and beliefs that a culturally underrepresented group goes through as it encounters the dominant culture.
- **Enculturation:** The socialization process by which individuals learn and acquire the cultural and psychological qualities of their own group.

## The Human Developing Process

As humans we develop in a variety of ways. There is physical development, cognitive development, social development, emotional development, and cultural development. Many scientists and theorists believe development is a process that occurs in stages. There is a threshold to meet at each stage before moving on to the next. This chapter will address the different forms of development specific to the adolescent stage of life. What can help or hinder development? How can culture, socialization, and environment affect or alter development? The length of adolescence and its demands and pressures vary greatly among cultures. Thus, researchers have often divided it into three phases: early adolescence (11 or 12 to 14 years) is the period of rapid pubertal change; middle adolescence (14 to 16 years) is when puberty is nearly complete; and during late adolescence (16 to 18 years) the teen reaches full adult appearance and prepares to assume adult roles (Berk, 2014; Rapport, 2016). The construct of adolescence was popularized by the work of Hall (1904) within his two-volume work *Adolescence*. Adolescence is a breaking away from one's childhood to prepare for adulthood, a period during which there are ever-present conflicting themes for the adolescent to confront (e.g., responsibility/irresponsibility, childlike ambitions/adultlike ambitions) in their social world (Scheer et al., 2007).

## PHYSICAL DEVELOPMENT

As children enter adolescence, ages 12 to 18, they experience growth spurts and sexual maturation called puberty. The growth spurts can occur rapidly and then slow during this 5-year time frame. Adolescents will experience changes differently. It is important to remember that some may show signs of maturity earlier or later than others. The onset of changes is influenced by environment, genetics, and diet (U.S. Department of Health and Human Services, n.d.; Kail & Cavanaugh, 2016). The start of puberty in boys and girls is influenced by both the mother and the father. In girls, signs of maturity such as breast development and pubic hair are strongly influenced by environmental factors. These environmental exposures include diet and obesity. In addition, chemicals that mimic human hormones have been linked to playing a role in the early onset of girls' puberty in developed countries.

The beginning of adolescence is loosely anchored to the onset of puberty, which brings dramatic alterations in hormone levels and a number of consequent physical changes. Puberty onset is also associated with profound changes in drives, motivations, psychology, and social life. These changes continue throughout adolescence (Blakemore et al., 2010). A first outward sign of puberty is the rapid gain in height and weight known as a growth spurt (Berk, 2014). Puberty is experienced as a series of events. The under- or overdevelopment of an adolescent can lead to increased risk of social and emotional problems. One study suggests that those who go through puberty early may be shorter than average because they stop growing at an early age following the initial growth spurt. These people are at an increased risk for obesity as adults.

There are 1.2 billion adolescents worldwide, the largest cohort of this age group in history (UNICEF, n.d.). We will explore separately the average physical changes that adolescent boys and girls experience.

### BOYS

Puberty on average starts between ages 9.5 and 14 years, with the enlargement of testicles followed 1 year later by enlargement of the penis. Pubic hairs develop around age 13, and nocturnal emissions start at age 14. **Spermarche**, or the first ejaculation, normally occurs around age 13.5. Facial hair, underarm hair, and voice changes occur at age 15 (Stanford Children's Health, n.d.; Rapport, 2016).

### GIRLS

Puberty on average starts between ages 8 and 13, with the development of breasts followed by pubic hair. **Menarche**, or the first menstruation, typically occurs around age 12.5 for North American girls, age 13 for western Europeans, and generally has a wide range from ages 10.5 to 15 years (Berk, 2014). Underarm hair begins to grow following breast development and pubic hair growth after menarche. Nature may delay sexual maturity until a girl's body is large enough for childbearing, and menarche will take place after the peak of the growth spurt (Stanford Children's Health, n.d.).

### WELLNESS GOALS

Physical activity is necessary in all facets of life. Adolescents should engage in 60 minutes of moderate to vigorous exercise daily. Research shows that only 30% of adolescent boys and 13% of girls get enough exercise. Activities should be varied and include tasks that will increase heart, bone, and muscle strength. Brisk walking, running, and swimming increase heart strength; jumping, and basketball are good for bone strength; and weight lifting increases muscle strength.

Nutrition is an important process within adolescent development. Adolescents are in the second largest growth stage after infancy, and the growth spurt during this stage of life requires the consumption of key nutrients and a healthy diet that includes calcium, iron, and vitamins A, C, and D. Adolescents who are more active may require additional nutrients. Being active can also protect against obesity. In 2019, the prevalence of obesity was 18.5% for adolescents and children (Centers for Disease Control and Prevention, 2019). Several factors contribute to children becoming obese, including heredity, parents, sedentary lifestyle, and too little sleep.

Dieting can become a common concern during adolescence. Diet trends can lead to unhealthy behaviors such as restricting intake, skipping meals, taking diet pills, or purging after a meal. **Anorexia nervosa** is a disorder marked by a persistent refusal to eat and an irrational fear of being overweight. Unfortunately, without treatment, as many as 15% of adolescents with anorexia have died (Berk, 2014). **Bulimia nervosa** is a disorder in which individuals alternate between binge eating (uncontrolled overconsumption of food) and purging (self-induced vomiting or the use of laxatives). Although less common, boys make up about 10% of diagnosed cases of eating disorders. A meta-analysis of studies of individuals with eating disorders, conducted by Jacob et al. in 2004 (Berk, 2014), identified risk factors unique to bulimia and anorexia. Obesity in childhood is associated with adolescent bulimia, but not anorexia. Conversely, overprotective parenting is associated with adolescents becoming anorexic, but not bulimic.

In the digital age we live in, adolescents spend a lot of time online. Larsen and Martey (2011) reported that 31% of the 93% of all U.S. adolescents online have used the internet to search information on general health, dieting, and physical fitness. In addition, 69% of adolescents with specific health concerns reported finding useful and correct health information. Parents can be a source of support by modeling healthy eating habits and exercise, leaving out snacks, limiting screen time and TV, encouraging family dinners, and including the adolescent in food choices for meals (Cincinnati Children's, 2018).

Consistent communication about eating habits, wellness, and exercise can help adolescents navigate the rough waters of their body's development. There are online tools available to assist parents and adolescents with learning and engaging in healthy eating habits when at home and when dining out. Two such tools are ChooseMyPlate.gov (https://www.choosemyplate.gov/) and Eatright (https://www.eatright.org/).

## COGNITIVE DEVELOPMENT

Along with the physical changes of adolescence, cognitive changes develop as well. Boys and girls at this age are able to think abstractly, seek autonomy, set goals, and begin to individuate from parents. Teens will likely gain interest in social issues, philosophy, and politics; they can think about long-term goals, and begin to compare themselves with their peers. During this stage of life, teens will want to have more independence from parents, will desire acceptance by peers, and will begin to focus on romantic and sexual relationships. Piaget would say that during adolescence (age 12 to adulthood) teens have entered the formal operational stage. In this stage, they gain the ability to think abstractly, think creatively, imagine possible outcomes, and manipulate ideas in their heads without dependence on concrete manipulation (McLeod, 2010). **Inferential reasoning** is a sign of the formal operational stage. An example would be the ability to answer the following question: If Jacob has more money than Edward, and Edward has more money than Bella, who has the most money? The child who can answer the question correctly has the ability to think about things not experienced and draw conclusions from his or her thinking.

Two additional core tenets of the formal operational stage are **abstract thinking** and **hypo-deductive reasoning**. **Abstract thought** is an individual's ability to think about concepts they have yet to experience; it is important for future planning. **Hypo-deductive reasoning** is the ability to think scientifically through generating predictions, or hypotheses, about the world and answering those questions.

Erikson's identity versus role confusion stage states that developing a sense of self and connecting to one's ability is important at this stage. It is the fifth of the eight stages, with the basic virtue to achieve being **fidelity**—the psychological virtue characterized by an individual's ability to relate to others and form genuine connections. Erikson believed that at each stage an individual faces a developmental conflict that must be resolved to develop the virtue of that stage. **Ego identity** is the conscious sense of self we gain from social interaction. Successfully completing this stage leads to a strong sense of self that will continue throughout life. If there are issues and an individual is not given opportunities to explore different identities, an adolescent may grow up struggling without knowing who they are or what they want, drift in and out of jobs and relationships, and have issues of self-esteem and self-worth.

In their search for identity, adolescents may move through four ways of thinking: adolescent egocentrism, imaginary audience, personal fable, and illusion of invulnerability (Kail & Cavanaugh, 2016). Adolescents during this time tend to be more self-oriented, caring mostly about their experiences and feelings, despite the fact they have developed the ability to understand that others have different viewpoints. The chart below defines and provides an example of each thought process.

TABLE 8.1    Features of Adolescent Thought

| FEATURE | DEFINITION | EXAMPLE |
|---|---|---|
| Adolescent egocentrism | Adolescents are overly concerned with their own thoughts and feelings. | Greg gets upset because he is forced to attend his father's work promotion event on the night he planned to attend Jacob's party. He ignores his father's excitement. |
| Imaginary audience | Adolescents believe that others are watching them constantly. | Tameka tripped while descending stairs as she left biology class. She KNEW her gymnastics friends saw the fall and would tease her. |

(Continued)

TABLE 8.1    (Continued)

| FEATURE | DEFINITION | EXAMPLE |
|---|---|---|
| Personal fable | Adolescents believe that their experiences and feelings are unique. | Corey tore his ACL and was out for the season. As he shared his anger with his dad, he thought, *He still doesn't understand.* |
| Illusion of invulnerability | Adolescents think that misfortune happens only to others. | Roshun was joyriding and speeding with friends. One suggested he slow down, but he thought there was no way he would get a ticket. |

## SUBSTANCE USE AND ADOLESCENCE

Cognitive development can be altered by the introduction of substances. The period of adolescence is vital to healthy cognitive function as an adult, so it is important to maintain a strict level of healthy behavior during these years. Drug abuse can affect the brain's ability to function in the short term and prevent proper growth and development later in life. Prescription drugs and opioid use are being accessed more by adolescents. The use of opiates is growing at an alarming rate (National Institute on Drug Abuse, 2018). Opioid overdoses increased 30% from July 2016 through September 2017 in 52 areas in 45 states (National Institute on Drug Abuse, 2018). According to the DSM 5 (APA, 2013), substance use disorders are patterns of symptoms resulting from the use of a substance that one continues to take despite experiencing problems as a result. Substance use disorders cover 11 criteria. A person suffering with substance use disorder may have mild, moderate, or severe usage, be in remission, or engaged in active use. Research suggests the use of substances can alter brain development (National Institute on Drug Abuse, 2018).

## SOCIAL AND EMOTIONAL DEVELOPMENT

As adolescent bodies grow and change, so do their hormones. Higher hormonal levels are modestly linked to increases in adolescent moodiness (Berk, 2014). Research has found that adolescent moodiness is often a result of the highs and lows of this stage of development, spurred by such events as arguments with parents, breakups with romantic partners, and conflicts with authority at school. Positive attitudes are fostered by spending time being active with friends and hanging out with them, while being home without activities to engage in can lead to loneliness (Berk, 2014; Kail & Cavanaugh, 2016).

During this stage of development, adolescents began to have more adultlike bodies and higher cognitive processing abilities. This change in physical and cognitive abilities can be a source of tension as adolescents try to assert themselves and become more autonomous. They may have more arguments with parents about curfew, dating, respect, and homework (Apter, 2009; Berk, 2014). The underlying desire of the adolescent is to be seen as mature, capable, and having value (Apter, 2009). **Individuation** is a developmental process involving an individual's successive and progressive negotiation of the balance between separateness and connectedness in relationship to the family of origin (Levpušček, 2006). Girls tend to have more successful individuation from parents and friends, while boys show more excessive autonomy strivings in their individuation. In cases of less satisfactory relations with parents, adolescents can compensate for the deprivation of their dependency needs by seeking support from their friends.

Adolescents also struggle with body image. Body image decreases significantly during adolescence, resulting in widespread body dissatisfaction and associated eating disturbances, particularly among adolescent females (Meier & Gray, 2013). Many adolescents spend more time looking in the mirror, checking for additional physical changes (Kail & Cavanaugh, 2016). Girls tend to compare their bodies with their peers and are more likely to be dissatisfied when appearance is a common topic of conversation. Conversely, boys' emotions around body image are less negatively influenced by peers and more negatively influenced by the expectation of having a physical appearance that is strong and muscular.

Pressure to have the perfect body is increased tremendously by living in the digital age and seeing the flood of media images. It is not the total time spent on Facebook (FB) or the internet, but the amount of FB time allocated to photo activity that is associated with greater thin-as-ideal internalization, self-objectification, weight dissatisfaction, and drive for thinness. Results are consistent with research findings on traditional media effects that conclude exposure to specific TV and magazine genres predicted body dissatisfaction when total media consumption did not (Meier & Gray, 2013). Research has also found that girls, already struggling with eating disorders, tend to view more social media images presenting the thin ideal body.

## SOCIAL CIRCLES AND CONFLICT

Cultivating and maintaining friendships is an important task during adolescence. Friendships are specific attachments that carry expectations such as loyalty, trust, and intimacy. Friendships are voluntary and must have common ground and affirmation for formation and maintenance (Bukowski et al., 1998). Although, friendships may not be permanent, their significance in adolescent development should not be discounted. As with other parts of adolescence, friendship building comes with conflicts and at times aggression. Aggression is a major concern not only because of the detrimental effects of aggression on its victims, but also because of the long-term negative developmental outcomes associated with being a perpetrator. Aggression can be either physical or relational. "Crick and Grotpeter (1995) coined the term "relational aggression" to designate directly or indirectly aggressive behaviors that harm social relationships, e.g., behaviors such as spreading rumors and excluding peers" (Lansford et al., 2012, p. 3).

Although boys were both directly and indirectly more aggressive than girls, cluster analysis revealed a group of highly aggressive adolescents whose use of aggression was predominantly indirect and they were girls. Many studies exist on gender differences in aggression and although girls tend to shy away from physical and relational aggression between 2 to 8 years old, girls demonstrate the most extreme relational aggression (Lansford et al., 2012). Age related shifts in aggression might lead to within group ostracism. Ostracism is the act or acts of ignoring and excluding of an individual or groups by an individual or group in social context to act aggressively and gain control over social relationships or to control contra-normative behavior and to regulate or protect the group (Wolfer, 2013). Boys or girls who do not follow group norms or demonstrate perceived correct physical or relational aggression may be ostracized to correct their behavior.

### PSYCHOSOCIAL STAGES

Sigmund Freud and Erikson believed that personality developed in a series of stages. Unlike Freud's theory of psychosexual stages, Erikson's theory described the effect of social experience across the whole life span. Erikson was interested in how social interaction and relationships played a role in the development and growth of human beings.

Each stage in Erikson's theory builds on the preceding stages and paves the way for following periods of development. In each stage, Erikson believed people experience a conflict that serves as a turning point in development. These conflicts are centered on either developing a psychological quality or failing to develop that quality. During these times, the potential for personal growth is high, but so is the potential for failure.

If people successfully deal with the conflict, they emerge from the stage with psychological strengths that will serve them well for the remainder of their lives. If they fail to deal effectively with these conflicts, they may not develop the essential skills needed for a strong sense of self.

Erikson also believed that a sense of competence motivates behaviors and actions. Each stage in Erikson's theory is concerned with becoming competent in an area of life. If the stage is handled well, the person will feel a sense of mastery, which is sometimes referred to as ego strength or ego quality. If the stage is managed poorly, the person will emerge with a sense of inadequacy in that aspect of development. See figure 8.1 below on Erikson's psychosocial stages.

**FIGURE 8.1**    Erik Erikson Psychosocial Stages Chart

Lev Vygotsky developed a sociocultural approach to cognitive development. Vygotsky believed social learning tends to precede development and that language has a strong influence on social learning. The social development theory leans on social and cultural interactions as a strong factor in childhood development. He strongly believed that community plays a central role in "making meaning" (Kail & Cavanaugh, 2016). For adolescents, that community consists of family members and peers. According to Vygotsky, during adolescence the system that directs functioning at each stage is motivated by different interests due to the sexual maturation of teens. In this sense, sexual maturation is the appearance of new needs and stimulations and the foundation for the whole change in the system of interest for adolescents. Vygotsky's zone of proximal development and scaffolding have been discussed in previous chapters. What follows is a chart comparing the theoretical components of Piaget and Vygotsky.

TABLE 8.2    Differences Between Piaget and Vygotsky

|  | PIAGET | VYGOTSKY |
|---|---|---|
| Sociocultural context | Little emphasis | Strong emphasis |
| Constructivism | Cognitive constructivist | Social constructivist |
| Stages | Strong emphasis on stages of development | No general stages of development proposed |
| Key processes in development and learning | Equilibration, schema, adaptation, assimilation, accommodation | Zone of proximal development, scaffolding, language/dialogue, tools of the culture |
| Role of language | Minimal—language provides labels for children's experiences (egocentric speech) | Major—language plays a powerful role in shaping thought. |
| Teaching implications | Support children to explore their world and discover knowledge | Establish opportunities for children to learn with the teacher and more skilled peers |

*Source*: McLeod, 2018

As adolescents strive to achieve an identity, they often progress through different phases or statuses. Those phases include diffusion, foreclosure, moratorium, and achievement (Kail & Cavanaugh, 2016). Unlike Piaget's stages, these stages may not occur in sequence. Diffusion and foreclosure most often occur in young adolescence, while teens may alternate between achievement and moratorium as they progress to older adolescence. Achievement of an adolescent's identity developing across various domains (religion, politics, and occupation) occurs at different times. The chart below defines and provides an example of each phase.

**TABLE 8.3**   Adolescent Identity Statuses

| STATUS | DEFINITION | EXAMPLE |
|---|---|---|
| Diffusion | The individual is overwhelmed by the task of achieving an identity and does little to accomplish the task. | Kyle has missed 40 days of school and, when asked by the counselor, said he only comes to school to socialize and talk to her. |
| Foreclosure | The individual has a status determined by adults rather than personal exploration. | Cherica is from a military family and when they came to the school to recruit she was one of the first in line. She hadn't considered other options. |
| Moratorium | The individual is examining different alternatives but has yet to find one that's satisfactory. | Jade enjoys a lot of things; some days she wants to be a tennis player, some days she thinks of being a veterinarian, other days she considers doing photography. |
| Achievement | The individual has explored alternatives and has deliberately chosen a specific identity. | Charity took art classes in eighth and ninth grades, then joined the soccer team in 10th grade, but after volunteering at a children's hospital, she knew she wanted to be a pediatrician. |

### RITES OF PASSAGE

As youth develop in their social context, they often are thought to experience what we subsequently refer to as a "rites of passage" in ways that create either a positive or negative orientation to their navigation through adolescence to adulthood. In general, these rites of passage have been the way our species have responded to individual and community stressors and the resulting imbalance that occurs during life transitions. Arnold van Gennep first used the term "rites of passage" in 1908 in his seminal work *Les rites de passage.* He noticed a pattern of events that contained similar activities, which he classified as (1) **Separation** from a previous status; (2) **Margin or liminality** as a period of uncertainty characterized by anxiety, "betwixt and between" two different states; and (3) **Reincorporation** as an integration of new attitudes, values, and/or behaviors that connoted a new status (Scheer et al., 2007, p. 2).

One such effort is the Rite Of Passage Experience©, ROPE®, which follows the guiding principles discussed earlier. Organizations such as the Boys and Girls Clubs of America, 4-H Youth Development, YMCA, Boy Scouts of America, and Girl Scouts of the USA aid in rite-of-passage-type opportunities for healthy adolescent transitions. Religious organizations also have been committed to youth and their healthy development for hundreds of years, whether through Sunday school programs or rite-of-passage rituals, including bar/bat mitzvahs, confirmations, and baptisms (Ream and Witt 2004). Studies indicate that these religious rites of passage have a positive influence on youth through spiritual development, supportive peer relationships, and mentorships (Scheer et al., 2007).

Rites of passage are powerful social events that help guide and affirm a transition from one status in life to another. One of the most critical transitions is from adolescence to adulthood, where youth will either progress into adulthood with life trajectories for success (responsibility, financial independence, healthy relationships) or difficulties (crime, unemployment, irresponsibility). For rites of passage to have lasting impact, they should be framed as events that have special meaning for the adolescent in the context of community and culture. Rites of passage are influenced by the culture of the adolescent. Below are a few rites of passage from different cultures (Nunez & Pfeffer, 2016). You can read the full list online at https://www.globalcitizen.org/en/content/13-amazing-coming-of-age-traditions-from-around-th/.

- The Sateré-Mawé Coming Of Age Tradition: Bullet Ant Initiation
  - In the Brazilian Amazon, young boys belonging to the indigenous Sateré-Mawé tribe mark their coming of age in a Bullet and Ant Initiation when they turn 13.
- Amish Coming of Age Tradition: Rumspringa
  - Rumspringa marks the time when youth turn 16 and are finally able to enjoy unsupervised weekends away from family. They are encouraged to enjoy whatever pleasures they like.
- Hispanic Coming of Age Tradition: Quinceanera
  - In many parts of Central and South America, young girls celebrate their Quinceanera when they turn 15 years old. She renews her baptismal vows and solidifies her commitment to her family and faith.
- Khatam Al Koran Coming of Age Tradition: Malaysia
  - In Malaysia, 11 is a special birthday for some Muslim girls, as it marks the time they can celebrate Khatam Al Koran, a prestigious ritual that demonstrates their growing maturity.

## KOHLBERG'S MORAL DEVELOPMENT

Moral reasoning and development occurs in stages much as other forms of development. Lawrence Kohlberg identified three levels of moral reasoning: **preconventional, conventional, and postconventional.** Each level is further divided into two substages.

Level One: Preconventional

- **Stage 1. Obedience and Punishment Orientation**. The child/individual is good in order to avoid being punished. If a person is punished, they must have done wrong.
- **Stage 2. Individualism and Exchange**. At this stage, children recognize that there is not just one right view that is handed down by the authorities. Different individuals have different viewpoints.

Level 2: Conventional

- **Stage 3. Good Interpersonal Relationships**. The child/individual is good in order to be seen as being a good person by others. Therefore, answers relate to the approval of others.
- **Stage 4. Maintaining the Social Order**. The child/individual becomes aware of the wider rules of society, so judgments concern obeying the rules in order to uphold the law and to avoid guilt.

Level 3: Postconventional Stage

- **Stage 5. Social Contract and Individual Rights**. The child/individual becomes aware that while rules/laws might exist for the good of the greatest number, there are times when they will work against the interest of particular individuals.
- The issues are not always clear-cut. For example, in Heinz's dilemma, the protection of life is more important than breaking the law against stealing.
- **Stage 6. Universal Principles**. People at this stage have developed their own set of moral guidelines that may or may not fit the law. The principles apply to everyone.
  - E.g., human rights, justice, and equality. The person will be prepared to act to defend these principles even if it means going against the rest of society in the process and having to pay the consequences of disapproval or imprisonment (McLeod, 2013).

For most children, the preconventional level is moral reasoning based on trusting authority figures to know what is right and wrong. For many adolescents and adults, stage 1 of moral reasoning is controlled almost exclusively by rewards and punishments. In the conventional level, moral reasoning is based more on societal norms and determined largely by others' expectations. Adolescents in stage 3 of the conventional level become focused on winning the approval of others. At the post-conventional level, moral reasoning is based on a personal code and no longer precipitated by rewards and punishments or social norms. Some limitations of Kohlberg's theory include dilemmas that are artificial and hypothetical, a biased sample, and a poorly constructed research design. However, many believe moral development during adolescence is a key as we move into adulthood.

## DIGITAL NATIVES AND THE IGENERATION

According to IGI Global (www.igi-global.com), the digital generation is a generation who has grown up with easy access to digital information and communication technologies. They are people whose generational location places their birth and developmental experiences during a time of widespread access to digital computing technologies—and whose exposure to and experience with those technologies led to a comfort and expertise with electronic devices that surpasses those of prior generations. Adolescents are avid users of mobile devices. Nearly 80% of adolescents in the United States now own a mobile phone, and they use them to send an average of 60 text messages per day (George & Odgers, 2014).

Having ease of access to so much information has changed the cognitive, social, and emotional landscape of adolescence. Gone are the days of going to the library, using the Dewey Decimal System to locate a book or encyclopedia to research the history of a country in Africa. Now, Google and Siri provide intel and data as quickly as a person can ask for it. Access to so much data and intel can have positive and negative effects on development. As the adolescent brain is developing, it works to be more efficient by eliminating unnecessary synapses and connections between different parts of the brain. This mental pruning allows the brain to be more focused and efficient. The potential overload of information and lack of regulation (either by parents or internet governing bodies) can lead to misinformation, misinformed actions, or altered path of development.

It may be that adolescents' frequent usage of new technologies, combined with their rapid cognitive, physical, and social development, makes them more vulnerable to the ill effects of technology (over)usage. Alternatively, the plasticity that characterizes this period may allow adolescents to optimize their potential within the digital world. Research is just beginning to emerge regarding how mobile technologies are influencing adolescents' still developing brains, bodies, and relationships.

More than 90% of children and teenagers in the United States play video games, and they spend substantial amounts of time playing. The increasing prevalence of digital media has led to growing public concerns about potential detrimental effects, including the possibility that video game play may be addicting. There is now a considerable body of research literature suggesting that some heavy users of video games indeed develop dysfunctional symptoms that can result in severe detrimental effects on functional and social areas of life (Gentile et al., 2017).

The American Psychiatric Association recently included internet gaming disorder (IGD) as a potential diagnosis. It is defined as "persistent and recurrent use of the Internet to engage in games, often with other players, leading to clinically significant impairment or distress" (Gentile et al., 2017, p. 82). Possible treatment options include various iterations of cognitive behavioral therapy that are most widely represented in published literature and practice, but other approaches, including family therapy and motivational interviewing, have also been used alone or in conjunction with cognitive behavioral therapy

As future counselors, we have to take into consideration the uniqueness of the iGeneration when we work with adolescents. From a systems perspective, one must consider the accompanying generations within the household, the parenting styles used, and the development of other children in the home. What pieces within an adolescent's mesosystem (Bronfenbrenner, 2005) are playing a role in how they develop? As you read this chapter, begin to think about how information from previous chapters connects with this information, and how you can use that knowledge to make an informed assessment of a potential client.

**FIGURE 8.2**    Social Engagement in a Digital World

# Obstacles and Oases

As individuals develop, there are a number of both positive and negative factors that may play a role. Consider socioeconomic status, homelessness, education level, parental unit (single parent, abusive parent, parenting style), trauma, and the justice system as obstacles or oases to healthy adolescent development. Developmental factors are influenced by environmental, cultural, and social allowances. Certain behaviors may be seen and characterized as deviant from one perspective but be characterized as resilient from another perspective. Some of the factors listed here cannot be escaped by adolescents who cannot legally leave negative situations. Here we will discuss a few of the obstacles that may arise in an adolescent's mesosystem.

## CAREER INTEREST

During adolescence, individuals often engage in and value the same activities as their friends in order to fulfill a need for relatedness, and such activity participation may lead them toward particular career paths. Part-time work during adolescence is also a key source of information about work and one's place in the workforce. Parents influence their children's values in four main ways: developing a socioemotional climate, acting as role models, providing key experiences, and transmitting their perceptions and expectations (Messersmith et al., 2008).

According to Rojewski and Kim (2003), social cognitive career theory is described as a complement or conceptual link to other theories of career behavior and provides a tentative explanation for (a) how occupational aspirations develop over time, (b) the influence of contextual variables like gender and SES on aspirations, and (c) the relationship between academic and occupational aspirations. SCCT posits that career self-efficacy, outcome expectations, and goals interact with personal, contextual, and learning factors to explain academic and career choices and attainment. Self-efficacy (situation-specific estimates of the ability to successfully perform a task or behavior) is a central factor in determining aspirations and subsequent behavior. The career choice process is seen as a dynamic one that is continuously modified by performance outcomes, such as academic achievement. As future counselors, it is imperative that you have tools to support various client needs. The U.S. Department of Labor's CareerOneStop (youth.gov) is a free online resource that provides employment information and inspiration. It is a place to manage careers, develop pathways to career success, and find tools to help job seekers, students, businesses, and career professionals. This resource and other tools are available at youth.gov.

## HOMELESSNESS

Homelessness is defined as an individual or family lacking a fixed, regular, or adequate nighttime residence which includes (1) a place not designed for or ordinarily used for nighttime accommodations, and (2) a publicly or privately operated shelter or transitional housing, including a hotel or motel, paid for by government or charitable donations.

Currently in America, nearly 40% of the homeless population is under 18 years old, 25% of former foster children become homeless within 2 to 4 years of leaving the system, and 50% of adolescents aging out of foster care and juvenile justice systems will be homeless within 6 months because they are unprepared to live independently and have limited education and no social support (U.S. Department of Health and Human Services, 2020). SAMHA reported that among homeless children, in one year 97% moved multiple times, 22% were separated from families, and 25% witnessed violence. Homeless children also experience higher rates of emotional and behavioral problems than children in low-income housing.

## ADVERSE CHILDHOOD EXPERIENCES

In 2007, Dr. Nadine Burke-Harris, began to see a correlation between traumatic experiences and health outcomes in the children she treated. After conducting research, she realized many were struggling with adverse childhood experiences (ACEs), and she founded the Bayview Child Health Center in San Francisco, California. ACEs are based on 10 categories discovered in a 1998 study by Kaiser Permanente and the Centers for Disease Control (CDC), including physical, emotional, and sexual abuse; physical and emotional neglect; a household where a parent was mentally ill, substance-dependent, or incarcerated; and parental separation or divorce, or domestic violence. This was the first large epidemiological study to document the association between adverse childhood experiences and heart disease, cancer, chronic lung disease, and Alzheimer's disease.

When we experience something frightening or traumatic, our body's flight-or-fight response releases stress hormones in our body, such as adrenaline and cortisol. The released hormones raise our blood pressure, raise our heart rate, and raise our blood sugar. These changes affect how our brains function. They also activate the amygdala, and that turns down the effectiveness of that part of the brain responsible for impulse control and judgment and executive functioning, which is the prefrontal cortex. When we activate our stress response, it also activates our immune system so that if you are in the ocean and you see the fin of a shark, your immune system is alerted to bring inflammation to stabilize the wound. The flight-or-fight response was designed to protect our lives and protect our health (Centers for Disease Control and Prevention, n.d.). When the shark appears night after night, what happens? When this system is activated repeatedly, it goes from being adaptive and life-saving to being maladaptive and health-damaging. Children are especially sensitive to high doses of adversity because their brains and bodies are just developing. So, adverse childhood experiences are associated with changes in the structure and function of children's developing brains, their developing hormonal systems, and even the way their DNA is read and transcribed (Centers for Disease Control and Prevention, n.d.).

### DATING AND DOMESTIC VIOLENCE

Dating or romantic relationships build from friendships, and often those in the relationship have things in common such as popularity and physical attractiveness (Kail & Cavanaugh, 2016). Adolescent relationships are at risk for dating violence. In 2007, 10% of adolescents nationwide reported being the victim of physical violence at the hands of a romantic partner during the previous year. Psychological victimization is even higher. Between two and three in 10 reported being verbally or psychologically abused in the previous year (Mulford & Giordano, 2008). Teens who perpetuate violence are influenced by parents and peers. Bandura's social learning theory suggests that adolescents learn to be violent toward dating partners by observing the behavior of important others model (such as parents or friends) and its positive consequences (Arriaga & Foshee, 2004). Dating violence is more common because of peer acceptance and peers being in their own abusive relationships (Arriaga & Foshee, 2004; Kail & Cavanaugh, 2016). Hispanics and Asian American adolescents may delay the initiation of romantic relationships because it's culturally seen as gaining independence while parents tend to value family and loyalty (Kail & Cavanaugh, 2016).

## Theoretical Considerations

Adolescence can be a confusing time of development for the child, parent, and clinician. Some theories work better in certain situations. Much of adolescence, according to Erikson, Vygotsky, and others, is an individual figuring out who they are separate from their parents. This growth process is differentiation. It is the process of growth where one becomes aware of what makes one different. Theories that would benefit those working through this ever-evolving process include narrative therapy, motivational interviewing, dialectical behavior therapy, acceptance and commitment therapy, and reality therapy. Similar among these theories is the autonomy for adolescents to tell their own story, adjust and move to acceptance of the current situation, and explore options for the choices they will have to make now and as they continue to develop. Expressive arts, music, bibliotherapy, and animal-assisted therapy have been helpful therapeutic interventions with adolescents.

## Strengths and Challenges from the "ISMs" Perspectives

Adolescence is a period of internalized and mental growth, along with physical growth. Development is influenced by factors that were not prevalent 20 years ago. Social media and the current political climate in the world have added to the strengths and challenges adolescents face.

### MULTICULTURAL

The developmental stage of adolescence is universal. How an individual navigates the adolescent stage is personal. Different cultures view adolescents and their roles in different ways. International students and adolescents who have immigrated to the country experience a different set of obstacles and oases. Oases may include bringing their language, culture, and traditions to share with their peers, which increases learning opportunities for those born in America. They may also bring a different perspective on human development, education, family, friendships, romantic relationships, marriage, and child rearing. Obstacles may include discrimination, bias, prejudice, stereotypes and microaggressions; learning a new language, culture, and tradition; and finding the ability to complete the citizenship process, work, and attend school. Many second-generation-immigrant adolescents serve as the liaison between the educational system and their parents due to a lack of resources and diversity of educational administration, faculty, and staff members. While experiencing the physical, cognitive, emotional, and social changes of adolescence, international and immigrated teens may vacillate between acculturation and enculturation. **Acculturation** is changes in behavior, cognition, values, language, cultural activities, personal relationship styles, and beliefs that a cultural minority undergoes as it encounters the dominant culture. **Enculturation** is the socialization process by which individuals learn and acquire the cultural and psychological qualities of their own group (Hays & Erford, 2018, p. 6).

### DIVERSITY

African American and Hispanic students are more likely to be sent home from school for behavior than their White counterparts. One study showed that Black boys are four times more likely to be suspended than their White counterparts and that the action is influenced by racial bias (Arends, 2019). A 2017 paper by researchers at the University of Texas, Austin, and Yale University and Stanford University found that Black and Hispanic students "who often bear the brunt of inconsistent school discipline, are less likely than white peers to trust their schools" (Arends, 2019).

Social circles are often formed similar to culture; that is, adolescents share similar values and beliefs that are shared across groups. Being in an environment that provides access to such connections can assist adolescents in discovering who they are among their peers and other adults outside the home. They are differentiating from their parents, while developing a sense of self and working through Erikson's stage of identity versus role confusion. When barriers prevent adolescents from successfully completing this stage, they may enter a stage of crisis that Erikson coined as an **identity crisis** (McLeod, 2010). Adolescence is a time of growth and exploration into self and how that self interacts with others and the world around them. It is a time period when growth is being affected by both the micro- and mesosystems of Bronfenbrenner's ecological system; therefore, exposure to diversity in many facets will influence the adolescent's development of self and their **worldview.**

### GENDER

By age 4, children's knowledge of gender stereotypes and gender-stereotyped activities is extensive. Gender stereotypes are beliefs and images about male and females that may or may not be true and exist across cultures (Kail & Cavanaugh, 2016). As children interact with parents, teachers, peers, and other people, messages are received that influence boys and girls to act differently. Children gradually begin to take on the specific behaviors associated with their gender and begin to identify with one group and develop their gender identity. Gender identity is a sense of oneself as male or female. Later, during adolescence, gender intensification occurs. Gender intensification is increased gender stereotyping of attitudes, behaviors, and movement toward a more traditional gender identity (Berk, 2014). By late adolescence, gender intensification declines. Adolescents who were encouraged to explore non-gender-typed options and question the value of gender stereotypes overall tended to be psychologically healthier, especially girls. Just as adolescents grow and develop a stronger sense of self, gender and gender identity are growing as well. The graphics that follow are to assist in understanding and talking about gender with the adolescent in your life.

# The Gender Person

**Gender Identity**

Woman — Man

A person's deeply felt internal and individual experience of gender, which may or may not correspond with the sex assigned at birth.

**Gender Expression**

Feminine — Masculine

The external display of one's gender, through a combination of appearance, disposition, social behavior, and other factors, generally measured on a scale of masculinity and femininity.

**Biological Sex**

Female — Male

A medical term used to refer to the chromosomal, hormonal, and anatomical characteristics that are used to classify an individual as female or male or intersex.

**Sexual Orientation**

Heterosexual — Homosexual

An enduring emotional, romantic, or sexual attraction primarily or exclusively to people of a particular gender.

USAID     PEPFAR     HEALTH POLICY PROJECT

**FIGURE 8.3**    Understanding Gender Better

| GENDER DEFINITIONS | |
|---|---|
| **Gender** | **Transgender** |
| The state of being male or female in typically regarding to social constructs rather than physical attributes. | Refers to someone who does not identify with the gender they were assigned at birth. |
| **Cisgender** | **Non-Binary** |
| Refers to someone who identifies with the gender they were assigned at birth. | Refers to someone who does not identify as exclusively male or female. |
| **Gender Fluid** | **Genderqueer** |
| Refers to someone whose gender identity changes over time from one end of the spectrum to the other. | Refers to someone whose gender identity falls on the spectrum between male and female. |

**FIGURE 8.4**    Gender Definitions

## SEXUAL ORIENTATION

Sexual orientation is the emotional, romantic, or sexual attraction that a person feels toward another person. There are several types of sexual orientation, including heterosexual, homosexual, bisexual, and asexual (Sexual Attraction and Orientation, n.d.). For people of all sexual orientations, learning about sex and relationships can be difficult. In early and middle adolescence, about 15% of teens experience sexual questioning and sometimes report emotional and sexual attraction to members of the same sex, while 5% of teen boys and girls identify their sexual orientation as gay or lesbian (Berk, 2014).

Questioning, identifying, and sharing one's sexual orientation with others may prove hard at times. A 2012 survey by the Human Rights Campaign found that 92% of LGBT teens had heard negative things about being lesbian, gay, bisexual, or transgender. Due to fears of prejudice, rejection, or bullying, people who aren't straight may keep their sexual orientation secret, even from friends and family who might support them. Whether gay, straight, bisexual, or just not sure, almost every adolescent has questions about physically maturing and about sexual health—such as whether certain body changes are "normal," what the right way to behave is, or how to avoid sexually transmitted infections (Sexual Attraction and Orientation, n.d.). It's important to provide resources and safe spaces with knowledgeable adults ready to discuss these issues.

## ABLEISM

Worldwide, people with disabilities have difficulty accessing education, health services, and employment. Disability is an economic development issue because it is linked to poverty; disability may increase the risk of poverty, and poverty may increase the risk of disability. A growing body of evidence indicates that children with disabilities and their families are more likely than their peers to experience economic disadvantage, especially in low- and middle-income countries (LMICs) (Graham et. al., 2017.). Among children 3–17 years of age, about 15% have one or more developmental disabilities, including autism spectrum disorder, cerebral palsy, intellectual disability, and other developmental delays (Boyle et al., 2011). Understandably, most adolescents with disabilities desire to have developmental experiences and social opportunities similar to their typically developing peers. However, when struggles related to their disabilities make it more difficult, or impossible, to participate in social activities at the same rate and level as their peers, negative psychosocial outcomes such as stress and loneliness can result (Maxey & Beckert, 2017). School attendance helps dispel the misconceptions about disability that serve as barriers to inclusion in other spheres. Education bolsters human capital, minimizes barriers to entering the workforce, and improves economic earning potential. Inclusive education is based on the belief that all children can learn and should have access to a curriculum and necessary adaptations to ensure meaningful educational attainment. Support for inclusive education is gaining momentum (Graham et al., 2017).

## MORTALITY AWARENESS

The number one cause of death in teens is motor vehicle accidents; 20,360 teens were killed in 2016 in such accidents (Cunningham et al., 2018). This may be attributed to adolescents needing to assert themselves and develop autonomy. Teens are more likely to engage in risk behaviors due to the continued development of the frontal cortex, the area of the brain that controls reasoning and helps us think before we act. Conversely, the amygdala develops early and controls immediate reactions that include fear and aggressive behaviors, skills we need to survive when threatened.

The early development of the amygdala may share responsibility for the second-highest cause of death, which involves use of firearms. Firearms were responsible for 3,140 adolescent deaths in 2016. Homicides account for 60% of those deaths, suicides about 35%, unintentional or accidental injuries about 1%, and mass shootings slightly less than 1% (Cunningham et al., 2018). This number has increased, while the number of motor vehicle accidents has decreased due to more federal regulations and training.

The third most common cause of death for adolescents is cancer; 1,853 teens died of cancer in 2016, a number that is decreasing due to more scientific studies. Suffocation and suicides by hanging are the fourth-leading causes of death in adolescents, and that number of cases is on the rise. Drownings, drug overdoses, and birth defects combine to be the fifth-leading causes of death among adolescents. Drug poisoning and overdoses have risen to be the sixth-leading causes of death for young people. This is largely due to increases in opioid overdoses, which the study shows account for more than half of drug overdoses among adolescents.

Knowing what leads to death among adolescents can provide a framework to help teens and parents better understand and communicate with one another. It is an opportunity to create a space for psychoeducation that teaches open and assertive communication of needs, expectations, boundaries, and consequences. Through education, adolescents and parents can make better and informed decisions and work through the emotions connected to death (Cunningham, Walton, & Carter, 2018).

Most adolescents understand the concept that death is permanent, universal, and inevitable. They may or may not have had past experiences with death of a family member, friend, or pet. Adolescents, similar to adults, may want to have their religious or cultural rituals observed. Most adolescents are beginning to establish their identity, independence, and relationship to peer groups. A predominant theme in adolescence is feelings of immortality or being exempt from death (Children's Hospital of Philadelphia, 2021). Denial and defiant attitudes may suddenly change the personality of a teenager facing death as they may feel as if they no longer belong or fit in with their peers. Additionally, they may feel as if they are unable to communicate with their parents.

Another important concept among adolescents is self-image. A terminal illness and/or the effects of treatment may cause many physical changes that they must endure. Adolescents may feel alone in their struggle, and scared, and angry. It is important for counselors and parents to realize that children of all ages respond to death in unique ways. Children need support and, in particular, someone who will listen to their thoughts and provide reassurance to alleviate their fears.

## Summary

Adolescence is the second-fastest growth stage after infancy. With 1.2 billion adolescents, they have the largest cohort of this age group in history. In the span of a few years, adolescents will reach full sexual maturity, cultivate romantic relationships, develop a sense of identity, become more autonomous, and increase their cognitive and emotional abilities. With so much happening, teens may also demonstrate varying levels of emotions. Parental and peer support and influence are key factors during this stage of development. By the end of adolescence, teens are still refining who they are, but they are ready to take on more adult responsibilities. A counselor can be a crucial support during a time of such change.

## CASE STUDIES

### CASE #1

Triton is a 43-year-old White male with six daughters, and his youngest, Ariel, is 16. Ariel is smart, funny, inquisitive, and curious enough to explore new things. Triton has very strict rules, however, and doesn't like to allow his daughters out of his sight. He has their lives planned for them, including who they are to marry. Triton keeps such control because he lost his wife, the girls' mother, from a heart attack while he was on a trip at sea. Her death forever changed him. Ariel knows that one day she will marry and have a family, but she wants to first travel the world to see and learn new things. Their differences constantly keep Ariel and Triton at odds. Recently, the girls decided to have a special dinner for their dad to show appreciation for all he had done. When it was time to bring out the cake and sing his favorite song, Ariel was nowhere to be found. She had run off with a guy, Eric, she had recently met. Triton was furious, but also worried. "What have I done?" he asked. "I only wanted to protect her and keep her safe from the dangers of the world outside our community." After a month had passed, Triton had not slept well, felt disconnected, and did not want to engage with others in the community. A few weeks later he began getting letters from Ariel, sharing stories of her adventures, pictures of new places, and updates about people she had met and what she was learning.

1. When you think of the four phases adolescents go through during identity development, which stage or stages is Ariel in?
2. What are some possible reasons Ariel and Triton are having so many arguments?
3. How would you help Triton and Ariel work through their relationship?

### CASE #2

Jasmine is a 19-year-female from Al-Bahah, Saudi Arabia. She is the only daughter of her parents, Ibrahim and Fatemah, who are considered Al-Bahah royalty. Jasmine was excited about turning 19 and had been researching colleges in London to attend. One day at breakfast, Ibrahim announced that at the end of the week he and Jasmine's mother would host a celebration for Jasmine's birthday, and at this gathering they would pick her husband. "Husband? Father, I am not ready to be married. There is so much I want to see and do. Why do I have to get married—and to someone I don't even know?" Jasmine said. Ibrahim scolded Jasmine and proclaimed that it is tradition and that she needed to accept it because it was happening. Later that night Jasmine was in the garden with Raja, her feline companion, ruminating on what her had father said and trying to figure out a way to help him understand that times are different, that she wants to marry for love and only when she is ready, rather than because some ancient tradition dictates it for her.

1. How would you approach this case from an advocacy perspective?
2. How would you help Jasmine navigate what she is going through? What should you make sure to consider when working with her?
3. What is occurring between Jasmine and her father, and how are their different stages of life affecting their relationship?

## Reflections and Targeted Discussion Questions

1. Think back to your adolescent years (13–18) and how you learned to handle conflict with your peers, parents, or teachers. How would having so much access to digital media help hinder you from being able to address that problem? As a counselor, how could you incorporate technology into helping an adolescent client communicate better with peers, parents, and teachers?

2. You have a client whose biological presentation does not match the individual's social and emotional presentation and who seems behind target for the psychosocial stage that aligns with the client's age. The client lives in a supportive and socially acceptable environment. What factors or criteria do you need to consider? What would you want to know first? How would you collect the information? How would knowing all this information help you better serve the client?

3. When thinking of working with adolescents, which theory from the previously cited cases do you believe would align with your counselor identity? How could you use either theory to help a 17-year-old client who is 6 months from graduating decide what to do next?

## References

American Counseling Association. (2014). ACA code of ethics. www.counseling. org

American Psychiatric Association. (2013). *Diagnostic and statistical manual of mental disorders* (5th ed.). American Psychiatric Publishing.

Apter, T. (2009). Teens and parents in conflict: Why does my teenager want to fight with me? In *Psychology Today*. https://www.psychologytoday.com/us/blog/domestic-intelligence/200901/teens-and-parents-in-conflict

Arends, B. (2019, October 16). Black kids more likely to be suspended than white kids over same behavior. *New York Post*. https://nypost.com/2019/10/16/black-kids-more-likely-to-be-suspended-than-white-kids-over-same-behavior/

Arriaga, X. B., & Foshee, V. A. (2004). Adolescent dating violence: Do adolescents follow in their friends', or parents' footsteps? *Journal of Interpersonal Violence, 19*(2), 162–184. doi: 10.1177/0886260503260247

Berk, L. E. (2014). *Development through the lifespan* (6th ed.) Pearson Education.

Blakemore, S-J., Burnett, S., & Dahl, R. E. (2010). The role of puberty in the developing adolescent brain. *Human Brain Mapping, 31*, 926–933.

Boyle, C. A., Boulet, S., Schieve, L. A., Cohen, R. A., Blumberg, S. J., Yeargin-Allsopp, M., Visser, S., & Kogan, M. D. (2011). Trends in the prevalence of developmental disabilities in US children, 1997–2008. *Pediatrics, 127*(6), 1034-1042. doi: https://doi.org/10.1542/peds.2010-2989

Bronfenbrenner, U. (2005). Ecological systems theory (1992). In U. Bronfenbrenner (Ed.), *Making human beings human: Bioecological perspectives on human development* (pp. 106–173). SAGE Publications.

Bukowski, W. M., Newcomb, A. F., & Hartup, W. W. (1998). *The company they keep: Friendships in childhood and adolescence.* Cambridge Studies in Social and Emotional Development.

Centers for Disease Control and Prevention. (n.d.). Prevention of adverse childhood experiences. What are adverse childhood experiences? https://www.cdc.gov/violenceprevention/aces/fastfact.html

Centers for Disease Control and Prevention. (2019). Childhood obesity facts. *Prevalence of childhood obesity in the United States.* https://www.cdc.gov/obesity/data/childhood.html

Children's Hospital of Philadelphia. (2021). A child's concept of death. https://www.chop.edu/conditions-diseases/childs-concept-death

Cincinnati Children's. (2018). Adolescent nutrition. https://www.cincinnatichildrens.org/health/a/adolescent#:~:text=Adolescence%20is%20the%20second%2Dfastest,vitamins%20A%2C%20C%20and%20D

Cunningham, R. M., Walton, M. A., & Carter, P. M. (2018). The major causes of death in children and adolescents in the United States. *New England Journal of Medicine, 379*(25), 2468. doi: 10.1056/NEJMsr1804754

Gentile, D. A., Bailey, K., Bavelier, D., Brockmyer, J. F., Cash, H., Coyne, S. M., Doan, A., Grant, D. S., Green, C. S., Griffiths, M., Markle, T., Petry, N. M., Prot, S., Rae, C. D., Rehbein, F., Rich, M., Sullivan, D., Woolley, E., & Young, K. (2017). Internet gaming disorder in children and adolescents. *Pediatrics, 140*(2), S81-S85. DOI: https://doi.org/10.1542/peds.2016-1758H

George, M. A., & Odgers, C. L. (2014). The risks and rewards of being an adolescent in a digital age: Should we rethink our ever-growing concerns that smart phones are terrible for teens? In *American Psychological Association.* https://www.apa.org/pi/families/resources/newsletter/2014/12/digital-age

Graham, N., Schultz, L., Mitra, S., & Mont, D. (2017, November 20). Disability in middle childhood and adolescence. In D. A. P. Bundy, N. de Silva, S. Horton, D. T. Jamison, & G. C. Patton (Eds.), *Child and adolescent health and development* (3rd ed). International Bank for Reconstruction and Development, The

World Bank (Chapter 17). https://www.ncbi.nlm.nih.gov/books/NBK525252/ doi: 10.1596/978-1-4648-04236_ch17

Hays, D. G., & Erford, B. T. (2018). *Developing multicultural counseling competence: A systems approach* (3rd ed.). Pearson.

IGI Global. (2018). *What is digital generation?* https://www.igi-global.com/dictionary/digital-generation/7631

Kail, R. V., & Cavanaugh, J. C. (2016). *Human development: A lifespan view* (7th ed.). Cengage Learning.

Lansford, J. E., Skinner, A. T., Sorbring, E., Di Giunta, L., Deater-Deckard, K., Dodge, K. A., Malone, P. S., Oburu, P., Pastorelli, C., Tapanya, S., Tirado, L. M., Zelli, A., Al-Hassan, S. M., Alampay, L. P., Bacchini, D., Bombi, A. S., Bornstein, M. H., & Chang, L. (2012). Boys' and Girls' Relational and Physical Aggression in Nine Countries. *Aggressive behavior, 38*(4), 298–308. https://doi.org/10.1002/ab.21433

Larsen, J. N., & Martey, R. (2011). Adolescents seeking nutrition information: Motivations, sources and the role of the internet. *International Journal of Information & Communication Technology Education, 7*(3), 74–85.

Levpušček, M. P. (2006) Adolescent individuation in relation to parents and friends: Age and gender differences. *European Journal of Developmental Psychology, 3*:3, 238-264, doi: 10.1080/17405620500463864

Maxey, M., & Beckert, T. E. (2017). Adolescents with disabilities. *Adolescent Research Review, 2*, 59–75. doi.org/10.1007/s40894-016-0043-y

McLeod, S. A. (2010, December 14). Formal operational stage. *Simply psychology.* https://www.simplypsychology.org/formal-operational.html

McLeod, S. A. (2013). Kohlberg's theory of moral development. In *Simply Psychology.* https://www.simplypsychology.org/kohlberg.html

McLeod, S. A. (2018, Aug 05). Lev Vygotsky. Simply psychology: https://www.simplypsychology.org/vygotsky.html

Meier, E. P., & Gray, J. (2013). Facebook photo activity associated with body image disturbance in adolescent girls. *Cyberpsychology, Behavior, and Social Networking, 17*(4), 1–8. doi: 10.1089/cyber.2013.0305

Messersmith, E. E., Garrett, J. L., Davis-Kean, P. E., Malanchuk, O., & Eccles, J. S. (2008). Career Development From Adolescence Through Emerging Adulthood Insights From Information Technology Occupations. *Journal of Adolescent Research, 23*(2), 206–227. https://doi.org/10.1177/0743558407310723

Mulford, C., & Giordano, P. C. (2008, October 26). Teen dating violence. A closer look at adolescent romantic relationships. In *National Justice Institute.* https://nij.ojp.gov/topics/articles/teen-dating-violence-closer-look-adolescent-romantic-relationships

National Institute on Drug Abuse (NIDA). (2018, March). *Opioid overdose crisis.* https://www.drugabuse.gov/drugs-abuse/opioids/opioid-overdose-crisis

Nunez, C. & Pfeffer, L. (2016, July 21). Thirteen amazing coming of age traditions from around the world. In Global Citizen. https://www.globalcitizen.org/en/content/13-amazing-coming-of-age-traditions-from-around-th/

Raphelson, S. (2014, October 6). *From GIs to gen z (Or is it iGen?): How generations get nicknames.* National Public Radio (NPR). https://www.npr.org/2014/10/06/349316543/don-t-label-me-origins-of-generational-names-and-why-we-use-them

Rapport, L. (2016, April 15). Puberty timing influenced by both parents. *In Reuters health care and pharma.* https://www.reuters.com/article/us-health-puberty-genetics/puberty-timing-influenced-by-both-parents-idUSKCN0XC1U1

Ream, G. L., & Witt, P. A. (2004). Organizations serving all ages. In Stephen F. Hamilton and Mary Agnes Hamilton, (Eds). *The youth development handbook* (pp.51–76). Sage.

Rojewski, J. W. & Kim, H. (2003). Career choice patterns and behaviors of work-bound youth during early adolescence. *Journal of Career Development, 30*(2), 89–108.

Scheer, S. D., Gavazzi, S. M. & Blumenkrantz, D. G. (2007). Rites of passage during adolescence. *The Forum Journal,12*(2), 2–20.

Sexual attraction and orientation. (n.d.)*In Teens Health.* https://nypost.com/2019/10/16/black-kids-more-likely-to-be-suspended-than-white-kids-over-same-behavior/

Stanford Children's Health. (n.d.). The growing child: Teenager (13 to 18 Years). https://www.stanfordchildrens.org/en/topic/default?id=the-growing-child-adolescent-13-to-18-years-90-P02175

UNICEF. (n.d.). Adolescent research briefs. https://www.unicef-irc.org/adolescent-research-methods/

U.S. Department of Health and Human Services. (n.d.). Physical activity in children https://www.hhs.gov/ash/oah/adolescent-development/physical-health-and-nutrition/healthy-behavior/physical-activity-in-adolescence/index.html#:~:text=Adolescents%20should%20get%20at%20least,others%20strengthen%20bones%20or%20muscles

U.S. Department of Health and Human Services. (n.d.). Physical development. https://www.hhs.gov/ash/oah/adolescent-development/explained/physical/index.html#:~:text=Many%20young%20people%20will%20reach,adolescence%20are%20related%20to%20fertility

U.S. Department of Health and Human Services. (2020, April 15). SAMHSA, Youth. https://www.samhsa.gov/homelessness-programs-resources/hpr-resources/youth

Wölfer, R. & Scheithauer, H. (2013) Ostracism in childhood and adolescence: Emotional, cognitive, and behavioral effects of social exclusion, *Social Influence,* 8(4), 217-236. doi: 10.1080/15534510.2012.706233

Youth.gov. Career exploration and skill development. https://youth.gov/youth-topics/youth-employment/career-exploration-and-skill-development

## Credits

# Young Adulthood Development

Stacy Speedlin Gonzalez, PhD; Chelsea Barron Davila Conaway, MS; and Jordan Elliott, MS

*I'm not lost for I know where I am. But however, where I am may be lost.* —A. A. Milne, *Winnie-the-Pooh*

## Learning Objectives

After reading this chapter, you should be able to

1. Define key concepts relevant to the developmental processes of young adults.
2. Describe human growth and development from an ecological and psychosocial developmental lens.
3. Infuse Bronfenbrenner's ecological theory and Erik Erikson's eight stages of development as a lens for effective counseling with this population.

# Introduction

Literature demonstrates that young adults constitute a unique population and require more insight with regard to their counseling needs (Jennifer et al., 2008; Park et al., 2006). In particular, adjustment issues such as relational, occupational, social, and familial stressors become more prevalent as adolescents transition into young adulthood. The effects of intrinsic (identity formation) and extrinsic (ecological systems) variables play a significant role in conceptualizing this transitional period in life (Bronfenbrenner, 1994). In this chapter, we focus on counseling and teaching young adults from an ecological and developmental perspective.

# Key Concepts

- **Young Adult:** For the purpose of this chapter, the term "young adult" is defined as an individual between the ages of 18 and 24.
- **Identity:** The term "identity" refers to an individual's own self-awareness and ability to self-reflect on experiences, values, and ideologies.
- **Interpersonal Relationships:** Refers to a close relationship with an associate or acquaintance between two or more people. Interpersonal relationships may result in short or lasting duration.
- **Emotional Intelligence:** Refers to "one's ability to perceive, understand, use and regulate emotions in self and others" (Kong & Zhao, 2013, p. 197).

# The Human Developing Process

Human development can be understood through a myriad of theories. For the purpose of capturing development as a flexible stage process, we examine growth using Erik Erikson's eight stages of psychosocial development theory (Erikson, 1963), which describes young adults through a social, cultural, and familial framework (Knight, 2017). Erikson utilizes the eight stages as a comprehensive theory of identity formation. One key factor posits that growth and development is ascertained through relational and interpersonal impact (Ogden, 2008). The eight stages describe the "sequential process that culminates when an individual moves away from adolescence into adulthood and beyond" (Knight, 2017, p. 1048). Congruent with other models, Erikson gives focus to the genesis and remediation of crisis and problems through life stages (Kivnick & Wells, 2013).

TABLE 9.1    Erikson's Eight Stages of Development (Erikson, 1963)

| AGE | CONFLICT | RESOLUTION OR "VIRTUE" | CULMINATION IN OLD AGE |
|---|---|---|---|
| Infancy (0–1 year) | Basic trust vs. mistrust | Hope | Appreciation of interdependence and relatedness |
| Early childhood (1–3 years) | Autonomy vs. shame | Will | Acceptance of the cycle of life, from integration to disintegration |
| Play age (3–6 years) | Initiative vs. guilt | Purpose | Humor, empathy, resilience |
| School age (6–12 years) | Industry vs. inferiority | Competence | Humility, acceptance of the course of one's life and unfulfilled hopes |
| Adolescence (12–19 years) | Identity vs. confusion | Fidelity | Sense of complexity of life; merging of sensory, logical, and aesthetic perception |
| Early adulthood (20–25 years) | Intimacy vs. isolation | Love | Sense of the complexity of relationships, value of tenderness and loving freely |
| Adulthood (26–64 years) | Generativity vs. stagnation | Care | Caritas, caring for others; and agape, empathy, and concern |
| Old age (65–death) | Integrity vs. despair | Wisdom | Existential identity, a sense of integrity strong enough to withstand physical disintegration |

*Source*: http://mrmcnabb.weebly.com/psychosocial-development.html

Through Erikson, we can comprehensively define how individuals develop unity and cohesion with others and attune to their own sense of self (McAdams, 1995). Each stage of life describes two binary dispositions, referred to as syntonic and dystonic (Erikson et al., 1994). Each stage is defined by a crisis in identity formation, rather than through chronological age (Erikson, 1993). Resolution of the crisis results in the integration of core development (Kivnick & Wells, 2013). When individuals do not integrate two opposing dispositions, the result is "maldevelopment" or "malignant tendencies" for growth (Erikson et al., 1986). In other words, individuals will move away from virtue-attainment into unhealthy relational and coping strategies.

Transitions in stages arise due to new dimensions in social interaction based on nuances of maturity. For example, the period of adolescence is viewed by Erikson as central to development (Rosenthal, 1981). During adolescence, identification as a mode of adjustment ends and identity formation begins. If adolescents do not succeed in formulating a strong identity, then adulthood is met with challenges (Rosenthal et al., 1981). In young adulthood, the challenge of whether to grow toward intimacy presents. From an Eriksonian perspective, young adulthood is the stage in which social norms dictate how individuals must form long-term romantic partnerships. Further, individuals should ascribe to social and cultural scripts of romantic relationships (Erikson, 1963). This can mean pressure to get married, remain monogamous, and have children. These expectations can also introduce additional pressure to achieve intimacy and avoid isolation (Erikson, 1963).

Considering social and cultural expectations for young adults, those who do not form long-term romantic partnerships during this stage may experience feelings of marginalization, failure, inadequacy, and shame (Bonilla-Silva, 2017). This social pressure may pose a risk to healthy development as young adults attempt to meet social expectations and remain congruent for intimate relationships. Exposure to older adults and discussion of social expectations and pressure may support healthy development at this stage (Erikson, 1963). Since this stage of development prepares individuals for middle and late adulthood, imperatively one should consider the cultivation of healthy relationships. Individuals who learn the skills of relational negotiation at this stage are healthier later in life. Further, the development of positive social and romantic relationships improves all facets of well-being (physical, emotional, spiritual, etc.).

Relationships also serve as a rite of passage in young adulthood. Young adults learn to resist societal pressures, external stressors, and culturally defined norms. For example, some young adults may feel pressure to get married, begin having children, or satisfy their family's perceptions of success. Additionally, young adulthood comes with many relational risks. Adults between the ages of 18 and 25 are at the second highest risk for experiencing intimate partner violence, which creates a multitude of complications for relationships later in life. The psychological (and often emotional or physical) aspect of abusive relationships creates long-term effects on an individual's social, emotional, and spiritual well-being. Therefore, psychoeducation on healthy intimate and social relationships is imperative for this age group.

Finally, as young adults emerge from adolescence into this adulthood stage, they are often heavily contemplative about the prospects of career and finances. Young adults may or may not be aware of their own strengths, skills, and capability with respect to joining the workforce. Some have strong ideas about their professional goals and dreams, which may not be realistic. For example, some young people desire to be a professional basketball player or to be a Supreme Court Justice. The odds of obtaining such a career goal are limited for most. At this stage, young people may become more cognizant of realistic worldly concepts surrounding career. Counselors can assist them with career planning through finding strengths and examining their values. Further, counselors can assist young people with accessing financial resources to pursue education, job training, etc.

## PHYSICAL AND COGNITIVE

Similar to any change of development, young adults experience age-related changes in their physical features. Several factors mediate physical growth (i.e., illness, genetic endowment/vulnerabilities, onset of puberty, etc.). Generalized physical features include completion of physical maturation, peak abilities in muscular strength, and developmental solidification of reaction times and sensory abilities (Boundless Psychology, n.d.). Despite physical attributes reaching full peak in young adulthood, cognitive features continue to develop. According to Jean Piaget's theory of cognitive development (1950), formal operational thinking occurs during early adolescence and continues through adulthood. Unlike earlier concrete thinking, formal operational thinking is characterized by grasping abstract concepts, engaging in deductive reasoning, and developing hypothetical ideas (Piaget, 1950).

Cognitive development in early adulthood formalizes well into the more latent portions of this stage. Individuals develop metaethical thinking (Markoulis, 1989), moral and value judgments, and solidification of reasoning. Jean Piaget (who wrote prolifically on cognitive development throughout his life) theorized a concept of a fifth stage of cognitive development, known as postformal operational thinking. He postulated that operational thinking creates opportunities for existential reflection and advanced moral reasoning (Markoulis, 1989). Gibbs (1979) reconceptualized that postformal operational thinking can be viewed as "reflective products of the human quest for meaning, rather than as natural standards for determining human moral maturity" (p. 109).

## SOCIAL AND EMOTIONAL

Social and emotional changes occur within young adulthood. For many young adults, finding meaning through career, social, and familial avenues carries higher value at this stage (Boundless Psychology, n.d.). Sterns and Huyck (2001) found that meaning for young adults is often actualized through career and professional development. Additionally, Ryff and Singer (2009) found that socializing with others and constructing positive interpersonal relationships was key to well-being for adults. Equally, being capable of formulating strong connections can solidify well-being for adults throughout all stages of life. These findings highly correspond with Erikson's sixth stage of *intimacy versus isolation* in which individuals face the crisis of being alone versus formulating true and meaning connections with others (Rosenthal et al., 1981).

Emotional intelligence (EI) has been widely examined within academic literature in the past decade (Kong & Zhao, 2013). Petrides et al. (2007) proposed two conceptualizations of EI: trait EI, and ability EI. Ability EI refers to "one's ability to perceive, understand, use and regulate emotions in self and others" while trait EI, "by contrast, is conceptualized as a trait which refers to a constellation of behavioral dispositions and self-perceptions located at the lower-levels of personality hierarchies" (Kong & Zhao, 2013, p. 197). Emotional intelligence demonstrates support for individual propensity for adaptation, social competence, and self-esteem (Mayer et al., 2004). Further, EI can also serve as an effective mediator in improving career and academic achievement (Lopes et al., 2004). Therefore, intentional development of emotional intelligence is supported within academic literature as having high value for young adults.

## Theoretical Considerations

While young adults experience a range of physical, cognitive, social, and emotional progress, counselors and educators can help their clients and students more effectively develop these skills. This begins with conceptualizing and assessing the current juncture at which the individual presently operates. Therefore, the authors infused Erikson's eight stages of development (1963) with Bronfenbrenner's ecological theory (1994) to conceptualize identity formation through social and environmental contexts. Erikson's stage model examines various intrinsic experiences (identity formation) of young adults, while Bronfenbrenner's ecological theory speculates more on extrinsic (external environmental) systems. Both play a significant role in this transitional period in life.

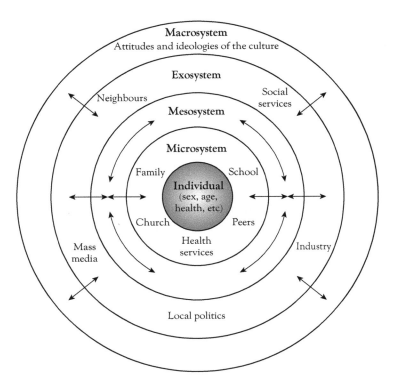

**FIGURE 9.1**    Bronfenbrenner's Ecological Model

## Strengths and Challenges from the "ISMs" Perspectives

The development processes previously described occur in the context of young adults'
extrinsic environments. Systems of social power operate within these environments
to subjugate the disempowered. These systems function to maintain privileges for the
cultural majority and manifest in the form of various ISMs. These ISMs can have a
significant influence on development in young adulthood. Examining the effects of
these ISMs on young adults' psychosocial development will strengthen counselors'
contextual understanding of this population. The following sections will explore
the influence of ISMs on young adults' development from an ecological systems and
Eriksonian perspective.

### MULTICULTURAL

Systems of racial dominance operate within the chronosystem and macrosystem in
the form of racist values, attitudes, and cultural norms with sociohistorical under-
pinnings (Bonilla-Silva, 2017). Racism maintains power and privileges for members
of dominant racial groups. Young adults are socialized in and must navigate racist

social systems as they interact with their environment. Racism manifests in young adults' experiences at the exo-, meso-, and microlevels (Bonilla-Silva, 2017). White and White-passing young adults experience power and White privilege because of racism. In turn, racialized young adults may encounter subtle and overt barriers, challenges, insults, hostility, and violence (Bonilla-Silva, 2017; Delgado & Stefancic, 2017). Racist values and beliefs can also have a profound effect at the individual level. Young adults of color may internalize racist attitudes and ideologies, which can provoke the perpetration of racism, colorism, and other systems of racial dominance. Moreover, these experiences affect interpersonal interactions that occur at the primary contextual level and can inform perceptions of safety, belongingness, and acceptance (Bonilla-Silva, 2017; Delgado & Stefancic, 2017).

Experiences of racism at all ecological stages inform relationship formation in young adulthood. Recall that the primary task for young adults from an Eriksonian perspective is to cultivate meaningful relationships with others (Rosenthal et al., 1981). Young adults must navigate racist attitudes, beliefs, and behaviors as they work to build these connections. Racism can also hinder the development of racially integrated social groups and inform how young adults select romantic partners and close friends (Bonilla-Silva, 2017). Racism, therefore, can limit young adults' ability to form intimate, cross-racial relationships.

Experiences of racism at the primary contextual level may be a risk to healthy development. Conversely, these experiences can enhance young adults' resiliency as they encounter and grow through racist experiences (Godsay, 2018). Additionally, young adults can use these experiences to build a supportive racial community, thereby enhancing psychosocial development at this stage (Bonilla-Silva, 2017). Processing the effects of racism on social interactions may assist young adults in working through the psychological barriers these systems create.

## DIVERSITY

As Bronfenbrenner (1994) suggested, the extrinsic environment profoundly affects individuals' psychosocial development. Experiences at the exo-, meso-, and micro-levels may contribute to the effect of diversity on this population (Bronfenbrenner, 1994). As young adults encounter various transitions at this stage, primary contextual experiences can shape how these individuals conceptualize experiences of diversity. This, in turn, introduces them to novel values, attitudes, and beliefs. The ways young adults conceptualize these experiences informs the effect of diversity on development at this stage. Negative views of diversity may inhibit young adults from seeking out interaction with diverse populations. This can enhance the perpetuation of the various ISMs described in this section (Bonilla-Silva, 2017). On the other hand, if a person finds value in interaction with diverse populations, that individual may seek to expand their social circle and reflect on personal values, attitudes, and beliefs (Boisjoly et al., 2006). In turn, this can strengthen development. Broaching the subject of diversity with young adults may also encourage dialogue about the effect of diversity on development.

## GENDER

Patriarchal power systems operate within the chronosystem and macrosystem to maintain gender-based oppression. These systems manifest in experiences of sexism and/or transphobia in the exo-, meso-, and microsystems of gender-diverse young adults. Exposure to sexism and transphobia varies depending on young adults' gender identity and expression. Cisgender women, transgender, nonbinary, gender queer, and other gender-diverse young adults encounter subtle and overt gender-based challenges and insults at the primary contextual level. This includes, but is not limited to, interpersonal rejection and lack of support, challenges to gender identity, barriers to access in all social and economic spaces (e.g., the job market, health care, housing), and even overt hostility and violence (Anderson, 2014; Bates, 2016). These experiences can contribute to the effects of sexism and transphobia on development at this stage.

Sexism and transphobia also affect young adults' quest for intimacy. Socially determined gender roles impose gender-based expectations for individuals in romantic and platonic relationships. Moreover, women and gender-diverse individuals may face hostility and violence in interpersonal relationships. These experiences may impede the development of intimacy with significant others; however, many gender-diverse individuals build strong connections with supportive individuals and groups, which supports healthy psychosocial development at this stage.

## SEXUAL ORIENTATION

Homophobia within the chronosystem and macrosystem manifests as anti-LGBTQ+ prejudice and discrimination in the lives of young adults. This can significantly affect social and relational experiences at this stage. Although pervasive, anti-LGBTQ+ prejudice and discrimination are not universal. One's sexual orientation and expression informs the privileges and discrimination they may encounter. As such, LGBTQ+ young adults have diverse encounters with homophobia based on their sexual orientation. Anti-LGBTQ+ prejudice and discrimination includes, but is not limited to, interpersonal rejection, rejection from social spaces such as places of worship, barriers to access and advancement in higher education and the workplace, and overt hostility and violence (Human Rights Campaign, 2009). Experiences of marginalization can also occur within the LGBTQ+ community, which may contribute to feelings of isolation and disconnection (Schimanski & Treharne, 2019). Finally, coming out during this period can influence development (Schimanski & Treharne, 2019). Young adults face varying interpersonal responses, ranging from rejection and hostility to enhanced support and feelings of belonging. All of these experiences can contribute to the effect of homophobia on the lives of young adults.

LGBTQ+ young adults may also face challenges in developing intimate relationships. Coming out during this stage can provoke rejection from friends and family members (Klein et al., 2015). Additionally, this population must navigate anti-LGBTQ+ prejudice and discrimination as they work through young adult dating. Lack of support at this stage may hinder healthy psychosocial development. Working toward authentic self-expression with the support of significant others and the LGBTQ+ community, however, can result in a sense of liberation and connection (Klein et al., 2015). Identifying these supports and processing experiences of homophobia may act as a protective factor to healthy development at this stage.

## ABLEISM

Young adults with disabilities face physical and social barriers at the exo-, meso-, and micro-levels. Physical barriers hinder this population's ability to access public and private spaces such as workplaces, schools, and places of worship. In turn, this may affect young adults' ability to gain independence during this transitional stage. Ability exists on a spectrum and can range from invisible conditions to cognitive or physical disabilities. The latter may affect physical appearance. Young adults with visible disabilities (wheelchair, crutches, hearing aids, etc.) may be more likely to experience microaggressions and other negative interpersonal interactions.

Ableism also influences relationship formation in young adulthood. Negative interpersonal encounters at the exo-, meso-, and micro-levels may interfere with the development of intimacy. In turn, the othering of young adults with disabilities can impede the development of romantic relationships and friendships. Moreover, the desexualization and dehumanization of individuals with visible disabilities can negatively affect this population's ability to form romantic relationships and may precipitate experiences of marginalization (Block et al., 2012; Hirschmann, 2013). Strengthening feelings of hope, optimism, resilience, meaning-making, and post-traumatic growth may contribute to successful psychosocial adaptation of these experiences (Martz & Livneh, 2015).

## AGEISM

Age influences the interaction between young adults and the environment. Ageism perpetuates attitudes and beliefs that value the young and devalue the aged. Manifestations of ageism in the exo-, meso-, and microsystems may remain invisible to young adults, as they are the beneficiaries of this power system. As such, this population may internalize ageist values and beliefs, which can inform their interactions with older adults at the primary contextual level. Individuals within this population who internalize ageist values and attitudes may believe that their worth as individuals will decrease as they age. Ageism can also lead to feelings of failure and inadequacy if a young adult has not met social and cultural expectations for this age group, such as gaining financial independence and entering a long-term romantic relationship.

## MORTALITY AWARENESS

Mortality awareness is low for young adults compared with individuals at other points in the life span. Death anxiety and mortality awareness, however, can increase due to death-related experiences at the primary contextual level, such as aging or death of parents and elder family members (Yalom, 2008). As older generations begin to age and die, the role of young adults in their ecological context begins to shift. These changes may provoke increased mortality awareness, death anxiety, and existential concerns as young adults are confronted with the impermanence of the self and others. If left unaddressed, death anxiety and increased mortality awareness may lead to negative mental health outcomes (Sherman et al., 2010; Whitehead et al., 2011), thereby hindering healthy development at this stage. Conversely, addressing death anxiety and discussing existential concerns enhances feelings of connectedness and enables individuals to make meaning out of difficult death and aging-related experiences (Chibnall et al., 2002; Chochinov et al., 2004; Ozanne et al., 2013). Building a supportive social network and processing feelings of mortality awareness and death anxiety may strengthen development at this stage. Further, being informed about the process related to death and dying, such as creating a living will or advanced directives, helps young people.

## Summary

Through the lens of ecological and psychosocial developmental theory, counselors can more effectively conceptualize intrinsic and extrinsic values for young adults and assist them with healthy life adjustments. Further, ecological theory offers a springboard of thought relative to multicultural and intersectional needs of young adult clients. The identity of young adults is multilayered and multifaceted. Young adulthood represents a significant period of transition in an individual's life. Counselors and educators can attempt to better understand young adults' needs and experiences using infused theories. Therefore, the authors recommend the synthesis of Bronfenbrenner's ecological theory and Erikson's eight stages of development as a modality for assisting young adult clients with identity formation and understanding the effects of multiple systems.

**CASE STUDY**

FIGURE 9.2    "Olivia"

Olivia is a 23-year-old Mexican woman living at home with her parents. After graduating from high school, she intended to go to college but felt pressure from her parents to remain at home. Olivia's parents migrated from Nuevo Leon, Mexico, in their 20s. They maintained their traditional culture and values while raising their children in the United States. Olivia grew up learning about the traditions of her ancestors and her father's native beliefs. She learned to speak English, Spanish, and some Nahuatl from her Indian grandmother. Every year, they would travel back to Mexico to see family and partake in the el Dia de Los Muertos celebration and the celebration of La Virgen de Guadalupe.

When Olivia began school in her formative years, she was bullied a lot. Kids teased her because of her accent and because her parents never attended high school. Kids at school would often go to her house and criticize her parents' traditional customs. Olivia would feel ashamed of her culture, and she wished her family were more American. She would watch TV news anchors and try to learn how to speak English more eloquently. At 9 years old, she wanted a cell phone like her friends at school used. Her parents were often frightened that she would pick up bad habits from others at school. They were alarmed at the way her peers addressed their parents with such disrespect. Olivia's parents attempted to keep her grounded in the traditional cultures and practices of Mexico for fear that she would go astray and pick up the poor habits they saw in American children. Every time they brought this to her attention, Olivia would get angry and tell them she did not care about her ancestors; she wanted to live her "best life" and be a pop star or a movie star.

When Olivia was 15, her mother asked her to quit school and help with the family business. Olivia cried and pleaded not to have to give up her friends. After long nights of arguing and pleading, she finally gave up and left school. Olivia obtained her GED from the local community college in hopes that she could go to the university. By the time she was 18, Olivia was still living at home with her parents. She had limited contact with friends who were leaving for college. She met her boyfriend on her 20th birthday at her friend's wedding. At first, she was not attracted to him. He asked for her phone number three times, and she eventually agreed.

They dated for one year prior to moving in together. While she did not mind living with her boyfriend, Olivia was afraid of being committed to him. Her boyfriend proposed to her several times, and she turned him down. Finally, he became frustrated and broke up with her. Afterward, Olivia moved in with her family. Since her family does not know how to help her, they suggest she go to the local counseling center.

## Reflections and Targeted Discussion Questions

1. Using Bronfenbrenner's ecological theory, how does Olivia's culture, family upbringing, neighborhood, and country of origin influence her developmental process?
2. From Erikson's stage theory, how would you conceptualize her experience with her boyfriend?
3. As her counselor, how would you work with Olivia while taking multiculturalism into consideration?

## References

Anderson, K. (2014). *Modern misogyny: Anti-feminism in a post-feminist era.* Oxford University Press.

Bates, L. (2016). *Everyday sexism.* Thomas Dunne Books.

Block, P., Shuttleworth, R., Pratt, J., Block, H., & Rammler, L. (2012). Disability, sexuality, and intimacy. In N. Pollard & D. Sakellariou (Eds.), *Politics of occupation-centered practice* (pp. 162–179). John Wiley & Sons.

Boisjoly, J., Duncan, G. J., Kremer, M., Levy, D. M., & Eccles, J. (2006). Empathy or antipathy? The impact of diversity. *American Economic Review, 96*, 1890–1905. doi:10.1257/aer.96.5.1890

Bonilla-Silva, E. (2017). *Racism without racists* (5th ed.). Rowman and Littlefield Publishers.

Boundless Psychology. (n.d.). https://courses.lumenlearning.com/boundless-psychology/chapter/early-and-middle-adulthood/

Bronfenbrenner, U. (1994). Ecological models of human development. *Readings on the Development of Children, 2*(1), 37–43.

Chibnall, J. T., Videen, S. D., Duckro, P. N., & Miller, D. K. (2002). Psychosocial-spiritual correlates of death distress in patients with life-threatening medical conditions. *Palliative Medicine, 16*, 331–338. doi:10.1191/0269216302pm544oa

Chochinov, H. M., Hack, T., Hassard, T., Kristjanson, J., McClement, S., & Harlos, M. (2004). Dignity and psychotherapeutic considerations in end-of-life care. *Journal of Palliative Care, 20*, 134–142. doi:10.1177/082585970402000303

Delgado, R., & Stefancic, J. (2017). *Critical race theory: An introduction* (3rd ed.). University Press.

Erikson, E. H. (1968). *Identity: Youth and crisis* (No. 7). W. W. Norton & Company.

Erikson, E. H. (1950). *Childhood and society* (2nd ed.). W. W. Norton & Company.

Erikson, E. H., Erikson, J. M., & Kivnick, H. Q. (1994). *Vital involvement in old age.* W. W. Norton & Company.

Gibbs, J. C. (1979). *Kohlberg's moral stage theory: A Piagetian revision. Human Development, 22*, 89–112.

Godsay, S. (2018). *Resilience and empowerment in the face of racism: From "resisting the stereotype" to "maintaining a movement"* (Doctoral dissertation). ProQuest (No. 10746074).

Hirschmann, N. J. (2013). Queer/fear: Disability, sexuality and the other. *Journal of Medical Humanities, 34*, 139–147. doi:10.1007/s10912-013-9208-x

Human Rights Campaign. (2009). *Hate crimes and violence against lesbian, gay, bisexual, and transgender people.* Human Rights Campaign Foundation.

Jennifer, W. Y., Adams, S. H., Burns, J., Brindis, C. D., & Irwin, Jr., C. E. (2008). Use of mental health counseling as adolescents become young adults. *Journal of Adolescent Health, 43*(3), 268–276.

Kivnick, H. Q., & Wells, C. K. (2013). *Untapped richness in Erik H. Erikson's rootstock. The Gerontologist, 54*(1), 40–50.

Klein, K., Holtby, A., Cook, K., & Travers, R. (2015). Complicating the coming out narrative: Becoming oneself in a heterosexist and cissexist world. *Journal of Homosexuality, 62,* 297–326. doi:10.1080/00918369.2014.970829

Knight, Z. G. (2017). A proposed model of psychodynamic psychotherapy linked to Erik Erikson's eight stages of psychosocial development. *Clinical Psychology & Psychotherapy, 24*(5), 1047–1058.

Kong, F., & Zhao, J. (2013). Affective mediators of the relationship between trait emotional intelligence and life satisfaction in young adults. *Personality and Individual Differences, 54*(2), 197–201.

Lopes, P. N., Brackett, M. A., Nezlek, J. B., Schutz, A., Sellin, I., & Salovey, P. (2004). Emotional intelligence and social interaction. *Personality and Social Psychology Bulletin, 30*(8), 1018-1034. doi:10.1177/0146167204264762

Markoulis, D. (1989). Postformal and postconventional reasoning in educationally advanced adults. *The Journal of Genetic Psychology, 150*(4), 427–439.

Martz, E., & Livneh, H. (2015). Psychosocial adaptation to disability within the context of positive psychology: Findings from the literature. *Journal of Occupational Rehabilitation, 26,* 4–12. doi:10.1007/s10926-015-9598-x

Mayer, J. D., Salovey, P., & Caruso, D. R. (2004). Emotional intelligence: Theory, findings, and implications. *Psychological Inquiry, 15*(3), 197-215. doi: 10.1207/s15327965pli1503_02

McAdams, D. P. (1995). What do we know when we know a person? *Journal of Personality, 63*(3), 365–396.

McNabb, M. (n.d.). *Erik Erikson 1902–1994.* Mr. McNabb. http://mrmcnabb.weebly.com/psychosocial-development.html

Ogden, T. H. (2008). On holding and containing, being and dreaming. *The International Journal of Psychoanalysis, 85*(6), 1349–1364.

Ozanne, A. O., Graneheim, U. H., & Strang, S. (2013). Finding meaning despite anxiety over life and death in amyotrophic lateral sclerosis patients. *Journal of Clinical Nurses, 22,* 2141–2149. doi:10.1111/jcon.12071

Park, M. J., Mulye, T. P., Adams, S. H., Brindis, C. D., & Irwin, Jr., C. E. (2006). The health status of young adults in the United States. *Journal of Adolescent Health, 39*(3), 305–317.

Petrides, K. V., Pita, R., & Kokkinaki, F. (2007). The location of trait emotional intelligence in personality factor space. *British Journal of Psychology, 98*(2), 273–289.

Piaget, J. (1950). *Psychology of intelligence.* Harcourt, Brace & World.

Rosenthal, D., Gurney, R. & Moore, S. (1981). From trust to intimacy: A new inventory for examining Erikson's stages of psychosocial development. *Journal of Youth and Adolescence, 10,* 545–537.

Ryff, C. D., & Singer, B. (2009). *Understanding healthy aging: Key components and their integration.* In V. Bengtson, D. Gans, N. M. Putney, & M. Silverstein (Eds.), *Handbook of theories of aging* (2nd ed., pp. 117–144).

Schimanski, I. D., & Treharne, G. J. (2019). Extra marginalisation within the community: Queer individuals' perspectives on suicidality, discrimination and gay pride events. *Psychology & Sexuality, 10,* 31–44. doi: 10.1080/19419899.2018.1524394

Sherman, D. W., Norman, R., & McSherry, C. B. (2010). A comparison of death anxiety and quality of life of patients with advanced cancer or AIDS and their family caregivers. *Journal of the Association of Nurses in AIDS Care, 21,* 99–112. doi:10.1016/j.jana.2009.07.007

Sterns, H. L., & Huyck, M. H. (2001). *The role of work in midlife. In M. E. Lachman (Ed.), Wiley series on adulthood and aging. Handbook of midlife development (pp. 447–486).*

Whitehead, B., O'Brien, M. R., Jack, B. A., & Mitchell, D. (2011). Experiences of dying, death and bereavement in motor neuron disease: A qualitative study. *Palliative Medicine, 26,* 368–372. doi:10.1177/0269216311410900

The Williams Institute. (2018). *The impact of stigma and discrimination against LGBT people in Arizona.* UCLA School of Law.

Yalom, I. (2008). *Staring at the sun: Overcoming the terror of death.* Jossey-Bass.

## Credits

# Middle Adulthood Development

Sharon Bowles, MA; Christopher Townsend, PhD; and Stacy Speedlin Gonzalez, PhD

*What a relief to find, in middle age, that there are still interests wait-ing inside of you to be discovered.* —*Alexis Schaitkin*

## Learning Objectives

After reading this chapter, you should be able to

1. Define key concepts relevant to the developmental processes of persons in middle adulthood.
2. Describe human growth and development from a bioecological and psychosocial developmental lens.
3. Illuminate inclusive practices and social-justice-oriented actions for working with this age group in clinical settings.

# Introduction

Persons in middle adulthood will experience significant life changes, accompanied by a reevaluation of values and needs. Furthermore, mid-aged adults grapple with challenges unique and specific to physiological, cognitive, and social adjustments. For this reason, this age group can benefit from counseling and clinical services. Clinicians working with this age group should familiarize themselves with the experiences and needs of their clients. Intersectionality and cultural context should also be considered in case conceptualization with this group.

# Key Concepts

Key concepts in this chapter are primarily related to the physical and cognitive aging process for middle adulthood. The following list is not comprehensive. Therefore, clinicians who work with this population should familiarize themselves with the specific needs of adults at this stage in life. Intersectionality of various cross-groups (age, gender, race, ability, and sexual/gender identity) is also unique and should be taken into consideration. For the purpose of conceptualizing terms within this chapter, the authors provide the terms that follow.

- **Middle Adulthood (or midlife):** Refers to the period of the life span between early adulthood and late adulthood. Although ages and tasks are culturally defined, the age definition for this textbook is from 40–65.
- **Crystallized Intelligence:** The accumulation of knowledge, facts, and skills acquired throughout life (Horn & Cattell, 1967).
- **Fluid Intelligence:** The capacity to think logically and solve problems in novel situations, independent of acquired knowledge (Horn & Cattell, 1967).
- **Presbyopia:** Gradual progression of losing the ability to see objects in near sight. This is typically described as a normal aging process.
- **Presbycusis:** Hearing loss that gradually occurs in most individuals and is associated with aging (NIH, 1997).

# The Human Developing Process

## ERIKSON'S EIGHT STAGES OF PSYCHOSOCIAL DEVELOPMENT

Erikson's model provides a psycho-developmental overview as a context for understanding client developmental processes and how this translates into the therapeutic relationship (Knight, 2017). Erikson's model examines various life stages from a binary perspective. For example, the adolescent stage is conceptualized through the lens of identity cohesion versus role confusion (Snarey et al., 1987). The stage of development for this age group is viewed from a perspective of generativity versus stagnation; a pertinent value system for understanding middle-aged adult experience (Table 10.1). Psychosocial development occurs as an individual navigates his or her own internal processes with respect to work productivity, physical capability, negotiating monetary needs and retirement, and social/familial connections (Erikson et al., 1994).

**TABLE 10.1**    Erikson's Psychosocial Development Model (1950)

| STAGES | STAGE DESCRIPTION (SYNTONIC TENDENCY–DYSTONIC TENDENCY) | ADAPTIVE STRENGTH/ VIRTUE | MALDEVELOPMENT (MALADAPTIVE TENDENCY–MALIGNANT TENDENCY) |
|---|---|---|---|
| Infancy | Basic Trust vs. Mistrust | Hope | Sensory Maladjustment–Withdrawal |
| Early Childhood | Autonomy vs. Shame and Doubt | Will | Shameless Willfulness–Compulsion |
| Play Age | Initiative vs. Guilt | Purpose | Ruthlessness–Inhibition |
| School Age | Industriousness vs. Inferiority | Competence | Narrow Virtuosity–Inertia |
| Adolescence | Identity Cohesion vs. Role Confusion | Fidelity | Fanaticism–Repudiation |
| Young Adulthood | Intimacy vs. Isolation | Love | Promiscuity–Exclusivity |
| Adulthood | Generativity vs. Stagnation/ Self–Absorption | Care | Overextension–Rejectivity |
| Old Age | Integrity vs. Despair | Wisdom | Presumption–Disdain |

Dissimilar to developmental stages that explain cognitive or growth milestones, Erikson's eight-stage model examines identification and relational growth. Personal needs and identity shifts can be better understood through the view of adulthood stage (generativity versus stagnation). Beyond employment, relationships, and physical well-being, persons at this stage must navigate mental health and create a microcosm of belonging (Snarey et al., 1987; Syed & McLean, 2017). The generativity versus stagnation stage can serve as a lens for navigating such adjustments. This psychosocial stage occurs when individuals reach a point in their life where they navigate care, empathy, and concern for themselves and others. Adults at this stage will create or nurture things and people expected to outlast them. Success in life can result in a sense of accomplishment, while failure can lead to shallow involvement with others (Erikson et al., 1994). Regarding this stage of life, individuals can often experience challenges based on cultural and personal demands (Knight, 2017). Personal and relational adversities are often shaped by self-centeredness and rigid value systems. Since mid-aged persons are often die-casted in their personality, they can require more flexibility from others while feeling less obligated to accommodate people around them.

## BRONFENBRENNER'S ECOLOGICAL STAGE MODEL

To better understand the influence of external systems, Bronfenbrenner developed the ecological stage model to explain how environmental experiences affect an individual's growth and development. Different aspects or levels of the environment that influence development were labeled to better conceptualize the effect, including the macro-, micro-, meso-, and exosystems (Bronfenbrenner, 1994). This theory examines how individuals experience life within their own various systems. Macrosystems include systems such as political and societal (Bronfenbrenner, 1994). Counselors or clinicians can understand how laws, politics, and policies can affect health care and community-based needs for middle-aged adults. Microsystems involve familial systems, whether nuclear or extended (Bronfenbrenner, 1994). Family involvement and engagement is often culturally sanctioned, therefore, it can be viewed as a vital construct for understanding middle-aged adults. Meso- and exosystems involve communities and culture (Figure 10.1). As stated previously, culture and community experience will mediate relational connections/disconnections with this age group. For example, women at this stage may seek more time with family and adapt a matriarchal role with children and grandchildren. Infused with Erikson's stage model, the ecological stage model demonstrates how relational connectivity evolves through developmental milestones. An example of this is shown through the number of micro- and meso-systemic connections an individual has and how well they transition from intimacy to generativity. Middle-aged adults who reach optimal development in their young adult years will go on to develop lifelong relationships with family, community, and friends.

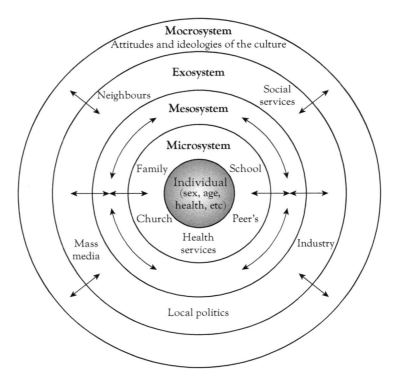

FIGURE 10.1   Bronfenbrenner's Ecological Stage Model

## PHYSICAL AND COGNITIVE

Given the broad spectrum of health, resources, and biology, middle-aged adults will experience physical and cognitive milestones differently. Culture (e.g., future orientation) and resources (e.g., affluence, funding, and access to health care) play a significant role in mediating physical and cognitive outcomes.

### PHYSIOLOGICAL PROCESSES

*Ages 40–50* mark the beginning of vision changes, hearing loss, and gray hair. Those in this age group will often experience face thinning and wrinkles, loss of skin integrity, and loss of muscle/bone mass. Women will encounter significant decline in estrogen, resulting in irregularity of the menstrual cycle and decreased ability to birth children. Men equally will produce lower levels of testosterone and, therefore, produce less semen and sperm. Both men and women's intensity of sexual response may decline. The risk of disease elevates at this stage.

*Throughout ages 50–65*, health concerns often persist. Individuals at this age will develop changes in the lens of their eyes (macular degeneration, glaucoma), more hearing loss, and bone mass further decreases. They may also lose height because of collapse in spinal column discs. Their skin loses significant integrity; wrinkles, age spots, and blood become visible. At this age, menopause and erection inability occurs. Cancer, heart diseases, and other diseases may occur more frequently.

## COGNITIVE PROCESSES

*At ages 40–50 and 50–65*, deeper awareness of aging increases. Crystallized intelligence also increases as fluid intelligence declines. Practical intelligence, otherwise known as "street smarts," also begins to solidify in middle adulthood. Midlife adults experience a decline in processing speed (compensated through experience and practice), while selectivity, attention to tasks, and memory retention declines. Further, they discover difficulties with retrieving from long-term memory. Meanwhile, metacognitive information, practical problem solving, the ability to integrate ideas, creativity, and self-expression will increase with this age group. Despite declines in various cognitive abilities, adults at this stage require stimulation and mental activities (Sterns & Huyck, 2001).

## SOCIAL AND EMOTIONAL

Similar to physical and cognitive processes, midlife adults will experience social and emotional milestones based on different contextual lifestyles (e.g., culture, relational values, gender roles, and familial supports). Psychosocially, individuals tend to desire more generativity, meaningful living, and self-acceptance. Persons at this stage develop more environmental/social awareness and may become a caregiver, especially of aged parents or parents-in-law and relatives. Due to end-of-life expectancy for parents, individuals may seek more relationships in their extended family and friends. They can experience more appreciation of others, develop closer relationships with siblings and relatives, and have increased job satisfaction as retirement looms in the future. Further, they experience relational stressors, including dating, marriage, and divorce. Familial systems may change or adjust according to relational restructuring (cohabitating, co-parenting, etc.). Job satisfaction or dissatisfaction plays a significant role in overall happiness and quality of life. Occupational crises may occur, depending on whether they experience workplace challenges (gender bias, racism, ageism, or ableism). Beyond age 50, parent-to-child assistance may decline, while child-to-parent assistance increases. After age 60, retirement may occur and assisted living may be necessary for individuals with chronic, degenerative diseases. At any point in middle adulthood, midlife crisis may occur. Individuals may realize they have not experienced all they intended, life looks different than what they had anticipated, or they experience a crisis of identification.

## Scientific Contributions

Historically, the scientific and research community often viewed midlife adults from a medicalized view. Therefore, the literature on middle adulthood is highly characterized by examining how the aging process impedes relationships, social roles, and work life.

## Theoretical Considerations

Professionals working with middle-aged adults can aid in the progression of health and well-being by acknowledging the effect of these processes on development. Moreover, it is critical for clinicians to conceptualize middle-aged individuals' experiences and development within the context of their salient experiences. To achieve these goals, the authors position this chapter within the framework of Erikson's (1950) psychosocial theory of human development and Bronfenbrenner's (1994) ecological stage theory. The authors examine both internal psychosocial processes and external environmental factors that influence social, cultural, familial, and communal processes for adults within this age group.

## Strengths and Challenges from the "ISMs" Perspectives

Ageism, racism, sexism, and all other isms are biases against particular sectors of society. Each ism targets a "defining" quality or characteristic considered a deficit by other groups. The ism restricts access and opportunities to those who are attempting to schematically operate and function in society in a meaningful capacity. ISM constructs are built on mechanisms of assumptions, discriminatory attitudes, oppression, and control.

The intersection of Erickson's middle adulthood stage and various domains of ISMs are relevant and persisting experiences for this group (Erikson et al., 1994). ISMs threaten the process of moving successfully through this developmental stage. In a stage in which "making your mark" is a focus of one's existence through caring for others, the meaning of life connects to making the world a better place for future generations. Failing to contribute creates disconnections and stagnant dispositions across ecological domains (Syed & McLean, 2017).

The clinician's awareness of the task for this developmental stage will provide insight into the overarching need to be helpful and caring. Understanding the surfacing of virtues, and perhaps the need to perpetuate life, provides the counselor with a framework to facilitate a meaning process for the client (Andrews, 2016). Validating the value of this role will very likely foster a deeper understanding of the cultural and social implications. Counselors may find themselves helping this age group work through dissatisfaction, disconnections, and sabotaging thoughts related to experiences of rejection, be it with an employer, connections with youth, or combating isms (Sterns & Huyck, 2001).

## DIVERSITY

Honoring a client's diversity and multicultural facets calls for a compilation of knowledge, skills, and abilities on the counselor's behalf. This implies having a mindset to consider and pursue an understanding of all differences with genuine intentions to empower those seeking help. In many instances, this could mean the client becomes the counselor's teacher as it relates to expanding the counselor's knowledge on topics that may be distant from the counselor's realities (Ratts et al., 2016).

For those in middle adulthood this is a period of pulling life experiences together in preparation for a "master's class." The contemplation of meaning and purpose of life along with consideration of mortality presses this group to be impactful across their systems of influence (Malone et al., 2016), particularly when it comes to advocating for equalities. For many marginalized groups, difference has symbolized deficits, creating a culture of biases and systemic barricades toward those who stand outside what has been considered the cultural standard of the majority.

Cross-culturally, the life experiences of this group will present a plethora of challenges and successes its members have worked through. The effects of cultural suppression, oppression, or racism is a detriment to psychosocial development. Inequalities hinder growth and development across life domains (Dutta et al., 2016). A counselor's awareness and sensitivity to cultural inequities and the effect on targeted groups are critical to the change process.

Application of multicultural and social justice counseling interventions and principles fosters a sense of validation, empowerment, and solidarity for the client (Caswell et al., 2017). Counselors will find themselves leveraging resources across ecological levels in meeting clients' needs as they move forward in the tasks of middle adulthood. Counseling for marginalized groups is not only about helping to manage internal conflicts but helping to challenge external forces that foster conflicts.

**FIGURE 10.2**    Living an Active Life

## GENDER

Contemporary scholarship suggests gender exists on a spectrum and encompasses a wide range of expressions and ideas about the self (Coleman et al., 2011; Yarbrough, 2018). Therefore, for the purpose of this chapter, the authors define gender as the gender in which an individual identifies, expresses the self, and lives. Gender is an expansive term; individuals can live as nonbinary, gender neutral, or gender fluid (Goodrich et al., 2017). Alternatively, individuals can exist within specific gender constructs, such as male, female, or transgender.

At this age, gender can be typically identified and experienced by an individual, though some persons may transition to a different gender later in life (White Hughto & Reisner, 2018). Regardless of the gender a person identifies or expresses, age affects one's experiences as hormonal and physical changes occur. While gender experience may mediate specific changes, individuals collectively will encounter noteworthy differences in their physical appearance, cognitive capabilities, and overall outlook on life. Thus, clinicians should work to understand the role of gender identity and potential marginalization that clients may experience and work from an affirming clinical role (Goodrich et al., 2017).

## SEXUAL ORIENTATION

For the purpose of this section, heterosexism is discussed. The authors define "heterosexism" as a system of attitudes and beliefs that maintain power for heterosexual individuals through the subjugation of non-heterosexual persons (Nunn & Bolt, 2015).

For LGBTQ-identifying individuals, heterosexism manifests in the form of biases, prejudice, and discrimination. Such experiences are more likely to impede personal and developmental growth at this stage in life.

More recently, research on palliative care shows how LGBTQ people are more susceptible to certain life-threatening conditions compared with their heterosexual and cisgender counterparts (Cartwright et al., 2012). Yet, LGBTQ persons may forego medical and clinical care out of fear of marginalization (Cartwright et al., 2012). While this can result in more complicated health conditions, LGBTQ persons at this age often experience civil rights violations at disproportionate levels compared with younger members of the community (Obradors-Campos, 2011). To be supportive, clinicians should familiarize themselves with the needs of more vulnerable middle-aged adults in accordance with their intersectionalities.

## ABLEISM

Ableism (disability discrimination) is a set of beliefs and practices that privilege the experiences and narratives of able-bodied individuals while perpetuating disempowerment. Ableism can hinder disabled individuals' ability to access physical and social spaces. These ideas are rooted in the notion that disabled people need to be fixed rather than considering the disability as a dimension of difference (Bogart & Dunn, 2019).

This is important because it highlights that disability intersects all other social identities including race, gender, and sexual orientation (Brault, 2012). A person can be born into a disability group or become a member at any time. People with disabilities often find themselves isolated, not having an in-group identity. They may be the only ones in their families or communities with a particular disability.

Historically, rehabilitation counselors have specialized in working with clients who have disabilities. These professional counselors are trained in medical aspects and have knowledge specific to accommodation technology and disability law. By using modifications and technology, people with disabilities are able to perform and meet expectations. Unfortunately, many decision makers remain uneducated regarding laws and resources for those with disabilities (Dirth & Branscombe, 2017). Therefore, the rooted ideals of ableism are perpetuated and the need for advocacy continues in order to foster equitable opportunities.

## AGEISM

For the sake of this discussion, ageism is a social construct wherein people are portrayed in stereotypical perspectives (Chasteen et al., 2020). As age increases, the factor of multiple jeopardies come into the equation, making this population more vulnerable to multiple isms simultaneously (i.e., ageism, sexism, etc.). Synchronizing success with opportunities to share and help others aids in buffering ism threats and moving through the developmental stage.

Developmental maturation and advancement in life allows this group to potentially operate in multiple levels of society. Their identities are not just individualistic but oriented toward their reference groups within society (Syed & McLean, 2017). These associations can ripple through all levels of the person's reference groups, including family, community, civic groups, and society. Making contributions establishes a positive sense of self.

### MORTALITY AWARENESS

Mortality awareness and fear of death are universal human experiences (Yalom, 2009). Individuals across all intersections will very likely experience varying levels of mortality awareness and death anxiety across the life span (Carstensen, 2006). As indicated in previous chapters, the intensity of mortality awareness varies across developmental stages. It tends to be highest in middle age and decreases during late adulthood and old age (Cicirelli, 2006). Therefore, this age group will very likely experience stressors as the result of getting older and developing chronic health conditions (Bellavia et al., 2013). Additionally, middle-aged adults may be tasked with caring for older family members and are challenged to alter their own life to accommodate this need. This may lead to intrinsic thinking about their own mortality, ability, or physical/cognitive challenges. Developing a supportive social network and connecting more with family members may strengthen development at this stage and assist with processing mortality concerns.

## Summary

Counseling and educating persons in middle adulthood requires knowledge beyond traditional counseling and teaching practices. When working with this population, counselors and educators should work to understand the needs of this group through a developmental and multicultural lens. The authors believe Bronfenbrenner's ecological theory infused with Erikson's stage of development model provides a unique lens for conceptualizing development. Further, counselors and educators can benefit from examining the intersectionality of race, gender, citizen status, and sexual/affectional orientation and how this affects the experiences of midlife adults.

**CASE STUDY**

Martina is a 58-year-old Black American woman who lives in Atlanta, Georgia, with her husband, her 30-year-old son, his wife, and their children. Her husband's mother (who is 82) also resides in the home. Martina is actively involved in her church and serves on the Deacon Board of Elders. She plays a significant role in her church and with members of the congregation, serving as a maternal figure to many of the youth and young adults who attend services. Additionally, she works part time at a local diner as a waitress to bring in extra money for the household. Her husband is the primary breadwinner of the family.

Recently, Martina came into the local counseling agency after a member of her church suggested that she talk with someone. She feels uncomfortable with the idea of talking to a counselor, worrying that the professional will "mess with her mind." She further vocalizes concerns that anything involving her mind is from God, and therefore she is concerned that

FIGURE 10.3    Aging Gracefully

counseling may be sacrilegious. The counselor who sees Martina assures her that she can attend a few sessions and stop coming if she prefers this. She apprehensively agrees.

In her first counseling session, she tells the counselor that her grandson (who is often left with her during the day) is sneaking out of the house and abusing drugs with his older friends. She attempts to control him by locking the doors or scolding him, but he leaves anyway. She once followed him and physically dragged him back to the house after she caught him hanging out with friends. She shakes her head in disdain, and says, "I would never have disrespected my elders this way. These children have no respect for anyone!" When asked about the grandson's parents, Martina reveals that she never liked her son's choice in women and does not get along with her daughter-in-law, who allows her children to get away with a lot without discipline. Her son constantly comes to his wife's defense. Martina tries to get support from her husband, but her husband is often too tired to deal with family issues after a long day at work.

The counselor asks Martina if she would be willing to invite her family to the next counseling session. Martina raises her eyebrows. "You are lucky that I came this time!" When the counselor asks Martina what she would like to get out of counseling, Martina quickly responds, "I want you to tell me how to get my grandson to behave. I want my daughter-in-law to stop disrespecting the family by dressing like a Jezebel! I can't believe my son chose her after I brought him up so well!" The counselor reminds her that counselors do not give advice. Martina replies, "Then why am I here?"

## Reflections and Targeted Discussion Questions

1. After reviewing this chapter, how would you conceptualize your client from a multicultural lens? How does intersectionality of various nondominant constructs (race, gender, citizen status, sexual/affectional orientation) play a role in identity and counseling needs?
2. If this client came in for her second session, how would you work with her? (Please take into account both developmental models. Include needs based on macro-, meso-, and micro-levels. Also, take into consideration where the client is now with her views on counseling, cultural needs, and concerns regarding her spiritual beliefs.)
3. What resiliency factors do you see that play a role in her ability to thrive and resolve her own challenges?

## References

Andrews, M. (2016). The existential crisis. *Behavioral Development Bulletin, 21*(1), 104.

Bellavia, A., Bottai, M., Wolk, A., & Orsini, N. (2013). Physical activity and mortality in a prospective cohort of middle-aged and elderly men—A time perspective. *International Journal of Behavioral Nutrition and Physical Activity, 10*(1), 94.

Bogart, K. R., & Dunn, D. S. (2019). Ableism [Special issue introduction]. *Journal of Social Issues, 75*, 650–664. doi:10.1111/josi.12354

Brault, M. (2012). *Americans with disabilities: 2010.* http://www.census.gov/prod/2012pubs/p70-131.pdf

Bronfenbrenner, U. (1994). Ecological models of human development. *International Encyclopedia of Education, 3*(2), 37–43.

Carstensen, L. L. (2006). The influence of a sense of time in human development. *Science, 312*(5782), 1913–1915.

Cartwright, C., Hughes, M., & Lienert, T. (2012). End-of-life care for gay, lesbian, bisexual and transgender people. *Culture, Health & Sexuality, 14*(5), 537–548.

Caswell, M., Migoni, A. A., Geraci, N., & Cifor, M. (2016): 'To be able to imagine otherwise': Community archives and the importance of representation, *Archives and Records, 38*(10), 1–22. DOI: 10.1080/23257962.2016.1260445

Chasteen, A. L., Horhota, M., & Crumley-Branyon, J. J. (2020). Overlooked and underestimated: Experiences of ageism in young, middle-aged, and older adults. *The Journals of Gerontology: Series B.*

Cicirelli, V. G. (2006). Fear of death in mid-old age. *Journal of Gerontology, 61B*, 75–81. doi:10.1093/geronb/61.2.p75

Coleman, E., Bockting, W., Botzer, M., Cohen-Kettenis, P., DeCuypere, G., Feldman, J., Green, J, . Monstrey, S. (2011). Standards of care for the health of transsexual, transgender, and gender-nonconforming people, Version 7. *International Journal of Transgenderism.* doi:10.1080/15532739.2011.700873

Dirth, T. P., & Branscombe, N. R. (2017). Disability models affect disability policy support through awareness of structural discrimination. *Journal of Social Issues, 73*, 413–442. https://doi.org/10.1111/josi.12224

Dutta, U., Sonn, C. C., & Lykes, M. B. (2016). Situating and contesting structural violence in community-based research and action. *Community Psychology in Global Perspective, 2*(2), 1–20.

Erikson, E. H., Erikson, J. M., & Kivnick, H. Q. (1994). *Vital involvement in old age.* W. W. Norton & Company.

Goodrich, K. M., Farmer, L. B., Watson, J. C., Davis, R. J., Luke, M., Dispenza, F., Griffith, C. (2017). Standards of care in assessment of lesbian, gay, bisexual, transgender, gender expansive, and queer/questioning (LGBTGEQ+) persons. *Journal of LGBT Issues in Counseling, 11*(4), 203–211.

Horn, J. L., & Cattell, R. B. (1967). Age differences in fluid and crystallized intelligence. *Acta Psychologica, 26*, 107–129.

Knight, Z. G. (2017). A proposed model of psychodynamic psychotherapy linked to Erik Erikson's eight stages of psychosocial development. *Clinical Psychology & Psychotherapy, 24*(5), 1047–1058.

Malone, J. C., Liu, S. R., Vaillant, G. E., Rentz, D. M., & Waldinger, R. J. (2016). Midlife Eriksonian psychosocial development: Setting the stage for late-life cognitive and emotional health. *Developmental Psychology, 52*(3), 496–508. https://doi.org/10.1037/a0039875

National Institute of Health. (1997). *What is presbycusis?* https://www.nidcd.nih.gov/sites/default/files/Content%20Images/presbycusis.pdf

Nunn, L. M., & Bolt, S. C. (2015). Wearing a rainbow bumper sticker: Experiential learning on homophobia, heteronormativity, and heterosexual privilege. *Journal of LGBT Youth, 12*(3), 276–301.

Obradors-Campos, M. (2011). Deconstructing biphobia. *Journal of Bisexuality, 11*, 207–226. doi:10.1080/15299716.2011.571986

Ratts, M. J., Singh, A. A., Nassar-McMillan, S., Butler, S. K., & McCullough, J. R. (2016). Multicultural and social justice counseling competencies: Guidelines for the counseling profession. *Journal of Multicultural Counseling and Development, 44*, 28–48. doi:10.1002/jmcd.12035

Snarey, J., Son, L., Kuehne, V. S., Hauser, S., & Vaillant, G. (1987). The role of parenting in men's psychosocial development: A longitudinal study of early adulthood infertility and midlife generativity. *Developmental Psychology, 23*(4), 593.

Sterns, H. L., & Huyck, M. H. (2001). *The role of work in midlife.* In M. E. Lachman (Ed.), Wiley series on adulthood and aging. Handbook of midlife development (p. 447–486). John Wiley & Sons.

Syed, M., & McLean, K. C. (2017, April 24). Erikson's theory of psychosocial development. https://doi.org/10.4135/9781483392271.n178

White Hughto, J. M., & Reisner, S. L. (2018). Social context of depressive distress in aging transgender adults. *Journal of Applied Gerontology, 37*(12), 1517–1539.

Yalom, I. (2009). *Staring at the sun: Overcoming the terror of death.* Jossey-Bass.

Yarbrough, E. (2018). *Transgender mental health.* American Psychiatric Association Publishing.

## Credits

# Late Adulthood Development

Tora N. Kincaid, MA, NCC, LCMHC, LCASA

*Aging is not lost youth but a new stage of opportunity and strength.* —Betty Friedan

## Learning Objectives

After reading this chapter, you should be able to

1. Recognize characteristics pertaining to the normal aging process.
2. Use techniques to support the emotional and adjustment of older adults to the experience of aging.
3. Describe key considerations for counseling individuals in late adulthood from an ecological and psychosocial perspective.

## Introduction

Although aging is a universal process that everyone goes through, the experience is different and deeply personal for each individual. As human beings develop into late adulthood, physiological changes occur along with psychological responses that can make it difficult to adjust. Situational conditions relative to one's environment, spirituality, social circles, and hereditary factors all play a significant role in our attitudes and perceptions about development later in life. In fact, developmental science shows that our lives continue to change situationally and behaviorally, based on multiple influences throughout the later stages of life. These days, being "old" is not what it used to be. There are much fewer age-related limitations, and people are living longer. Emphasis is placed not only on the quantity of years but also on the quality of life during longer life spans (Ackerman & Kanfer, 2020; Diehl et al., 2020; Freund, 2020; Staudinger, 2020).

Society is growing aware of the increasing numbers of baby boomers. In fact, researchers have predicted that by 2030, 72.1 million Americans will be 65 years of age or older (Administration on Aging, 2014). In 2011, the U.S. Census Bureau predicted that by 2020 longevity rates would reach 72 years for males and 88 years for females. By today's standards, the average American is no longer considered "young" and the prospectus for the next 30 years indicates that the number of older adults is expected to double (United Nations, 2020). With the onset of the population majority being in the late stages of adulthood, there is an urgent need for counselors to understand the interaction of perceptions, attitudes, and developmental theories of aging. This chapter focuses on concepts and various theories with an emphasis on positive and negative narratives that affect the aging process and how they influence cognitive and behavioral differences during late adulthood.

## Key Concepts

- **Positivity Bias:** Refers to the theory that elderly people remember positive things better than negative or neutral things (Thomas & Hasher, 2006).
- **Cultural Variation:** Refers to the rich tapestry of diversity in social practices that different cultures exhibit around the world.
- **Neuroplasticity:** The ability of the brain to undergo biological changes, ranging from the cellular level (i.e., individual neurons) all the way to large-scale changes involving cortical remapping.

## The Human Developing Process

According to traditional research, every human being goes through the same cycle of development—from the beginning physical inception, to a maturation process, and then the eventual final stages of decline (Niemczyński, 2017). In developmental science, this continuous series of stages over time is called the "life span" (Magnusson, 1996; Whitbourne & Whitbourne, 2016) and is a multidimensional process. Emerging research, however, shows that not everyone ages at the same rate (Stevenson, 2014). These empirical studies (Hertzog et al., 2008; Lindenberger, 2014) show there are patterns to the developmental changes that all people experience as they age, along with other factors that are present and specific to each individual. Because we are all different, counselors need to integrate a tailored approach in utilizing clinical interventions with older adults in the counseling setting. A tailored approach assessing client perceptions about aging and the developmental challenges they face can help to mitigate negative mental health factors such as age-related depression and anxiety.

## PHYSICAL AND COGNITIVE

How we view aging largely depends on a variety of factors, including our perspective (Rakoczy et al., 2018). As more studies are conducted in cognitive neuroscience, both perspective (Foster et al., 2015) and the correlational roles of the relationship between the nervous system and the brain have been shown to play a vital role in the concept of resiliency for human development. As the brain ages, many positive and negative psychological changes occur that coincide with changes appearing within the social and physical realm.

Since aging is subtle, we may be surprised when we see the visual signs, such as a few more gray hairs or wrinkles. These physical signs of aging are equated by most individuals with negative connotations. In addition, cognitively, relatively healthy people do not tend to feel their age; however, many people can optimize the aging process both physically and cognitively in order to continue being healthy and productive during this process. Studies have shown there is a link between cognitive memory processes and positive circumstances in an individual's life span. This link is termed positivity bias and posits that, cognitively, older adults tend to remember positive things instead of neutral or negative things (Thomas & Hasher, 2006). Although there is negativity surrounding the aging process (Lindland et al., 2015), biomedical and psychological research has shown that positive attitudes can and do affect the aging process (Levy, 2017; Tucker-Drob & Briley, 2014).

As middle-aged adults begin to move into late adulthood, they may feel powerless over how they age when, in fact, research suggests that individuals have more influence over how they age than previously thought (Carstensen et al., 2011; Charles & Carstensen, 2014). In other words, it is not all about genetics, loss, and decline (Schaie, 2013). Many physical issues that plague those in the phase of late adulthood, such as osteoporosis and sarcopenia, have been shown to be delayed, minimized, or even reversed (Hong & Kim, 2018) because they are malleable with continuing exercise, nutrition, and positive perceptions and attitudes (Willis & Belleville, 2016). Additionally, there are several recent studies confirming exercise as an alternative therapy in reducing depression and anxiety (Lee et al., 2018). Engaging in diverse activities (e.g., household chores, paid work, and leisure activity) can enhance older individuals' social networks and knowledge, which are fundamental elements of sound mental well-being. There are even more promising studies correlating the positive effects of physical activity in late adulthood and protection against terminal illnesses like dementia and Alzheimer's disease. Regular physical activity and exercise for older adults helps improve mental and physical health, both of which will help maintain independence throughout the aging process.

Nutritionally, we really are what we choose to put in our bodies. The risk for certain diseases associated with aging, such as heart disease, osteoporosis and diabetes, can be reduced with a lifestyle that includes healthy eating. Good nutrition also helps in the treatment and recovery from illness. While healthy living can't turn back the clock, it can help you feel good longer. Good nutrition is important, no matter what your age. It gives you energy and can help you control your weight. It may also help prevent some diseases, such as osteoporosis, high blood pressure, heart disease, type 2 diabetes, and certain cancers. As we age, our bodies and lifestyle changes, and so does what we need to stay healthy. For example, as we become older, the body may need fewer calories, but older adults still need to get enough nutrients. Some older adults need more protein. Older adults need more calcium and vitamin D to help maintain bone health. To meet these needs, calcium-rich foods and beverages are important to the daily caloric intake. Older adults should aim for three servings of low-fat or fat-free dairy products daily. Other sources of calcium include fortified cereals and fruit juices, dark green leafy vegetables, canned fish with soft bones, and fortified plant-based beverages. Good sources of vitamin D include fatty fish (such as salmon), eggs, and fortified foods and beverages. Calcium supplements and multivitamins that contain vitamin D are also good choices. Eating right and staying fit are important no matter what your age.

Just as nutrition and exercise have positive and negative effects on overall well-being in older adulthood, so too does the social environment. One of the pioneers in developmental science, Urie Bronfenbrenner (1979, 1986), proposed an ecological perspective to the aging process in which he believed that environmental systems affect us in many ways over the development of our lives. Although the ecological model specifically focuses on environmental systems, his theory can be applied to health and cognitive processes as well. For example, many people consider biological health to be an autonomous function operating within each person individually; however, researchers working within the Whitehall II study (Kouvonen et al., 2011) have found that relationships with other people affect our cognitive and biological functioning more than was previously thought. In the study (Kouvonen et al., 2011), it was discovered that individuals who reported negative characteristics within their close relationships had a higher probability of being overweight, which is just one example of how our social environment can affect our biological and cognitive health. The implications for this social and environmental context within treatment modalities can help clinicians to understand the tremendous role that the environment and perspective reactions play on physical and cognitive processes within the cycle of the aging process.

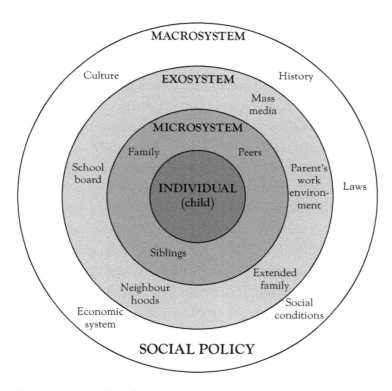

**FIGURE 11.1** Bronfenbrenner's Ecological Model

## SOCIAL AND EMOTIONAL

Regardless of our age, fulfilling and positive social relationships form a crucial aspect of personal development across the life span. In recent years, developmental psychology has begun to focus on studies highlighting the significance of social and emotional factors that influence memory processes in older adults (Schmitt et al., 2017). Across longitudinal and cross-sectional studies of older adults and social relationships, it has been shown that a person's social relationship network tends to decrease while the quality and satisfaction of those relationships have a tendency to increase (Luong et al., 2011; Wrzus et al., 2013). This is significant because the suicidality rates among older adults could be correlated to social isolation, which indicates loneliness and less community support for those in late adulthood. Loneliness and isolation can lead to depression and other risk factors for mental illnesses. The suicide rate for those over the age of 85 was noted to be caused most often by depression and other forms of mental illness (Xu et al., 2016). According to the social activity theory, older adults who are able to remain involved in meaningful social activities tend to be more satisfied with their life overall and able retain their sense of identity (Cavan et al., 1949).

These days, due to longevity, many older adults are still living and thriving into the third and fourth generations within families (Bóné, 2018) and take on the social role of being a grandparent who is also a caregiver. Many grandparents are in the position of being a caregiver or custodial parent to their grandchildren and their great grandchildren. Custodial grandparents face a variety of stressors stemming from increases in substance abuse, mental illness, negligence, and emotional problems (Choi, Sprang, & Eslinger, 2016; Saxena & Brotherson, 2021) of the parents. This type of supporting behavior can be especially beneficial for all parties involved in the rearing and upbringing of children in the family. Some nontraditional roles that place the grandparents at the heart of the nuclear family, especially in underrepresented communities, can decrease instances of social isolation and loneliness for older adults. In order to be active grandparents, the older adults must have good cognitive and emotional capacities that may increase their physical and mental fitness (Burns, 2010). Unfortunately, custodial grandparents can also be affected negatively as well.

Another influencer of well-being in older adults is the prospect of retirement. Retirement is often the first major transition faced by older adults. Its effects on physical and mental health differ from person to person, depending on attitude and reason for retirement. Some choose to retire, having looked forward to quitting work, while others are forced to retire because of health problems or job loss. Many retirees have difficulty adjusting to certain aspects of retirement, such as their reduced income, altered social role, and entitlements Appropriate preparation for retirement and counseling for retirees and families who experience difficulties may help. As individuals retire for many reasons, retirement can be a celebration in which people choose to travel and do the things they have always wished they had time to do. Others may become disenchanted as they realize retirement may not be as they dreamed. Some people reorient their lives and engage in rewarding activities like volunteer work or finding new hobbies. Finally, others may adjust to their new routine and decide how to best enjoy and spend their time. Unfortunately, some older adults can become stuck in the disenchantment of retirement and either reenter the workforce or experience a decline in mental health.

Research indicates that mental health issues occur relatively infrequently postretirement, but physical health problems are relatively common and often associated with aging rather than retirement. Issues that may affect health outcomes in retirement include social connectedness/support, participation in physical exercise, lifestyle (e.g., changes in smoking or alcohol use), gender, and postretirement activities, marital status, and whether retirement was voluntary or earlier than the normative age. Poor health can occur when retirees experience loneliness and social isolation. While not specifically a problem of retirees, retirement could trigger increased loneliness and a sense of decreased social connections.

Social isolation and loneliness can heighten the risk for premature mortality in older adults. Researchers have shown that loneliness can be a bigger killer than obesity and is considered a major public health issue. A review of 218 studies on the health effects of social isolation and loneliness found that lonely people have a 50 percent higher chance of premature death, while obesity increases the chance of early death by 30 percent (Zhu, 2016). The team found that the risk of early death associated with loneliness, social isolation, and living alone was equal to or greater than the premature death risk associated not only with obesity but also with other major health conditions.

Providing emotional support for culturally diverse members of the older adult population can be challenging because sociocultural perspectives on aging fail to consider the racial disparities of underrepresented cultures within the traditionally defined psychological processes. These processes include the importance of familial and cultural obligations and how their interdependence can affect retirement decisions. Clinicians and caregivers should be aware that these inequalities would influence the emotional and social well-being of older adults in underrepresented communities and their decisions on retirement.

## Scientific Contributions

Over the years, many significant research contributions made to the field of aging focused on successfully navigating late adulthood. Researchers examine several variables empirically, according to theoretical interests. As we have seen, successful aging is linked to many factors, such as environment, personal perspective, cognitive, social, emotional, and physical influences. Interestingly, researchers who study late adulthood have also found that participation in leisure activities plays a significant role in overcoming deficits in intellectual and physical functioning (McPhee et al., 2016). These findings suggest that cognitively challenging leisure activities can increase feelings of well-being and positivity and lower the risks of dementia in late adulthood.

Other influences regarding late adulthood resiliency and cognitively aging successfully include increased studies on more complex cognitive, social, and physical engagements. When older adults engage in social activities that increase complex cognitive functions in a sustained way (such as learning a new language, digital photography, quilting, etc.) and in physical activity (such as water aerobics and yoga), memory and cognitive ability are enhanced, thus decreasing the chances of declining functioning (Park et al., 2014; Lindenburger, 2014; Stillman et al., 2016). Volunteering has been linked with many health benefits, from increased cognitive functioning to less depression, higher morale, and enhanced longevity (Pilkington et al., 2012; Breheny et al., 2020). All of the aforementioned activities increase the brain's neuroplasticity. Neuroplasticity refers to the ability of the brain to undergo biological changes, ranging from the cellular level (i.e., individual neurons) all the way to large-scale changes involving cortical remapping. Neuroplasticity shows that, although we do not have complete control over the aging process, we can decrease susceptibility in developing chronic diseases by positively choosing our own lifestyle and behavior so that it becomes more beneficial to us as we move into later adulthood.

Even more exciting than neuroplasticity findings are the longitudinal studies indicating that some aspects of age-related losses are, in fact, not permanent but can be reversible. Emergent research on previously cited osteoporosis and sarcopenia, for example (Hong & Kim, 2018), and other age-related disabilities (Crimmins et al., 2016), indicates that a person's view on the aging process can be a determinant in reversing some losses related to aging. This is important because negative age-related stereotypes and discrimination, or ageism (Levy, 2017; Nelson, 2016), have become more prevalent in the United States in recent years, despite the fact that people are living longer, being more productive longer, and making choices that can and do affect the aging process. As a society, it is more important than ever that collective individuals focus on a narrative filled with opportunity and challenges rather than decline and loss of functioning. Clinicians have an ethical responsibility to help the community and their clients understand the current research on positive outcomes relative to developmental aging in a collective society and assist in decreasing negative stereotypes.

## Theoretical Considerations

There are many theoretical considerations when discussing the aging process. We will look at two. Keep in mind that all biological theories of aging recognize that, to a certain extent, our genes play a crucial role in how we age. Just as we have genes that determine our developmental features and aging processes, so too do we have genes that may determine our life span. This is called programmed aging theory (Whitbourne & Whitbourne, 2016), which proposes that aging and death are "hardwired" into all organisms. This is made evident by the fact that all species have varying life spans that are consistent within the species, barring unusual circumstances such as premature death or disease. According to biologists, this theory is supported because it is indicative of the systematic variances across species (Whitbourne & Whitbourne, 2016). Researchers believe that genetics account for the life span of humans living to be 100 in nearly 33% in women and 48% in men (Perls, Kunkel, & Puca, 2002) which is different from that of other species. Although this in itself is remarkable, environment and numerous other evolutionary theories play a factor in the genetic bases of aging and longevity across species (Kirkwood & Austad, 2000).

Terror management theory proposes that when unconscious or conscious thoughts of death are triggered, one can experience a wide range of benefits. For example, people may become more altruistic and turn their focus onto the more meaningful things in life. Their perspectives may broaden into a focus on deeper values, morals, spirituality, and attitudes. They may adopt more compassion, develop better health habits, create intrinsic rather than extrinsic goals, become less likely to have prejudices and hold stereotypes, and have an increased desire to develop closer relationships with family members and their community. As clinicians working with older populations that do not spontaneously engage in this process, life-review therapy could be especially beneficial to help older adults reframe negative events that occurred in their lives into a more acceptable and positive light (Korte et al., 2012; Whitbourne & Whitbourne, 2016).

## Strengths and Challenges from the "ISMs" Perspectives

Multiculturally competent counselors, psychologists, and psychiatrists have a major role to play in promoting healthy and productive aging for individuals entering late adulthood. Through more research, they can be at the forefront of generating the needed empirical evidence to show that we have much more control over aging factors than we previously believed. Such research can highlight the theories and techniques on how to truly optimize healthy aging. Translational research related to healthy behaviors such as physical activity, social support, goals, and self-regulation of beliefs and attitudes would be an instrumental educational tool for reducing negative stereotypes about the aging process (Lindenberger, 2014; Stillman et al., 2016; Lachman et al., 2018). Counselors, psychologists, and psychiatrists can use these positive ageing research strategies to promote a healthy perspective in their client outcomes. Although the public continues to perpetuate the negative effects regarding the aging process, individuals now more than ever have the personal responsibility, the wherewithal, and the opportunity to take control of their own aging.

## MULTICULTURAL

How could any studies on majority populations be complete without including underrepresented groups in the discussion? Most of the current research models incorporate a traditionally westernized cultural, contextualized frame of reference that fosters more independence related to outcomes in later life (Kitayama et al., 2020). In most Asian countries, however, achieving attunement with age-graded social roles and interdependence is more important culturally (Kitayama et al., 2020; Fung, 2013). For researchers to gain a more comprehensive understanding of how aging and later adulthood affects the physical, social, and cognitive functioning within multicultural groups, more systematic and representative studies of the variation within ethnic groups must be included in empirical cultural studies. This research would help to form a stronger foundation for understanding developmental outcomes; mental, physical, and behavioral resiliency and plasticity; the role and effect of social relationships on aging; and the specific service needs of multicultural populations in the latter stages of late adulthood (Ferraro et al., 2017; Torres-Gil & Angel, 2018). By studying cultural traditions, practices, and the strengths and weaknesses of underrepresented groups from a multicultural perspective, researchers can gain deeper insights into pathways of resilience and understand risk factors that could help the entirety of the projected aging population (Fredriksen-Goldsen et al., 2017).

There are significant cultural differences in beliefs about aging into late adulthood. Cultural competency training is essential for health-care professionals to adequately work with the increasing diversity of this population. As clinicians integrate successful outcomes in changing the narratives on ageism, they will play a vital role in educating and changing perceptions and attitudes about working with diverse populations of older and aging adults (Agness-Whittaker & Macedo, 2016).

## DIVERSITY

The work of Carol Gilligan (1993) and her theories of moral development were ground-breaking views of diversity within the concepts of late adulthood; they included her perspectives on the importance of the female voice in psychology. During that transformative time, she introduced her ethics of care theory as an alternative to Lawrence Kohlberg's (1969) hierarchical and male-dominated approach to ethics. Like her pioneering work, so too must the societal narratives on aging evolve to include the increasing diversity of the United States (Torres-Gil & Angel, 2018). Oftentimes, diversity is regulated into categories of race and ethnicity; however, there are many other parameters that should be included in that definition. Specifically, cultural background, sexual orientation, religious affiliation, socioeconomic status, gender, and many other broad categories should be included in the concept of diversity. This is essential because group identities influence how cultural groups approach aging and have access to resources (Mehrotra & Wagner, 2019). Disparities in access to resources will expose certain groups and cultures to negative risk factors that will impede their ability to enter late adulthood successfully (Mehrotra & Wagner, 2019). Current studies on diversified groups have found that not only do different cultural groups have unique risk profiles, including resiliency factors regarding aging, but they also require different planning structures for aging successfully (Alvarez et al., 2019; Fredriksen-Goldsen et al., 2017).

## GENDER

In looking at the need for more diversity in life-span developmental techniques, Carol Gilligan (1993) was a staunch advocate for the need of tailored research studies for women. As a research assistant, Gilligan believed there were two moral voices: masculine and feminine. She argued that androgyny, or incorporating both the masculine and feminine, was the best way to reach full potential as a human being. With her groundbreaking work she fueled the call for researchers to broaden the scope of empirical studies and diversify their investigations. Gender-related studies into age-related issues have revealed several gaps in our aging society. For example, the number of older women in modern society significantly outnumbers older men (Austen, 2016). What is the cause of this disparity? Another dramatic difference is that older women are more likely than older men to live out their later years unmarried (Austen, 2016). Why? Indeed, there are emergent studies showing that disparities exist in the types of care provided for women and men in health-care settings. Could this be a major cause for the differences between the genders and the aging process? Unfortunately, only a few studies have been conducted involving gender-tailored interventions for managing negative aging effects (Whiteman et al., 2016; Vanoh et al., 2019).

## SEXUAL ORIENTATION

Counselors may learn from studies in the LGBTQ community that although exposure to stigma and discrimination has its challenges and risks, under certain conditions it may become a source for stronger identity affirmation, formation of stronger social relationships, and the impetus for resilience during the aging process (Fredriksen-Goldsen et al., 2017). Unfortunately, as with other underrepresented populations, the Institute of Medicine (2011) reports that little is known about the health trends of LGBTQIA+ older adults. The reasons behind this lack of information are many, and it is unfortunate because, as a group with increasing diversity, LGBTQIA+ adults comprise 3.4% of the population (Gates & Newport, 2012). More research is needed to inform the exact health needs and profiles regarding the aging needs of this population (U.S. Department of Health and Human Services, 2012).

## ABLEISM

Ableism is discrimination or intolerance toward a particular group in favor of a more able-bodied group. Ableism toward the elderly is an ongoing and prevalent problem in western European culture. In fact, studies show that the perceptions against aging are so problematic that some middle-aged study participants fear aging enough that they implicitly blame themselves or others for failing to age successfully (Calasanti, 2016). In many cultures, especially heteronormative cultures that create conditions laden with disapproval and unacceptance of the natural aging process, women in particular are susceptible to this insidious standard if they do not meet the standard of beauty set by this society. This can lead self-blame that affects their sense of self-worth and gives them negative perceptions of their identities and their bodies (Berridge & Martinson, 2018).

## AGEISM

Ageism can apply to anyone, regardless of a person's age. It is mostly used, however, to describe negative stereotypes geared toward the negative defense mechanisms often portrayed by those in late adulthood. Ageism continues to be a form of institutionalized prejudice in the United States and around the world (Officer & de la Fuente-Núñez, 2018). This is due, in part, to the ongoing stereotypical narratives on aging becoming self-relevant as we get older. Negative stereotypes promote poorer health outcomes for individuals and can become a self-fulfilling prophecy that can affect physical and mental health. One way to change the narrative of negative aging stereotypes is to educate adults in the middle-age range of 40 to 64 about the common misconceptions of aging. Giving them knowledge and behavioral tools while they are still in good health can effectively reduce the negative stereotyping they could encounter. This middle-aged group has the most to gain from ending the narratives based on declining health and cognitive abilities as they will be enabled to continue being productive and healthy in later stages of adulthood (Crimmins, 2016).

Several groups within the United States raising awareness and fighting these negative misconceptions and stereotypes. Collectively, these organizations have joined to sponsor the Reframing Aging initiative (www.reframingaging.org) and fight the ageism and implicit bias perpetuated against older adults by reframing the current societal narratives on aging (Diehl et al., 2020). Although systemic change does not happen overnight, initiatives to promote awareness of ageism's decline-oriented histories are moving toward facilitating positive views on aging. Well-trained and motivated counselors, psychologists, and researchers who are actively engaged in research and promotion of multicultural competencies will be vital to the success of positive aging initiatives in the future.

## MORTALITY AWARENESS

In late adulthood, it is typical for individuals to think about their own mortality. Psychologically, as discussed previously, people focus on their own mortality increasingly as they reach the age when friends and loved ones have already died. Erik Erikson (1963) emphasized that it is during awareness of one's impending demise that reflection and self-evaluation occurs by attempting to put life into perspective. In his eight stages of psychosocial development, late adulthood is characterized by ego integrity versus despair. Ego integrity involves the older adult looking back through the events of the individual's life with intentionality and accepting mistakes and successes. In direct contrast, an individual can feel a sense of despair when taking this life assessment because of a failure to resolve these issues before death comes. Therapeutic interventions that help the client to focus on acceptance and acknowledgement of mistakes and successes can help to mitigate the feelings of despair in older adults.

It is also important to assess the possibility of abuse in older adulthood. Abuse can happen to anyone regardless of the person's age, sex, race, religion, or ethnic or cultural background. Unfortunately, hundreds of thousands of adults over the age of 60 are abused, neglected, or financially exploited each year. This is called elder abuse. Abuse can happen to any older adult, but often affects those who depend on others for help with activities of everyday life—including bathing, dressing, and taking medicine. The majority of abuse victims are women. Targets are older adults who have no family or friends nearby and people who have disabilities, memory problems, or dementia. People who are frail may appear to be easy victims. There are many places where abuse can happen, including the older person's home, a family member's house, an assisted living facility, or a nursing home. Abuse and mistreatment of older adults can be by strangers, family members, health care providers, friends, or caregivers.

If you see signs of abuse, try talking with the older adult to find out what is happening. For instance, the abuse may be from another resident and not from someone who works at the nursing home or assisted living facility. It is critically important to get help or report what you have witnessed to adult protective services. You do not need to prove that abuse is occurring; professionals will investigate.

If you think someone you know is being abused—physically, emotionally, or financially—talk with him or her when the two of you are alone. You could say you think something is wrong and you are worried. Offer to take him or her to get help at a local adult protective services agency. Many local, state, and national social service agencies can help with emotional, legal, and financial abuse. The Administration for Community Living has a National Center on Elder Abuse where anyone can find information about how to report abuse, where to get help, and applicable state laws that deal with abuse and neglect. More information may be found at https://ncea.acl.gov.

## Summary

Although human developmental theories have seen many changes over the years, current findings indicate that attitudes and perceptions are also important factors in the quality of life during the aging process. The consensus of the past has been one of negative stereotypes and negative outcomes featuring cognitive and physical decline. Growing older into late adulthood, however, is not the same as it used to be. We know that a unique set of factors, including genetics, environment, and sociocultural influences, shape each individual's aging process, and the good news is that biomedical and psychological research shows that growing older is more developmentally open than we previously thought (Hertzog et al., 2008; Lindenberger, 2014; Levy, 2017; Lindland et al., 2015).

Although social and cultural changes take time, negative stereotypes on aging into late adulthood can be dangerous if they do not allow the individual to engage in positive, healthy behaviors and outcomes. Middle-aged adults need to be educated on the choices and opportunities they have without minimizing the challenges that accompany the universal process of growing older.

Choyce is a 67-year-old African American female in Atlanta, Georgia. She was married to her husband Chance for 32 years, until he died recently from heart failure after an extended period of declining health. The couple did not have any children and spent a significant amount of time traveling after they both retired, until Chance became too ill to travel. At that time, Choyce became his caretaker and spent her time attending to his needs. After his death, she occupied herself for several weeks getting their affairs in order and taking care of personal estate matters. Then life settled into a routine, and Choyce found herself adrift in a sea of uncertainty, which left her with feelings of anxiety and depression. Because of the COVID-19 pandemic, she could not travel as she used to, and she found herself just going through the motions of social activities, such as attending church and going out with friends. Slowly, she began to decline social invitations and church obligations until she spent most of her days at home, staring out the window. Eventually, she became unaware of time and just slept or ate whenever she felt like it. It seemed the only thing she really wanted to do was drink. Choyce had never been a heavy drinker, but now she feels it is the only thing that numbs her pain. Choyce realizes she is becoming an alcoholic, but she feels powerless to stop drinking. One day she received a visit from her pastor, who had become concerned because she had not been attending to her church duties. Her pastor, shocked at Choyce's level of physical decline, decided to take her to the emergency room. She agreed to go. The hospital staff decided to keep Choyce a few days for observation and schedule an appointment for her with a counselor.

## Reflections and Targeted Discussion Questions

1. Think about Choyce's age and history and the disparities between cultures receiving care in clinical settings. Given the lack of research involving culturally competent care for ethnic groups, how would you approach case conceptualization with Choyce, who is an older African American Christian woman with limited natural supports?

2. What risk factors and concerns would a counselor have while working this client, and what interventions could be used to support Choyce's recovery and promote successful aging?

# References

Ackerman, P. L., & Kanfer, R. (2020). Work in the 21st century: New directions for aging and adult development. *American Psychologist, 75*(4), 486–498. https://doi.org/10.1037/amp0000615

Administration on Aging. (2014). *Aging statistics.* http://www.aoa.acl.gov/Aging_Statistics/index.aspx

Agness-Whittaker, C. F., & Macedo, L. (2016). Aging, culture, and health communication: Exploring personal cultural health beliefs and strategies to facilitate cross-cultural communication with older adults. Med Ed PORTAL, *The Journal of Teaching and Learning Resources, 12,* 10374. https://doi.org/10.15766/mep_2374-8265.10374

Alvarez, K., Fillbrunn, M., Green, J. G., Jackson, J. S., Kessler, R. C., McLaughlin, K. A., Sadikova E., Sampson, N., Alegría, M. (2019). Race/ethnicity, nativity, and lifetime risk of mental disorders in U.S. adults. *Social Psychiatry and Psychiatric Epidemiology, 54,* 553–565. https://dx.doi.org/10.1007/s00127-018-1644-5

Austen, S. (2016). Gender issues in an ageing society. *Australian Economic Review, 49*(4), 494–502.

Berridge, C. W., & Martinson, M. (2018). Valuing old age without leveraging ableism. *Generations, 41*(4), 83–91.

Bóné, V. (2018). Grandparenting: Created by evolution revised by history: Still in use today. *European Journal of Mental Health, 13*(1), 82–105. doi:10.5708/EJMH.13.2018.1.7

Breheny, M., Pond, R., & Lilburn, L. E. R. (2020). What am I going to be like when I'm that age? How older volunteers anticipate aging through home visiting. *Journal of Aging Studies, 53,* 100848. https://doi:10.1016/j.jaging.2020.100848

Bronfenbrenner, U. (1979).*The ecology of human development.* Cambridge, MA: Harvard University Press.

Calasanti, T. (2016). Combating ageism: How successful is successful aging? *The Gerontologist, 56*(6), 1093–101.

Carstensen, L. L., Turan, B., Scheibe, S., Ram, N., Ersner-Hershfield, H., Samanez-Larkin, G. R., Nesselroade, J. R. (2011). Emotional experience improves with age: Evidence based on over 10 years of experience sampling. *Psychology and Aging, 26,* 21–33. http://dx.doi .org/10.1037/a0021285

Charles, S. T., & Carstensen, L. L. (2014). Emotion regulation and aging. *In J. J. Gross (Ed.), Handbook of emotion regulation (2nd ed., pp. 203–218).* New York, NY: Guilford Press.

Choi, M., Sprang, G., and Eslinger, J.G. (2016). Grandparents raising grandchildren. *Family and Community Health, 39*(2), 120–128. https://doi.org/10.1097/FCH.0000000000000097

Cavan, R. S., Burgess, E. W., Havighurst, R. J., & Goldhamer, H. (1949). *Personal adjustment in old age.* Science Research Associates.

Crimmins, E. M., Zhang, Y., & Saito, Y. (2016). Trends over 4 decades in disability-free life expectancy in the United States. *American Journal of Public Health, 106,* 1287–1293. https://dx.doi.org/10.2105/AJPH.2016.303120

Diehl, M., Smyer, M. A., & Mehrotra, C. M. (2020). Optimizing aging: A call for a new narrative. *American Psychologist, 75*(4), 577–589. https://doi.org/10.1037/amp0000598

Ferraro, K. F., Kemp, B. R., & Williams, M. M. (2017). Diverse aging and health inequality by race and ethnicity. *Innovation in Aging, 1*(1), igx002. http://dx.doi.org/10.1093/geroni/igx002

Foster, T., Galjour, C., & Spengel, S. (2015). Investigating holistic wellness dimensions during older adulthood: A factor analytic study. *Journal of Adult Development, 22*(4), 239–247. https://doi:10.1007/s10804-015-9215-4

Fredriksen-Goldsen, K. I., Shiu, C., Bryan, A. E. B., Goldsen, J., & Kim, H.-J. (2017). Health equity and aging of bisexual older adults: Pathways of risk and resilience. *Journals of Gerontology: Series B, Psychological Sciences and Social Sciences, 72,* 468–478. https://dx.doi.org/10.1093/geronb/gbw120

Freund, A. M. (2020). The bucket list effect: Why leisure goals are often deferred until retirement. *American Psychologist, 75*(4), 499–510. https://doi.org/10.1037/amp0000617

Fung, H. (2013). Aging in Culture. *The Gerontologist, 53*(3), 369–377. https://doi.org/10.1093/geront/gnt024

Gates, G. J., Newport, F. (2012). *Special report: 3.4% of U.S. adults identify as LGBT. Gallup.* http://www.gallup.com/poll/158066/special-report-adults-identify-lgbt.aspx

Gilligan, C. (1993). *In a different voice: Psychological theory and women's development.* Harvard University Press.

Hertzog, C., Kramer, A. F., Wilson, R. S., & Lindenberger, U. (2008). Enrichment effects on adult cognitive development: Can the functional capacity of older adults be preserved and enhanced? *Psychological Science in the Public Interest, 9,* 1–65. https://dx.doi.org/10.1111/j.1539-6053.2009.01034.x

Hong, A. R., & Kim, S. W. (2018). Effects of resistance exercise on bone health. *Endocrinology and Metabolism, 33*, 435–444. https://dx.doi.org/10.3803/EnM.2018.33.4.435

Institute of Medicine. (2011). *The health of lesbian, gay, bisexual, and transgender people: Building a foundation for better understanding.* The National Academies Press.

Kirkwood T, Austad S.N. (2000). Why do we age? *Nature, 408*, 233–238.

Kitayama, S., Berg, M. K., & Chopik, W. J. (2020). Culture and well-being in late adulthood: Theory and evidence. *The American Psychologist, 75*(4), 567–576. https://doi:10.1037/amp0000614

Korte, J., Cappeliez, P., Bohlmeijer, E.,T., Westerhof, J. (2012). Empirical validation of a model of reminiscence and health in later life. *European Journal of Ageing.* 9(4):343–351. doi: 10.1007/s10433-012-0239-3

Kouvonen, A., Stafford, M., De Vogli, R., Shipley, M. J., Marmot, M. G., Cox, T., … Kivimäki, M. (2011). Negative aspects of close relationships as a predictor of increased body mass index and waist circumference: The Whitehall II study. *American Journal of Public Health, 101*, 1474–1480.

Lachman, M., Lipsitz, L., Lubben, J., Castaneda-Sceppa, C., & Jette, A. M. (2018). When adults don't exercise: Behavioral strategies to increase physical activity in sedentary middle-aged and older adults. *Innovation in Aging, 2*(1). https://dx.doi.org/10.1093/geroni/igy007

Lee, H., Yu, C., Wu, C., & Pan, W. (2018). The effect of leisure activity diversity and exercise time on the prevention of depression in the middle-aged and elderly residents of Taiwan. *International Journal of Environmental Research and Public Health, 15*(4), 654. https://doi.org/10.3390/ijerph15040654

Levy, B. R. (2017). Age-stereotype paradox: Opportunity for social change. *Gerontologist, 57*, S118–S126. https://dx.doi.org/10.1093/geront/gnx059

Lindenberger, U. (2014). Human cognitive aging: Corriger la fortune? [Correct fortune?]. *Science, 346*, 572–578. http://dx.doi.org/10 .1126/science.1254403

Lindland, E., Fond, M., Haydon, A., & Kendall-Taylor, N. (2015). *Gauging aging: Mapping the gaps between expert and public understandings of aging in America.* Frame Works Institute.

Luong, G., Charles, S. T., & Fingerman, K. L. (2011). Better with age: Social relationships across adulthood. *Journal of Social and Personal Relationships, 28*, 9–23. https://dx.doi.org/10.1177/0265407510391362

Magnusson, D. (1996). *The lifespan development of individuals: Behavioral, neurobiological, and psychosocial perspectives: A synthesis.* Cambridge University Press.

McPhee, J. S., French, D. P., Jackson, D., Nazroo, J., Pendleton, N., & Degens, H. (2016). Physical activity in older age: perspectives for healthy ageing and frailty. *Biogerontology, 17*(3), 567–580. https://doi.org/10.1007/s10522-016-9641-0

Mehrotra, C. M., & Wagner, L. S. (2019). *Aging and diversity: An active learning experience* (3rd ed.). Routledge.

Nelson, T. D. (2016). Promoting healthy aging by confronting ageism. *American Psychologist, 71*, 276–282. https://dx.doi.org/10.1037/a0040221

Niemczyński, A. (2017). Autonomy of human mind and personality development. *Polish Psychological Bulletin, 48*(1), 7–19. https://doi:10.1515/ppb-2017-0002

Officer, A., & de la Fuente-Núñez, V. (2018). A global campaign to combat ageism. *Bulletin of the World Health Organization, 96*, 295–296. http://dx.doi.org/10.2471/BLT.17.202424

Park, D. C., Lodi-Smith, J., Drew, L., Haber, S., Hebrank, A., Bischof, G. N., & Aamodt, W. (2014). The impact of sustained engagement on cognitive function in older adults: The Synapse Project. *Psychological Science, 25*, 103–112. http://dx.doi.org/10.1177/0956797613499592

Perls, T., Kunkel, L., & Puca, A. (2002). The genetics of exceptional human longevity. *Journal of Molecular Neuroscience 19*(1-2):233-8. https://doi:10.1007/s12031-002-0039-x

Pilkington, P., Windsor, T., Crisp, D. (2012). Volunteering and subjective well-being in midlife and older adults: The role of supportive social networks. *The Journals of Gerontology, Series B: Psychological Sciences and Social Sciences, 67*(2), 249–260. https://doi/10.1093/geronb/gbr154

Rakoczy, H., Wandt, R., Thomas, S., Nowak, J., & Kunzmann, U. (2018). Theory of mind and wisdom: The development of different forms of perspective taking in late adulthood. *British Journal of Psychology, 109*(1), 6–24. https://doi:10.1111/bjop.12246

Saxena, D., & Brotherson, S. (2021). *When grandparents become parents to their grandchildren.* https://www.ag.ndsu.edu/publications/home-farm/when-grandparents-become-parents-to-their-grandchildren

Schaie, K. W. (2013). *Developmental influences on adult intelligence: The Seattle longitudinal study* (2nd ed.). New York, NY: Oxford University Press.

Schmitt, Kray, & Ferdinand. (2017). Does the effort of processing potential incentives influence the adaption of context updating in older adults? *Frontiers in Psychology, 8*. https://doi.org/10.3389/fpsyg.2017.01969

Staudinger, U. M. (2020). The positive plasticity of adult development: Potential for the 21st century. *American Psychologist, 75*(4), 540–553. http://dx.doi.org/10.1037/amp0000612

Stevenson, B. (2014). *NZLSA measures. Summary report for the New Zealand Longitudinal Study of Aging (NZLSA)*. Massey University.

Stillman, C. M., Cohen, J., Lehman, M. E., & Erickson, K. I. (2016). Mediators of physical activity on neurocognitive function: A review at multiple levels of analysis. *Frontiers in Human Neuroscience, 10*, 626. http://dx.doi.org/10.3389/fnhum.2016.00626

Thomas, R. C., & Hasher, L. (2006). The influence of emotional valence on age differences in early processing and memory. *Psychology and Aging, 21*, 821–825.

Torres-Gil, F., & Angel, J. L. (2018). *The politics of a majority-minority nation: Aging, diversity, and immigration*. Springer. https://dx.doi.org/10.1891/9780826194794

Tucker-Drob, E. M., & Briley, D. A. (2014). Continuity of genetic and environmental influences on cognition across the life span: A meta-analysis of longitudinal twin and adoption studies. *Psychological Bulletin, 140*, 949 –979. http://dx.doi.org/10.1037/a0035893

United Nations. (2020). *World population prospects: The 2017 revision, volume II: Demographic profiles (ST/ESA/SERA/400)*. https://population.un.org/wpp/Publications/Files/WPP2017_Volume-II-Demographic-Profiles.pdf

U.S. Census Bureau. (2011). *Age and sex composition: 2010*. http://www.census.gov/prod/cen2010/briefs/c2010br-03.pdf

U.S. Department of Health and Human Services. (2012). *Healthy people 2020 objectives*. http://www.healthypeople.gov/2020/topicsobjectives2020/overview.aspx?topicid=31

Vanoh, D., Shahar, S., Razali, R., Manaf, Z. A., & Hamid, T. A. (2019). Influence of gender disparity in predicting occurrence of successful aging, usual aging, and mild cognitive impairment. *International Journal of Gerontology, 13*(3). https://doi:10.6890/IJGE.201909_13(3).0005

Whitbourne, S. K., Whitbourne, S. B. (2016). *Adult development and aging: Biopsychosocial perspectives* (6th ed). VitalSource Bookshelf version. vbk://9781119298984

Whiteman, K., Ruggiano, N., & Thomlison, B. (2016). Transforming mental health services to address gender disparities in depression risk factors. *Journal of Women & Aging, 28*(6), 521–529. https://doi:10.1080/08952841.2015.1072027

Willis, S. L., & Belleville, S. (2016). *Cognitive training in later adulthood*. In K. W. Schaie & S. L. Willis (Eds.), *Handbook of the psychology of aging* (8th ed., pp. 219–243). https://dx.doi.org/10.1016/B978-0-12-411469-2.00012-1

Wrzus, C., Hänel, M., Wagner, J., & Neyer, F. J. (2013). Social network changes and life events across the life span: A meta-analysis. *Psychological Bulletin, 139*, 53–80. https://dx.doi.org/10.1037/a0028601

Xu, J., Murphy, S. L., Kochanek, K. D., & Bastian, B. A. (2016). Deaths: Final data for 2013. *National Vital Statistics Reports, 64*(2). National Center for Health Statistics.

Zhu, R. (2016). Retirement and its consequences for women's health in Australia. *Social Science & Medicine, 163,* 117–125.

# End of Life

Chelsea Barron Davila Conaway, MS; Stacy Speedlin Gonzalez, PhD; and Brittany Hudson, MS

*Live as if you were going to die tomorrow, learn as if you were going to live forever.* —*Mahatma Gandhi*

## Learning Objectives

After reading this chapter, you should be able to

1. Define key concepts related to human development at the end of life.
2. Outline end-of-life development within the context of Erik Erikson's eight stages of psychosocial development and Bronfenbrenner's ecological theory.
3. Describe key considerations for counseling individuals at the end of life from an ecological and psychosocial perspective.

## Introduction

The end of life is a dynamic stage of human development that often encompasses self-discovery, reflection, and a need for interpersonal connection (Goodcase & Love, 2017; Wiesmann & Hannich, 2011; Yalom, 2009). Despite the universality of death, end-of-life experiences are as unique and diverse as the individuals who encounter them. Characteristics of the end of life can vary from peace and death acceptance, to anger, regret, and terror (Gawande, 2017; Nuland, 1995). The surging population of adults over 65 in the United States underscores the need for counselors and educators to understand the factors that affect maturation during this stage. This chapter will utilize Erik Erikson's (1950/1963) eight stages of psychosocial development and Bronfenbrenner's (1994) ecological theory to explore the intrinsic and extrinsic variables that influence growth during the final phase of life.

## Key Concepts

- **End of Life:** This term refers to the final stage of the life span that occurs either after age 65 or following the diagnosis of a life-limiting illness.
- **Life-Limiting Illness:** For the purpose of this chapter, this phrase will be used to identify terminal injuries or diseases that will likely result in death within the next 10 years.
- **Death Anxiety:** The authors will use this term to refer to "an unpleasant emotion of multidimensional concerns that is of an existential origin provoked on contemplation of death of self or others" (Nyatanga & de Vocht, 2006, p. 413).
- **Existential Concerns:** This term refers to matters related to existence and the meaning of life.

FIGURE 12.1   Having support while in the hospital is beneficial.

# The Human Developing Process

As indicated in previous chapters, human development is a progressive phenomenon that begins at conception and continues until death. Development encompasses both psychosocial and environmental factors and occurs within the context of social and cultural settings. As such, both intrinsic and extrinsic factors influence growth and development throughout the life span. These factors can have a powerful effect at the end of life as individuals confront impermanence and the various changes that take place at this stage.

The end of life is a transitional stage often characterized by profound self-reflection and existential contemplation (Goodcase & Love, 2017; Gawande, 2017). These internal processes occur within the context of considerable life changes, such as the deaths of significant others, retirement, a shrinking social network, an increased need for physical assistance, and decreased autonomy (Gawande, 2017; Goodcase & Love, 2017; Nuland, 1995). Moreover, as individuals at this stage confront mortality, they must begin making social, emotional, and practical end-of-life arrangements; additionally, family systems are tasked with preparing for lives in which the dying are no longer present (Detering et al., 2010; Emanuel et al., 2004; Heyland et al., 2006).

# Theoretical Considerations

This complex developmental process can be understood within the context of Erikson's eight stages of psychosocial development (Erikson, 1950/1963) and Bronfenbrenner's ecological theory (1994).

## ERIKSON'S EIGHT STAGES OF PSYCHOSOCIAL DEVELOPMENT

Erikson's final stage of development, *integrity versus despair*, begins in late adulthood and continues until death. The psychosocial crisis at this stage is defined by self-reflection and life assessment (Goodcase & Love, 2017). Through the reflection process, individuals confront past decisions, relationships, successes, and failures, and they must reconcile how these and other events shaped the course of their life. The goal of self-reflection at this stage is to derive meaning from one's existence (Goodcase & Love, 2017; Wiesmann & Hannich, 2011). Those who successfully resolve this conflict develop a sense of integrity associated with a well-lived, meaningful life. Failure to resolve this conflict engenders a feeling of despair related to regrets and unreconciled conflicts (Goodcase & Love, 2017). Achieving integrity inspires wisdom, described as the sum of the resilience, understanding, compassion, and humanity learned in previous stages (Goleman, 1988).

## BRONFENBRENNER'S ECOLOGICAL THEORY

Bronfenbrenner's (1994) ecological theory emphasizes the effect of environmental factors throughout the life span. External influences may be particularly salient at this stage as social and family roles change, compelling those at the end of life to rely on others for physical assistance. Further, contemporary literature indicates that the setting in which a person spends his or her final months (e.g., in a hospital, in a nursing home, or at home) can have a tremendous effect on whether one experiences a good or bad death—concepts discussed later in this chapter (Gawande, 2017; Nuland, 1995; Zitter, 2017).

Together, Erikson's theory of psychosocial development and Bronfenbrenner's (1994) ecological theory provide a holistic perspective on end-of-life maturation. It is important to remember that death is not limited to late adulthood. The diagnosis of a life-limiting illness can initiate the dying process at any point throughout the life span. Arriving at the end of life prior to the final stage of psychosocial development presents unique challenges to mental health professionals working with the dying. It is critical for counselors and educators to conceptualize end-of-life experiences within the context of an individual's current level of psychosocial maturity.

### PHYSICAL AND COGNITIVE

The typical person's physical and cognitive functions begin to decline years prior to death at a rapid pace (Burns et al., 2015). Terminal decline typically begins approximately 3 to 5 years prior to death (Gerstoff et al., 2016), with the decline including physical, cognitive, and social digressions. The declining of such imperative functions can result in formidable challenges for the individual, requiring mild to substantial levels of care. Counselors who work with clients at end-of-life stages should have a working knowledge of accessible resources for clients and families should physical challenges supersede their financial or collective capabilities. Through the utilization of Bronfenbrenner's ecological theory (1994), a counselor can assess existing resources for clients and their families and encourage them to utilize what is congruent with their value system (e.g., church supports, community charities, other family members, etc.).

While Erikson's theory discusses the final stage of *integrity versus despair* as being typically experienced in later adulthood (Goodcase & Love, 2017), the principles can also apply to younger persons who are dying. For example, the aging adult may examine the problems of mortality. This can manifest as existential contemplation through such life events as the loss of a spouse and acquaintances, facing a terminal illness, and other changes to major roles in life (Perry et al., 2015). While younger terminally ill clients may not resonate with some of these factors (e.g., retirement, changes to major roles in life), they can relate to the adjustments that occur naturally when an individual loses certain capacities. Such losses, regardless of age, have a significant effect on physical and emotional health (Burns, 2010; Dow et al., 2012). Counselors who work with this population should be cognizant of the correlation between physical limitations and overall emotional health and assess for potential emotional disorders (i.e., depression, anxiety, and agoraphobia). Further, due to increased grief factors, counselors should also assess periodically for risk of harm.

### SOCIAL AND EMOTIONAL

Shortly before his death, Erikson described wisdom in *integrity versus despair* as a collection of insights from each stage of psychosocial development. With regard to wisdom garnered during the *intimacy versus isolation* stage, he posited that individuals at the end of life might begin to appreciate the complexity and importance of meaningful relationships (Goleman, 1988). This assertion is consistent with evidence that social and relational factors can shape the dying experience (Kirby et al., 2014). For many, this is characterized by a deep sense of disconnection—from others, the world, and one's corporeal existence (Collett & Lester, 1969; Gawande, 2017; Yalom, 2009). People tend to distance themselves from the dying in response to heightened mortality salience and death anxiety, and this further contributes to feelings of isolation for individuals at the end of life (Menzfeld, 2017; Smith & Kasser, 2014). As stated by Yalom (2009), "The lesson here is simple: connection is paramount" (p. 80). Individuals at the end of life seek and find meaning in relationships (Fenwick & Brayne, 2011; Ozanne et al., 2013; Prado, 2017). Therefore, counselors have the responsibility to foster connection and healing in interactions with their dying clients.

Both tension and possibility are present during each stage of psychosocial development (Erikson, 1950/1963; Goleman, 1988). Individuals at the end of life encounter both existential conflict and the opportunity for profound emotional growth as they navigate *integrity versus despair*. Proponents of positive psychology view this tension as constructive. They argue, "it is the life-enhancing and life-expanding quest for meaning that enables us to live fully in the light of death" (Wong & Tomer, 2011, p. 104). Recent research supports the notion that individuals can and do experience positive emotions as they near death (Goranson et al., 2017). At the same time, this journey often includes fears related to the anticipation and ambiguity of death (Choron, 1964; Conte et al., 1982; Whitehead et al., 2011). Death anxiety, when unaddressed at the end of life, can have detrimental effects on mood (Chibnall et al., 2002; Sherman et al., 2010) and quality of life (Whitehead et al., 2011). Suggested interventions for mitigating death anxiety and promoting resilience at the end of life are described in the following section.

# Scientific Contributions

There is a growing body of research related to life in late adulthood. This is not surprising considering the steadily increasing population of Americans over the age of 65. Unlike previous generations, contemporary older adults are more likely to seek out and engage in counseling (Goodcase & Love, 2017). The growing number of older adults utilizing mental health services demonstrates the need for clinical competency in working with this population. This section will explore research related to the strengths and challenges associated with late adulthood and describe the characteristics of good and bad deaths.

FIGURE 12.2    Life's Simple Pleasures

## STRENGTHS AND CHALLENGES OF LATE ADULTHOOD

Many people over 65 live long, healthy, and productive lives well into late adulthood. Life at this stage can include enjoyable volunteer and leisure activities, a lively social network, and an active sex life (Berk, 2017). Moreover, the so-called "golden years" have been identified as a period in which individuals experience an enhanced sense of self and the opportunity to redefine priorities and cultivate a renewed sense of purpose (Fisher & Simmons, 2007). Considering the myriad strengths and opportunities present at the end of life, it is critical for counselors and educators to avoid defaulting to negative stereotypes about the aged. Nevertheless, professionals working with this population must remain cognizant of the challenges that are often present at the end of life.

Gerontological research has found an alarming prevalence of depression among older adults (Munk, 2011; Taylor, 2014). Unfortunately, mental health providers may dismiss this concern as a natural condition of aging (Goodcase & Love, 2017; Taylor, 2014). Experiences of death anxiety are also common and may diminish quality of life and enhance suffering (Gonen et al., 2012; Whitehead et al., 2011). Variables such as maintaining health, remaining active, and having a positive self-reflection may serve as protective factors against adverse mental health experiences for older adults (Wiesmann & Hannich, 2011). Grief and bereavement at this stage of life has several complications, and individuals who lose friends and family members are more physically and emotionally vulnerable themselves.

Counselors can assist end-of-life processes by normalizing and creating space in sessions to talk about grief and loss. Kubler-Ross (1972) described the process of grief using a stage model. In her model, she described five stages of grief for clients: denial, anger, bargaining, depression, and acceptance. While these stages are nonlinear, they serve as an educational tool for counselors to normalize client reactions to loss. Further, stage models can assist clients with understanding the influence of grief on their normal functioning.

## GOOD AND BAD DEATH

Death and dying have been the subject of art, literature, music, and scientific inquiry for many millennia (Ariès, 1974). Historical and contemporary death scholars alike have pondered the components of a good and bad death. In a literature review on the subject, Read and MacBride-Stewart (2018) found that a good death in western culture typically encompasses six primary characteristics: the absence of pain and discomfort; inclusion in end-of-life decision making; preparedness; finalization of unfinished business; posterity; and holistic end-of-life care. Bad death, on the other hand, is defined by pain and suffering, loss of autonomy, lack of physical and emotional connection with significant others, terror, anxiety, and unresolved interpersonal conflicts (Gawande, 2017; Nuland, 1995; Zitter, 2017).

Based on this conceptualization of the good and bad death, the need for person-centered, holistic care at the end of life is clear. The experience of a bad death may intensify death anxiety for the dying and contribute to feelings of suffering and anguish. Empowering the dying to maintain reasonable control, cultivating interpersonal connection, and advocating for the inclusion of mental health services in palliative and hospice care may contribute to a good death and serve as a protective factor against death anxiety (Menzfeld, 2017; Ozanne et al., 2013; Whitehead et al., 2011).

# Strengths and Challenges from the "ISMs" Perspectives

Systems of power and oppression affect development throughout the life span. Biases and prejudice within the chronosystem and macrosystem can have a tremendous influence at the primary contextual level as individuals confront the various challenges outlined in this chapter. The following sections will discuss the effect of various ISMs on end-of-life experiences from a psychosocial and ecological perspective.

## MULTICULTURAL

Experiences of death and dying are culturally sanctioned. An individual can perceive death as a positive or negative experience, depending on their cultural, familial, and communal worldview. Certain cultures, for example, may have traditions around death that entail celebration, while others invite mourning. Mourning and grief processes are also dependent on cultural traditions and practices. Some may feel that "getting over" grief is highly disrespectful to the deceased. Others perceive carrying grief beyond a certain period as a "stuckness" or pathology. Therefore, counselors should always consider the role of culture, tradition, and sanctioned practices when discussing grief and loss with clients.

Both life and death occur in proximity to systems of racial power and dominance in the United States (Rosenblatt, 2009). Dying individuals experience racism as it is embedded within their ecological environment. Although racism permeates all developmental contexts, the current literature highlights its influence on both microsystems and macrosystems at the end of life (Payne, 2016; Rosenblatt, 2009). Within these systems, racial patterning creates barriers to optimal development (Rosenblatt, 2009). It is critical that counselors attend to such manifestations of racism in their dying clients' lives.

Racism often surfaces in microsystems such as end-of-life care settings. Racially charged conflicts are common in these facilities and may present substantial challenges for both patients and staff members; however, these conflicts can create opportunities for racial healing (Rosenblatt, 2009). Exploring this possibility in the counseling relationship may promote constructive developmental experiences for racialized clients. In addition to discussing racist encounters at the end of life, counselors must also acknowledge how racism at the macro-level generates systemic disparities in racialized individuals' access to relevant and culturally responsive care (Payne, 2016).

## DIVERSITY

Death is a universal phenomenon but not a universal experience. Using Bronfenbrenner's (1994) ecological perspective, diversity can be conceptualized as a factor that influences the proximal processes driving development. Individuals at the end of life exist within a White-dominated macrosystem and chronosystem characterized by both death avoidance and "an insatiable appetite for the long good-bye as long as it is not [one's] own" (Samuel, 2013, p. 9). Although popular in the United States, White western notions of death and dying are not ubiquitous. There are significant cultural differences in death-related beliefs, education, and rituals that may affect development at the end of life (Irish et al., 1993). In contrast with western narratives, individuals in many cultures understand dying as positive and transformative. The realization of pure enlightenment in Buddhism is just one of many examples (Irish et al., 1993). Counselors must remain open to variations in the dying experience and address gaps in culturally sensitive support during the final stage of life.

## SEXUAL ORIENTATION AND GENDER

Research into lesbian, gay, bisexual, and transgender (LGBT) end-of-life care is limited, with most studies stemming from gay men's experiences of HIV/AIDS in the 1980s (Almack et al., 2010). Most LGBT persons experience end-of-life care unrelated to HIV/AIDS, and it occurs alongside their experience of growing older and accessing health- and aged-care services (Almack et al., 2010). More recent research on palliative care shows how LGBT people are more susceptible to certain life-threatening conditions compared with their heterosexual and cisgender counterparts (Cartwright et al., 2012). Such illnesses may occur earlier in life and become more chronic as life persists.

Lesbian, gay, bisexual, and transgender individuals express concern about end-of-life support (Sprik & Gentile, 2019). This is congruent with concerns expressed in the research on how little awareness exists of the needs of this population at the end of life (Sprik & Gentile, 2019). Despite more LGBT persons presenting in palliative care settings, individuals still experience stressors such as disenfranchised grief (Doka, 1989), forced outing of gender or sexual identity by medical staff members (Almack et al., 2010), previous discrimination by medical professionals to the point of avoiding seeking health care (Bristowe et al., 2016; Henderson & Almack, 2016), and homophobia and transphobia from caregivers (Lambda Legal, 2010; Bristowe et al., 2016).

## ABLEISM

Ableism precludes individuals from having power over their growth and development at the end of life. Dying persons with perceived or actual reduced capacities may not be invited to fully participate in or direct their end-of-life care (Kirby et al., 2014; Read & MacBride-Stewart, 2018). This dispossession of autonomy positions individuals with disabilities to experience a bad death and despair (Read & MacBride-Stewart,

2018). Inclusion in medical decision-making processes is associated with positive mental health outcomes such as enhanced dignity and decreased death anxiety (Chochinov et al., 2004; Menzfeld, 2017; Whitehead et al., 2011). Still, the concept of a good death is situated within ableist macrosystems and assumptions about ability (Read & MacBride-Stewart, 2018). Counselors might explore creative strategies for promoting the humanity and freedom of dying clients beyond these oppressive constructs. Developmentally targeted interventions should build on the adaptive strengths of clients with disabilities, employing, for instance, hope, resilience, and meaning-making (Martz & Livneh, 2015).

## MORTALITY AWARENESS

End-of-life scholarship has consistently demonstrated that both mortality awareness and death anxiety tend to be lower in late adulthood than at other points throughout the life span. While thoughts of death are present during this period, late adulthood is often characterized by a move from death denial and anxiety to death acceptance (Cicirelli, 2006). Reminders of one's impermanence, however, can still stimulate fear and existential angst (Arndt et al., 2003; Major et al., 2016). Both health maintenance and generativity can function as protective factors against uncomfortable feelings associated with mortality awareness at this stage (Arndt et al., 2003; Major et al., 2016).

## Summary

Carl Jung (1959) considered the end of life as one of the most meaningful milestones. Thus, careful consideration should be taken when working with clients at the final stage. The authors believe Erikson's stage model of development (1950/1963) to be an ideal model for conceptualizing end-of-life experiences. Further, Bronfenbrenner's ecological theory (1994) well describes the effect/support of environmental factors on death and dying. When counselors and educators infuse these models, a broad and inclusive theoretical lens results.

FIGURE 12.3    Walking the Road Less Traveled

Catalina is a 36-year-old Mexican-American woman living in the Rio Grande Valley, the southern-most region of Texas along the United States/Mexico border. She has been married to her high school sweetheart, Miguel, for 9 years, and the couple has three elementary-age children. Catalina is a first-generation U.S. citizen. Her family immigrated to Texas from Mexico before she was born. As their parents, Catalina and Miguel are deeply Catholic and hope to pass their religious values and traditions on to their children. Catalina feels a strong sense of pride for her Mexican heritage and iden-tifies culture as a primary strength. She particularly connects with collectivistic values and considers it an obligation to adhere to the advice of elders and ancestors.

There is a significant history of breast cancer in Catalina's family. Her mother was diagnosed with the disease at age 32 and died at 41, when the cancer metastasized to her spine. Catalina's maternal grand-mother and one maternal uncle also died of breast cancer before the age of 60, and one maternal aunt is currently in remission. Following genetic testing in her early 20s, Catalina was informed that she pos-sesses a rare gene mutation that increases the risk for the disease. She had the option of undergoing a preventative double mastectomy to decrease her breast cancer risk. After consulting with family and clergy, however, she decided against the procedure as she felt it would diminish her womanhood. Instead, she chose to leave her fate in the hands of God. After the discovery of her gene mutation, she underwent annual mammograms and regularly visited with a *curandero* (native healer) for preventative care.

At age 33, Catalina was diagnosed with an aggressive form of cancer in her left breast after a rou-tine mammogram. During the past 3 years, she underwent three rounds of chemotherapy and two rounds of radiation. During each 6-week treatment regimen, Catalina experienced debilitating nausea and vomiting, immobilizing fatigue, anemia, and a severe loss of appetite. She is now significantly underweight and malnourished because of these symptoms. Her inability to care for her children and feelings of being a burden have led to depression and a profound sense of shame and isolation.

A recent MRI revealed that her cancer has metastasized to her liver and bladder. Her onclogist indi-cated that her cancer is no longer curable. Catalina was given a prognosis of 6 to 8 months to live. The oncologist offered Catalina an 8-week, high-dose radiation treatment. There is a chance that this treat-ment will prolong Catalina's life by a couple of months, but there is an equal probability it will have no effect on the progression of her illness. This round of radiation would produce the same side effects as previous treatments. As an alternative, Catalina's palliative care team offered an in-home hospice pro-gram that would focus on pain reduction and comfort care. The hospice program would not administer any life-prolonging treatment or prevent the progression of the disease. Catalina is unsure about which option to choose, and her family is in conflict over the decision. Catalina's father and other elders in her family believe she should accept whatever treatment will offer hope for the longest possible survival. On the other hand, her husband and Catholic clergy believe she should let God's will prevail and focus on remaining comfortable during her final months. Regardless of the treatment option she chooses, she will continue to visit the *curandero* and the Catholic Church for mental and physical healing as long as she is able. She has been referred to counseling by her palliative care team and presents in session seeking answers to her current dilemma.

## Reflections and Targeted Discussion Questions

1.  Consider that Catalina was diagnosed with an aggressive form of breast cancer and is nearing the end of her life during young adulthood (the *intimacy versus isolation* stage of development). How might Catalina's prognosis during this stage of development influence your conceptualization of this case?

2.  Recall the importance of end-of-life interpersonal connection discussed in this chapter. What theoretical approach or intervention could be used to support relational connection in Catalina's life, and how might a strong sense of connection affect Catalina's developmental process?

## References

Almack, K., Seymour, J., & Bellamy, G. (2010). Exploring the impact of sexual orientation on experiences and concerns about end of life care and on bereavement for lesbian, gay and bisexual older people. *Sociology, 44,* 908–24.

Ariès, P. (1974). *Western attitudes towards death: From the Middle Ages to the present.* (P. M. Ranum, Trans.). Johns Hopkins University Press.

Arndt, J., Schimel, J., & Goldenberg, J. L. (2003). Death can be good for your health: Fitness intentions as a proximal and distal defense against mortality salience. *Journal of Applied Social Psychology, 33,* 1726–1746. doi:10.1111/j.1559-1816. 2003.tb01972.x

Berk, L. E. (2017). *Exploring lifespan development* (4th ed.). Pearson.

Bristowe, K, Marshall, S, Harding, R. (2016). The bereavement experiences of lesbian, gay, bisexual and/or trans* people who have lost a partner: A systematic review, thematic synthesis and modelling of the literature. *Palliat Med, 30*(8), 730–744.

Bronfenbrenner, U. (1994). Ecological models of human development. *International Encyclopedia of Education, 3*(2), 37–43.

Burns, S. T. (2010). Counseling adult clients experiencing chronic pain. *Journal of Counseling & Development, 88*(4), 483–490.

Burns, R. A., Byles, J., Magliano, D. J., Mitchell, P., & Anstey, K. J. (2015). The utility of estimating population-level trajectories of terminal wellbeing decline within a growth mixture modelling framework. *Social Psychiatry and Psychiatric Epidemiology, 50*(3), 479-487. doi:10.1007/s00127-014-0948-3

Cartwright, C., Hughes, M., & Lienert, T. (2012). End-of-life care for gay, lesbian, bisexual and transgender people. *Culture, Health & Sexuality, 14*(5), 537–548.

Chibnall, J. T., Videen, S. D., Duckro, P. N., & Miller, D. K. (2002). Psychosocial-spiritual correlates of death distress in patients with life-threatening medical conditions. *Palliative Medicine, 16*, 331–338. doi:10.1191/0269216302pm544oa

Chochinov, H. M., Hack, T., Hassard, T., Kristjanson, J., McClement, S., & Harlos, M. (2004). Dignity and psychotherapeutic considerations in end-of-life care. *Journal of Palliative Care, 20*, 134–142. doi:10.1177/082585970402000303

Choron, J. (1964). *Death and modern man.* Collier Books.

Cicirelli, V. G. (2006). Fear of death in mid-old age. *Journal of Gerontology, 61B*, 75–81. doi:10.1093/geronb/61.2.p75

Collett, L., & Lester, D. (1969). The fear of death and dying. *The Journal of Psychology, 72*, 179–181.

Conte, H. R., Weiner, M. B., & Plutchik, R. (1982). Measuring death anxiety: Conceptual, psychometric, and factor-analytic aspect. *Journal of Personality and Social Psychology, 43*, 775–785. doi:10.1037//0022-3514.43.4.775

Detering, K. M., Hancock, A. D., Reade, M. C., & Silvester, W. (2010). The impact of advance care planning on end of life care in elderly patients: Randomised controlled trial. *British Medical Journal, 340*, 1–9. doi:10.1136/bmj.c1345

Doka, K. J. (Ed.). (1989). *Disenfranchised grief: Recognizing hidden sorrows.* Lexington Books, 3–1.

Dow, C. M., Roche, P. A., & Ziebland, S. (2012). Talk of frustration in the narratives of people with chronic pain. *Chronic illness, 8*(3), 176–191.

Emanuel, E. J., Fairclough, D. L., Wolfe, P., & Emanuel, L. L. (2004). Talking with terminally ill patients and their caregivers about death, dying, and bereavement. *Archives of Internal Medicine, 164*, 1999–2004. doi:10.1001/archinte.164.18.1999

Fenwick, P., & Brayne, S. (2011). End-of-life experiences: Reaching out for compassion, communication, and connection—meaning of deathbed visions and coincidences. *American Journal of Hospice & Palliative Medicine, 28*, 7–15. doi:10.1177/1049909110374301

Fisher, J. C., & Simmons, H. C. (2007). *A journey called aging: Challenges and opportunities in older adulthood.* Routledge.

Gawande, A. (2017). *Being mortal.* Metropolitan Books.

Gerstorf, D., Hoppmann, C. A., Lockenhoff, C. E., Infurna, F. J., Schupp, J., Wagner, G. G., & Ram, N. (2016). Terminal decline in well-being: The role of social orientation. *Psychology and Aging, 31*(2), 19-165. doi:10.1037/pag0000072

Goleman, D. (1988, June 14). Erikson, in his own old age, expands his view of life. *The New York Times.* https://www.nytimes.com

Gonen, G., Kaymak, S. U., Cankurtaran, E. S., Karslioglu, E. H., Ozlap, E., & Soygur, H. (2012). The factors contributing to death anxiety in cancer patients. *Journal of Psychosocial Oncology, 30,* 247–358. doi:10.1080/073477332.2012.664260

Goodcase, E. T., & Love, H. A. (2017). From despair to integrity: Using narrative therapy for older individuals in Erikson's last stage of identity development. *Journal of Clinical Social Work, 45,* 354–363. doi:10.1007/s10615-016-0601-6

Goranson, A., Ritter, R. S., Waytz, A., Norton, M. I., & Gray, K. (2017). Dying is unexpectedly positive. *Psychological Science, 28,* 988–999. doi:10.1177/0956797617701186

Heyland, D. K., Dodek, P., Rocker, G., Groll, D., Gafni, A., Pichora, D., Lam, M. (2006). What matters most in end-of-life care: Perceptions of seriously ill patients and their family members. *Canadian Medical Association Journal, 174,* 627–633. doi:10.1503/cmaj.05062

Irish, D. P., Lundquist, K. F., & Nelsen, V. J. (Eds.). (1993). *Ethnic variations in dying, death and grief: Diversity in universality.* Routledge.

Jung, C. G. (1959). The soul and death. In Feifel, H. (Eds.), *The meaning of death,* 3–15. McGraw-Hill.

Kirby, E., Broom, A., Good, P., Wootton, J., & Adams, J. (2014). Families and the transition to specialist palliative care. *Mortality, 19,* 323–341. doi:10.1080/135762 75.2014.916258

Kübler-Ross, E., Wessler, S., & Avioli, L. V. (1972). On death and dying. *Jama, 221*(2), 174-179.

Lambda Legal. (2010). When health care isn't caring: Lambda Legal's survey on discrimination against LGBT people and people living with HIV. Accessed January 3, 2019, from www.lambdalegal.org/health-care-report

Major, R. J., Whelton, W. J., Schimel, J., & Sharpe, D. (2016). Older adults and the fear of death: The protective function of generativity. *Canadian Journal on Aging, 35,* 261–272. doi:10.1017/S0714980816000143

Martz, E., & Livneh, H. (2015). Psychosocial adaptation to disability within the context of positive psychology: Findings from the literature. *Journal of Occupational Rehabilitation, 26,* 4–12. doi:10.1007/s10926-015-9598-x

Menzfeld, M. (2017). When the dying do not feel tabooed: Perspectives of the terminally ill in western Germany. *Mortality, 22,* 308–323. doi:10.1080/13576275.2016.1270261

Munk, K. (2011). Depression in the late life. In L. Larsen (Ed.), *Geropsychology: The psychology of the ageing person* (pp. 199–215). Aarhus University Press.

Nuland, S. B. (1995). *How we die: Reflections on life's final chapter.* Alfred A. Knopf.

Nyatanga, B., & de Vocht, H. (2006). Towards a definition of death anxiety. *International Journal of Palliative Nursing, 12,* 410–413. doi:10.12968/ijpn.2006.12.9.21868

Ozanne, A. O., Graneheim, U. H., & Strang, S. (2013). Finding meaning despite anxiety over life and death in amyotrophic lateral sclerosis patients. *Journal of Clinical Nursing, 22,* 2141–2149. doi:10.1111/jocn.12071

Payne, R. (2016). Racially associated disparities in hospice and palliative care access: Acknowledging the facts while addressing the opportunities to improve. *Journal of Palliative Medicine, 19,* 131–133. doi:10.1089/jpm.2015.0475

Perry, T. E., Ruggiano, N., Shtompel, N., & Hassevoort, L. (2015). Applying Erikson's wisdom to self-management practices of older adults: Findings from two field studies. *Res Aging, 37*(3), 253–274. doi:10.1177/0164027514527974

Prado, A. M. (2017). *Understanding the lived experiences of counseling professionals in a hospice setting: A phenomenological study* (Publication No. 10604459) [Doctoral dissertation]. PsychInfo.

Read, S., & MacBride-Stewart, S. (2018). The "good death" and reduced capacity: A literature review. *Mortality, 23,* 381–395. doi:10.1080/13576275.2017.1339676

Rosenblatt, P. C. (2009). Racism and Black-White relationships in end-of-life care in the United States: A speculative analysis. *Illness, Crisis, & Loss, 17,* 113–124. doi:10.2190/IL.17.2.c

Samuel, L. R. (2013). *Death, American style: A cultural history of dying in America.* Rowman & Littlefield Publishers.

Sherman, D. W., Norman, R., & McSherry, C. B. (2010). A comparison of death anxiety and quality of life of patients with advanced cancer or AIDS and their family caregivers. *Journal of the Association of Nurses in AIDS Care, 21,* 99–112. doi:10.1016/j.jana.2009.07.007

Smith, L. M., & Kasser, T. (2014). Mortality salience increases defensive distancing from people with terminal cancer. *Death Studies, 38,* 44–53. doi:10.1080/07481187.2012.725449

Sprik, P., & Gentile, D. (2019). Cultural humility: A way to reduce LGBTQ health disparities at the end of life. *American Journal of Hospice and Palliative Medicine* (1049909119880548).

Taylor, W. D. (2014). Depression in the elderly. *The New England Journal of Medicine, 371,* 1228–1236. doi:10.1056/NEJMcp1402180.

Whitehead, B., O'Brien, M. R., Jack, B. A., & Mitchell, D. (2011). Experiences of dying, death and bereavement in motor neuron disease: A qualitative study. *Palliative Medicine, 26,* 368–372. doi:10.1177/0269216311410900

Wong, P. T. P., & Tomer, A. (2011). Beyond terror and denial: The positive psychology of death acceptance. *Death Studies, 35,* 99–106. doi:10.1080/07481187.2011.535377

Yalom, I. (2009). *Staring at the sun: Overcoming the terror of death.* Jossey-Bass.

Zitter, J. K. (2017). *Extreme measures: Finding a better path to the end of life.* Avery.

## Credits

# Futuristic Counseling

Jacqueline Kroemer, MA, and Noréal F. Armstrong, PhD

*Education is our passport to the future, for tomorrow belongs to the
people who prepare for it today.* —Malcolm X

## Learning Objectives

After reading this chapter, you should be able to

1. Understand the seven principles of the 20/20 Vision initiative and what has
   been accomplished to date.
2. Discuss the usage, strengths, and limitations of virtual learning.
3. Gain awareness of therapies of the postmodern era and their usefulness to human
   development.

## Introduction

In 2005, a collection of focused counseling professionals convened to develop a plan
for the growth of the counseling profession into the second decade of the 21st century.

The initiative that developed was 20/20: A Vision for the Future of Counseling, and it listed seven main principles (ACA, n.d; Kaplan, 2014). The seven principles of the American Counseling Association's initiative include the following: (1) Sharing a common professional identity is critical for counselors; (2) Presenting ourselves as a unified profession has multiple benefits; (3) Working together to improve the public perception of counseling and to advocate for professional issues will strengthen the profession; (4) Creating a portability system for licensure will benefit counselors and strengthen the counseling profession; (5) Expanding and promoting our research base is essential to the efficacy of professional counselors and to the public perception of the profession; (6) Focusing on students and prospective students is necessary to ensure the ongoing health of the counseling profession; and (7) Promoting client welfare and advocating for the populations we serve is a primary focus of the counseling profession.

FIGURE 13.1    Virtual Learning in the Digital Era

This chapter will highlight those principles, share what has been accomplished and how the principles were met through the use of theory, technique, and innovative ideas, as well as and where counseling may go from here. As the world has grown, counseling has adapted to meet the needs of the profession and clients. Currently, telehealth counseling and distance counseling and teaching are quickly becoming the new normal within the counseling profession. There are more than 85 CACREP-accredited online master's degrees in counseling programs (CACREP, 2020). The use of technology has become a key component in the delivery of instruction and care for our clients.

## Key Concepts

- **Biofeedback:** The use of medical instruments to provide real-time feedback of physiological changes in the body to help individuals monitor and treat a variety of disorders and symptoms (Bulhuis, 2017).
- **Deconstruction:** The practice of breaking down a large or overwhelming task or concept into smaller, more manageable parts.
- **Distance Education:** Educational program or course in which at least 50% of instruction and interaction are provided via technology (e.g., internet, phone, video or audio recordings, or email).
- **Externalization:** The practice of viewing the problem (e.g., behavior or thought) as separate from the person.
- **Hybrid Programs:** Educational program or course that utilizes both residential and virtual instruction and interaction.
- **Neurofeedback:** A branch of biofeedback that specifically focuses on brain wave activity to treat neurological conditions (Bulhuis, 2017).
- **Residential Learning:** Educational program or course in which at least 50% of instruction and interaction is in-person at a physical site.
- **Telepsychology:** Psychological services provided via telecommunication including, but not limited to, video conferencing, phone calls, texting, apps, and email.
- **Theraplay:** Theraplay is a dyadic child and family therapy to support healthy child/caregiver attachment.

## Virtual Learning

Virtual education programs are becoming increasingly popular. According to the United States Department of Education (2020), distance education is the use of technology (e.g., internet, phone, and recordings) as a method for delivering instruction to students who are separate from the instructor to support routine and significant interaction of students and instructor. A course is considered a distance learning course if 50% or more of instruction is given via technology (Snow et al., 2018). In March 2018, the Council for Accreditation of Counseling and Related Educational Programs (CACREP) reported 64 online degree programs at 36 CACREP-accredited institutions (Snow et al., 2018). CACREP is also responsible for accrediting these online programs to ensure they meet the same standards as residential programs. In response to the distance education trend, the Association for Counselor Education and Supervision (ACES) has developed guidelines for providing online instruction.

These guidelines include dependable technology, frequent communication, and interactive support (Snow et al., 2018).

## STRENGTHS

Prospective students pursue online education for a variety of reasons. Some of the most common reasons students prefer virtual learning to residential learning are work requirements, childcare commitments, physical limitations, and geographic location (Snow et al., 2018). This flexibility in schedule allows students to maintain their current work schedules and family commitments without major adjustments. The use of technology can also assist in cases of weather or other events that may prevent the students or the instructor from meeting at a physical site.

## LIMITATIONS

As with any learning format, distance education has its limitations. Technological proficiency of students and faculty members will greatly affect the effectiveness and success of a distance learning course (Snow et al., 2018). Distance learning may also be incompatible with certain learning styles and preferences (Snow et al., 2018). Similarly, a feeling of connection with the school or institution has been reported as a challenge related to distance education (Snow et al., 2018). This lack in feel of connection may be related to the lack of access to various resources and activities for virtual students that residential students have readily available on campus (Snow et al., 2018).

## Distance Counseling and Virtual Services

Technology has become an incredible tool for everyday activities. It can be used to wake us in the morning, remind us about appointments, communicate with friends, family, and, yes, even our boss from just about anywhere. Just doing a search for virtual jobs or work-from-home jobs will render an abundance of search results. The field of counseling has also been working to take advantage of these tools. Virtual counseling exists in a variety of formats, including text or chat, phone call, and video call (BetterHelp, n.d.).

According to the American Psychological Association (n.d.), laws surrounding the practice of telepsychology are behind the changes and availability of technology. Therefore, many laws and standards are developed by individual states (American Psychological Association, n.d.). That said, certification of distance counseling requires the provider to have a master's degree in counseling, mental health or a related field, and pass a credible distance counselor certification course (National Board for Certified Counselors, n.d.).

Guidelines have been proposed to develop a structure and professional compass for telepsychology service providers, with these guidelines intended to exist in addition to laws, standards, and ethical guidelines currently in place (American Psychological Association, 2013). The American Psychological Association's (2013) proposed guidelines include:

- Practitioners providing virtual services should demonstrate competence of the technology they work with and an understanding of risks and risk management involving those technologies.
- Practitioners should maintain both the standards of care outlined in the law and also their ethical and professional guidelines.
- Informed consent should include telepsychology-specific information. The practitioner should also be aware of laws and regulations regarding telepsychology practice.
- Practitioners must make reasonable efforts for the protection and maintenance of confidentiality; they must inform clients of the potential increased risk due to the nature of telecommunication.
- Practitioners must make reasonable efforts to protect and secure client data and information.
- Practitioners must make reasonable efforts to securely dispose of client data and information.
- Practitioners must be aware of the effect of telecommunication on tests and assessments.
- Practitioners must be aware of jurisdictional and international border laws.

By having these guidelines, practitioners are able to better provide fully informed, high-quality care.

## EFFECTIVENESS OF TELEPSYCHOLOGY (TELEMENTAL HEALTH COUNSELING)

Some diagnoses and treatments may be compatible and successful with telepsychology treatment. Participants in a randomized study for treatment of panic disorder were divided into two groups. One group participated in cognitive behavior therapy (CBT) while the other group received internet CBT (Bergström et al., 2010). Both groups showed significant improvement based on the Panic Disorder Severity Scale, or PDSS (Bergström et al., 2010).

A study on the effectiveness of mobile assessment and treatment of schizophrenia (MATS) used texting to help monitor and improve medication compliance, hallucination severity, and socialization (Granholm et al., 2012). The study found significant improvement in these areas, but not in general symptoms or functioning (Granholm et al., 2012). Telepsychology can be an important tool in supplementing standard treatment of mental health issues such as schizophrenia.

**FIGURE 13.2**    Connecting and Engaging Virtually

## STRENGTHS

Telepsychology allows for more freedom in scheduling due to the lack of time restrictions for telecommunication (Novotney, 2017). Similarly, telepsychology does not require a physical location, which saves practitioners money and time (Bergström et al., 2010; Novotney, 2017). Without the need for a physical site, practitioners save on facility fees. Practitioners also save on time because travel is unnecessary. Saving on time also allows for a better work-life balance (Novotney, 2017). Practitioners are able to dedicate more time to their lives.

## LIMITATIONS

Some telepsychology companies have restrictions on what counselors are allowed to do. BetterHelp (n.d.) states that counselors are unable to provide a diagnosis. Due to the nature of telecommunication, some treatments may not be appropriate (BetterHelp, n.d.). Treatment of more serious disorders may be better suited to traditional therapy; however, supplemental telepsychology may be beneficial with specific symptoms (Granholm et al., 2012; Novotney, 2017). Similarly, there is concern with how telepsychology practitioners address risk assessment and crisis intervention. The concern with risk assessment is how to determine suicidality via text or chat (Novotney, 2017). Standards will need to be developed for risk assessment and crisis scenarios so that practitioners can do what is best for their clients in these situations. Standards will also need to be developed for anonymous telepsychology to address any ethical or legal issues (Novotney, 2017).

## Theoretical Considerations

The following theories are relatively new to counseling. There is empirical data showing the success of each theory. Regarding human development, the theories that follow have been widely used with clients at various stages of development.

### ACCEPTANCE AND COMMITMENT THERAPY

Unlike traditional cognitive behavior therapies, acceptance and commitment therapy (ACT) states that coping by trying to change thoughts and feelings can be counterproductive (Hayes, n.d.). Therefore, symptoms reduction is not the goal of treatment (Harris, 2011). Instead, ACT focused on mindfulness, acceptance, values, cognitive diffusion, and committed action (Hayes, n.d.). With ACT, individuals focus on altering the effect of an event mentally rather than attempting to reduce or avoid the event (Hayes, n.d.). In short, the individual learns to change how he or she relates to thoughts (Harris, 2011). This technique has been successful in treating a variety of mental health issues and preventing burnout in practitioners (Hayes, n.d.). ACT encourages and empowers individuals to accept the inevitable pains and discomforts of life while taking action in mindful pursuit of their values (Harris, 2011).

ACT has been successful in individual and group settings with both brief and long-term therapy (Harris, 2011). Many populations have found success with ACT (Harris, 2011). While ACT has been successful with a variety of age groups, practitioners should consider the ability of young children to grasp and understand certain topics. That being said, ACT can still be used to treat young children, but the techniques may need to be tailored to fit the client's needs and capabilities.

### BIOFEEDBACK

Biofeedback is a form of treatment that uses tools specifically designed to monitor physical changes in the body (Mayo Clinic, 2019). There are various forms of biofeedback designed to address different physical functions. These various monitors can help individuals monitor and control physical functions (e.g., breathing, heart rate) and can improve health and physical performance (Mayo Clinic, 2019).

An electroencephalograph (EEG) can be used to monitor brain waves (Mayo Clinic, 2019). The use of an EEG in biofeedback treatment is typically referred to as neurofeedback, which specifically focuses on neurological functions and treatment of neurological disorders, such as traumatic brain injuries and concussions, post-traumatic stress disorder, anxiety, sleep disturbances, and Parkinson's and other related movement disorders (Stoler, 2014).

Elastic bands on the chest and abdomen can measure respiratory rates while heart rate can be measured using a variety of devices (Mayo Clinic, 2019). Other physical functions measured include muscle contraction, sweat gland activity, and temperature (Mayo Clinic, 2019). Biofeedback can be delivered in a facility through a computer-based program, or at home on devices (Mayo Clinic, 2019). Biofeedback is now commonplace and available with apps on smart watches and smartphones (Peake et al., 2018). These technologies monitor biological functions including heart rate, perspiration, sleep, steps, pace, and other physical responses and activities (Peake et al., 2018). However, the Food and Drug Administration (FDA) only monitors and approves of facility-based biofeedback treatment (Mayo Clinic, 2019).

FIGURE 13.3    Biofeedback Therapy

Biofeedback has been successful with physical and mental health issues including asthma, anxiety, chronic pain, and high blood pressure, and the treatment is noninvasive and can be a supplement or replacement to medication (Mayo Clinic, 2019). Biofeedback has very few risks to the individual; however, individuals with heart or skin conditions may have technological issues with the receptors (Mayo Clinic, 2019). As biofeedback may require the individual to be stationary (e.g., EEG), not all forms are suited for young children or individuals who may find it difficult to remain still for the extent of the treatment.

## CRITICAL RACE THEORY

Critical race theory (CRT) views race as a social construct used to serve the interests of those who created it, typically those in the White population (Curry, 2018). Racial inequality stems from generations of social, economic, and legal discrepancies between races (Curry, 2018). Although CRT has been around since 1989, people in the wider population are seeing the biased treatment of underrepresented populations (Curry, 2018). CRT operates from a social justice and advocacy platform (Curry, 2018). The theory was originally based on the thoughts of Martin Luther King, Jr., Malcom X, and the Black Panthers, but it has since evolved to include all marginalized groups (Curry, 2018).

Practitioners should be aware of a client's racial identity development. Cross's racial identity development model breaks down the five stages of racial identity development for individuals of color (Venngage, n.d.). By understanding the client's developmental stage, practitioners will be able to better help the client with awareness, and can better understand and advocate for the client.

## DIALECTICAL BEHAVIORAL THERAPY

Dialectical behavior therapy (DBT) is a form of cognitive behavioral therapy (CBT) that works to identify and address unhelpful thoughts, beliefs, and assumptions (Grohol, 2019). While addressing these unhelpful cognitions, DBT also focuses on identifying and building on the client's strengths (Grohol, 2019). A large focus is put on the development of problem-solving skills and adaptive behaviors (Grohol, 2019). Therefore, the focus of treatment is on managing emotional response to events rather than avoiding or eliminating those events (Grohol, 2019). The therapeutic relationship is a very important part as DBT is a collaborative therapy (Grohol, 2019).

DBT has four modules: mindfulness, interpersonal effectiveness, distress tolerance, and emotional regulation (Grohol, 2019). Mindfulness includes practices that help the individual be present and accepting (Grohol, 2019). Interpersonal effectiveness focuses on being assertive and having the ability to work through disagreements and emotionally charged situations (Grohol, 2019). Distress tolerance is a module focused on helping the individual develop resilience and the ability to cope with stressful events (Grohol, 2019). Emotion identification and understanding are key to emotion regulation (Grohol, 2019). Each of the four modules of DBT feeds into and off of the others (Grohol, 2019).

DBT has been shown to be successful with adolescents and young adults (Child Mind Institute, n.d.). DBT has also been the most researched form of treatment for borderline personality disorder, or BPD (Kliem et al., 2010). Many studies show that DBT is effective in treating symptoms of BPD (Kliem, et al., 2010), with research also done with DBT as a treatment for eating disorders, or ED (Wisniewski & Ben-Poarth, 2015). In both BPD and ED, clients can appear compliant or defiant (Wisniewski & Ben-Porath, 2015). By appearing compliant, the attention is taken off the disorder, whereas defiance typically results in relaxed treatment requirements (Wisniewski & Ben-Porath, 2015). Rather than address these issues head-on, DBT focuses on the underlying or secondary issues, such as staying alive/healthy, emotional regulation, and the therapeutic relationship (Wisniewski & Ben-Porth, 2015).

## MINDFULNESS-BASED COGNITIVE THERAPY

Mindfulness-based cognitive therapy (MBCT) branched off of mindfulness-based stress reduction (MBSR), which has been shown to be effective with physical ailments (e.g., chronic pain, heart disease, gastrointestinal issues) and psychological ailments (e.g., anxiety, panic disorders) (MBCT, n.d.). MBCT adapted the concepts of MBSR to be effective in treating recurrent depression. The goal of MBCT is not to avoid the emotion but to change the individual's understanding and perception of the emotion (Psychology Today, 2020). MBCT helps the individual address the high standards and pressures placed on oneself that are ultimately creating misery (MBCT, n.d.). MBCT also helps the individual be more present with what makes life worth living. The individual is given tools to mindfully experience their emotions and change negative thought processes to positive thought processes (Psychology Today, 2020).

Studies have shown that MBCT is effective in preventing relapse in depressive episodes (MBCT, n.d.). While MBCT was adapted for recurrent depression, it has been found to be an effective supplement or replacement to attention deficit hyperactivity disorder (ADHD) medications (Aadil et al., 2017). The MBCT techniques that are effective in preventing relapse in depressive episodes have also been effective in relapse prevention and treatment of generalized anxiety disorder and addictions, and for reducing symptoms of physical health conditions, such as traumatic brain injury (Psychology Today, 2020).

## NARRATIVE

Narrative therapy empowers clients as the experts and authors of their own lives (Clarke, 2020). Externalization separates the individual's problem from the person

(Clarke, 2020). By externalizing the problem, the focus is shifted from changing or fixing the *person* to addressing the unwanted thoughts or behaviors (Clarke, 2020).

Narrative therapy also believes that reality is an individual experience and is based on an individual's interaction with the world (Clarke, 2020). A narrative or story can help individuals make sense of their reality (Clarke, 2020). When an individual is experiencing problems with their dominant story, problems will arise in various aspects of life (decision-making, problem-solving, behavior issues, and emotional/psychological distress) (Clarke, 2020). When analyzing an individual's dominant story, deconstruction of the story may help the individual better understand their story and address personal challenges (Clarke, 2020).

## RADICAL ACCEPTANCE

In short, radical acceptance is accepting life as it is (Hall, 2012). Pain and discomfort are inevitabilities in life, but acceptance can prevent suffering (Hall, 2012). Suffering stems from an individual attempting to change or fight against something one has no control over, such as natural disasters or someone else's behavior (Hall, 2012). Radical acceptance encourages individuals to accept the painful experiences and the emotions that come with those experiences, rather than avoiding negative feelings and events (Hall, 2012). Acceptance of an experience or event does not mean that the individual approves of or enjoys the experience or event; the person is simply accepting that negative, unenjoyable, or uncomfortable events happen (Hall, 2012). Refusing to accept the pains of life does not change the event but increases the emotional suffering of the individual (Hall, 2012).

Radical acceptance can be practiced anywhere and anytime discomfort occurs. While radical acceptance may seem an abstract concept, it can be effective in teaching children and adolescents to handle stressful or undesirable events (Beck-Garcia, 2019). Radical acceptance is a concept that is applied as a mindfulness technique in theories such as DBT (Beck-Garcia, 2019).

## THERAPLAY

Theraplay was originally designed as an interactive therapy focused on the development of a healthy attachment between a child and caregiver (Theraplay Institute, 2020). Strong attachments promote trust, resilience, and overall good mental health (Theraplay Institute, 2020). Theraplay uses practitioner guidance to create playful and caring child–adult interactions that foster joyful shared experiences. These activities build attunement and understanding of each other—replicating early relationship experiences proven to lead to secure attachment.

The four foundations of theraplay are structure, nurture, engagement, and challenge (Theraplay Institute, 2020). **Structure** refers to organization and predictability; **nurture** refers to caring support both physically and emotionally; **engagement** refers to feeling seen, heard, understood, and accepted; and **challenge** refers to building confidence and competence. With each foundation, there is a balance between too much or too little (Theraplay Institute, 2020). For example, too little structure can lead to chaos and feelings of insecurity, while too much structure can lead to rebellion and feelings of imprisonment.

Theraplay can be beneficial to children and adolescents who have experienced trauma (e.g., adoption, foster care, abuse, neglect, divorce) by helping promote secure attachment, trust, and resilience (Nelson, 2017). Theraplay and its four foundations can benefit people at any age of development.

## Strengths and Challenges for the 20/20 Vision

The 20/20: A Vision for the Future of Counseling program was created to develop a strategic plan for the growth and sustainability of the counseling profession. Cosponsored by ACA and the American Association of State Counseling Licensing Boards (AASCB), 20/20 involved 31 major counseling organizations that combined a broad range of viewpoints to realize a set of goals to aid all counselors and advance the counseling profession. Professional counseling is approaching its 100th anniversary of the founding of the first counseling association. We have since become an established profession and made significant progress, and as the profession expands and develops, continued attention to a unified counselor identity is important.

### ADVOCACY AND PUBLIC PERCEPTION OF COUNSELORS

Working together to improve the public perception of counseling and to advocate for professional issues will strengthen the profession. The 20/20 delegates were able to create a central definition for counseling: Counseling is a professional relationship that empowers diverse individuals, families, and groups to accomplish mental health, wellness, education, and career goals (www.counseling.org/20-20/index.aspx). Through the development of one core definition of counseling, the perception of *who* counselors are and *what* they do becomes clear and consistent across states. As students are challenged to develop their counselor identity, the profession met the challenge to develop and solidify what counseling does to help erase the stigma and better serve clients.

## UNITY AND PROFESSIONAL IDENTITY

As the counseling profession has now reached a couple of decades beyond 100 years in existence, it has become even more pertinent that there is a unified front within the profession and that its members stay current as the profession grows. Similar to the growth and development of a person, the counseling profession considers all facets of the profession and what is needed to ensure successful growth over time. The profession's growth process has had its share of growing pains. Some people associate counseling with educational institutions or equate the word "guidance" with counseling because they are unaware of counseling's evolution. As a consequence, outdated ideas linger in their minds in contrast with reality; they misunderstand the essence of the profession and those who work in it. Even among counselors themselves, those who fail to keep up in their professional development may become confused as to exactly what counseling is, where it has been, and how it is moving forward (Gladding, 2009, p. 5). Presenting ourselves as a unified profession has multiple benefits. The principles created during the 20/20 Vision delegation meeting have been implemented, there is a core definition of counseling, counselors are engaged in ongoing professional development, and more people are seeking counseling with a better understanding of what counseling is. According to the National Alliance on Mental Illness (NAMI, 2020), a study conducted in 2018 showed that 43% of adults with mental illness sought counseling. This is an increase over the last 7 years.

## PAVING NEW PATHWAYS

In the NAMI study, BARNA study, and other studies, access to counseling is one of the barriers people mentioned. A large barrier is insurance companies not covering mental health (*Americans feel good*, 2018). A barrier within the profession is the lack of license portability, which is the ability of a professional counselor licensed at the independent practice level to transfer the license to another state or United States. jurisdiction when the counselor moves to a new state or jurisdiction. The American Counseling Association has developed an inclusive definition of a license portability model and has presented the model to state licensing boards during a presentation at the American Association of State Counseling Board's annual conference (*ACA license portability. n.d*). This process is ongoing and appears to be needed even more in the midst of the current pandemic.

## RESEARCH

Expanding and promoting our research base is essential to the efficacy of professional counselors and to the public perception of the profession. Evidence-based and practice-based research strengthens the efficacy of our profession by providing knowledge in areas such as autism, trauma, adverse childhood effects (ACEs), dementia, and Alzheimer's disease. The more we actively engage with clients of diverse populations, the more we study and test ideas, the more we are able to learn about what ails our clients and ways to help. As counselors within the profession have developed knowledge, skills, and awareness, they have also ventured to explore all facets of the human condition. Currently, that exploration has included more investigation into neuroscience and counseling. Myers and Young (2012) shared that Ivey and others cited five concepts that demonstrated how counseling can change the brain in positive ways. Knowing more about these positive brain changes and other data has propelled the profession forward, and in a new direction that developed from conducting research. As the profession continues into the future, expanding our research and evidence-based practices will increase counseling's efficacy.

## SUPPORTING STUDENT CARE

Focusing on students and prospective students is necessary to ensure the ongoing health of the counseling profession. The counseling profession engages in student care and support by encouraging self-care, offering educational outreach for students, and current counselors modeling healthy behaviors and mentorship from a developmental perspective. Supervision can be viewed as a form of Vygotsky's scaffolding (Kail & Cavanaugh, 2016) technique in which a more skilled professional assists the counseling student and/or intern in developing their skills. In the classroom, counselor educators are a part of students' micro- and mesosystems (Kail & Cavanaugh, 2016) and are there to teach and challenge students as they analyze, synthesize, and evaluate the structures and beliefs within their exo- and macrosystems. This experience can correlate with the roles and responsibilities students will have when they transition into the role of counselor and begin seeing clients. The behavior has been modeled for them and, in return, they are able to demonstrate the skills learned while working with clients. This cycle of student engagement and care, along with support for students who struggle, will continue to propel the profession forward.

## CLIENT AND COMMUNITY WELFARE

Promoting client welfare and advocating for the populations we serve is a primary focus of the counseling profession. The formal definition of counseling (ACA, 20/20 Consensus Definition, n.d.) states that counselors work in relationship with clients to help empower them to achieve their desired goals. To help empower, we at times need to advocate for the needs of the diverse populations served. According to the

Multicultural Social Justice Counseling Competencies or MSJCC (Ratts et al., 2016), counselors seeking cultural competence must traverse the outer level that includes action and advocacy. In the 2 years during this book's development, the counseling profession has addressed a variety of issues using various forms of advocacy (white papers, letter writing, workshops, webinars, and community outreach) to address the growing client need. The world has endured seeing children ripped from their parents' arms and put into detention centers, areas destroyed by natural disasters made worse by a lack of government support, continued injustice of unarmed Black men and women killed at the hands of those sworn to protect them, and the spread of a pandemic that has forever changed how the world functions. In this time, the world has also seen the surviving high school students of the Parkland, Florida, shooting become advocates for better gun control, the DACA program upheld by the Supreme Court, international students able to continue their education even with classes being online, and members of the LGBTQ community being included in the Civil Rights Act of 1964 and being protected from unfair termination based on sex. The ebb and flow of the world will not change, but as agents of change, counselors have a great responsibility to advocate for the welfare of clients and to empower them to advocate for themselves.

## Summary

This chapter discussed the seven principles of the 20/20 Vision, what has been accomplished, and how the profession is still working toward growth and improved client experiences. As our world changes, the counseling profession must adapt how research is conducted and disseminated, how and where counseling is offered, and how to gain and exhibit cultural competence. Human development is a combination of nature and nurture connected by cognitive, physical, social, emotional, and environmental processes. The many theories discussed in this book are the foundation for which trains of different therapies may run on. Learning how humans develop, what influences positive and negative development, and how those developments affect optimal living are essential to the counseling process. As this book was being written, the world witnessed a health crisis that no one has seen before. After the initial shock wore off, the resiliency of human nature and necessity ignited and we were able to pivot and find ways to succeed in the midst of a pandemic. This environmental and social event will have lasting effects on the development of current and future generations, and the counseling profession will be there to offer guidance, care, and support as this new normal unfolds.

> *Life can only be understood backwards; but it must be lived forwards.*
> —Søren Kierkegaard

---

**CASE STUDIES**

### CASE #1

Frances is a 65-year-old counselor whose license is grandfathered, which means she does not have to provide continuing education hours to renew her license. Frances is a White woman who has been a middle-school counselor for 40 years in a southern state with mostly Black and White students. In the last 2 years, there has been had an influx of Hispanic and Mexican students and who need services more than other students. Frances has not attended any workshops or webinars in years and believes that what works for one student will work for all. One day, Elijah, 12, is sent to her office because he has his hoodie on and will not participate in any class activities. Once in the office with Frances, she gives him space to share his feelings, and Elijah says, "I really don't know how I feel, but I don't feel good. I think I am sad about the kids being locked in detention centers and separated from their families." Frances responded, "Well that isn't happening here so you don't need to worry. Instead, let's look at some positives in your life. What are five good things that you are grateful for?"

1. What would you have done differently as Elijah's counselor?
2. How could Frances have been more open to what Elijah was experiencing and validated his feelings?
3. What message is Elijah receiving about his feelings from the teacher and Frances's actions?

### CASE #2

Jefferson, a 26-year-old counseling student, is seeing clients virtually for practicum. Due to the recent pandemic, all his clients were switched from in-person to virtual communication, which works well for Jefferson since his undergrad major was computer science. He has noticed some of his clients aren't as engaged; they log on late, and at times have multiple distractions, from the phone ringing to kids and pets popping up on screen. Jefferson has reminded his clients of confidentiality and the need to find a quiet place for sessions, but some clients have not listened. Jefferson shared, in supervision, that he was unsure what to do next. His supervisor, Monique, suggested that he remind his clients of his charge to practice care and concern for their welfare, and that in the midst of a pandemic he needs their help to ensure that confidentiality is met. His peer, Maya, shared that she attended a free webinar on how to conduct virtual counseling well and that she learned many helpful tools. One tool was to create a short PowerPoint presentation that can be shared with clients while in session, to share resources they can review during their own time to really understand the technology being used and the importance of staying safe on their end. Jefferson appreciated the feedback and decided to research upcoming webinars he could attend.

1. What struggles have you had with doing things virtually?
2. Think of one or two skills or activities you do well in person, and share how you would adapt them to the virtual format?
3. Due to the increased number of people seeing the value in counseling, where do you see the future of counseling going? Is virtual our new normal? Will in-person counseling therapy be a thing of the past?

## Reflections and Targeted Discussion Questions

1. Think about who you want to be as a counselor in the next 5 years. What would that look like? What do you need to develop your counselor identity? What do you need from peers, professors, and personal relationships? Be as specific as possible.
2. Should distance counseling certification be included in counselor education in the future? Why or why not?
3. With the current worldwide health and racial pandemics, what would you like to see more of within the curriculum of the counseling profession? What do you feel would be helpful, and how would you advocate for it?

## References

Aadil, M., Cosme, R. M., & Chernaik, J. (2017). Mindfulness-based cognitive behavioral therapy as an adjunct treatment of attention deficit hyperactivity disorder in young adults: A literature review. *Cureus, 9*(5). doi:10.7759/cureus.1269

American Counseling Association. (n.d.). *20/20 Consensus definition of counseling.* https://www.counseling.org/about-us/about-aca/20-20-a-vision-for-the-future-of-counseling/consensus-definition-of-counseling

American Counseling Association. (n.d.). *20/20 Principles for unifying and strengthening the profession.* https://www.counseling.org/about-us/about-aca/20-20-a-vision-for-the-future-of-counseling/statement-of-principles

American Counseling Association. (n.d.). ACA license portability model faqs. https://www.counseling.org/knowledge-center/aca-licensure-portability-model-faqs#:~:text=Licensure%20portability%20refers%20to%20the,hear%20the%20word%20%E2%80%9Creciprocity%E2%80%9D

American Counseling Association. (n.d.). What is professional counseling? https://www.counseling.org/aca-community/learn-about-counseling/what-is-counseling

American Psychological Association (Ed.). (2013). Guidelines for the practice of telepsychology. *American Psychologist, 68*(9), 791–800. Doi: 10.1037/a0035001

American Psychological Association (Ed.). (n.d.). What are telehealth and telepsychology? https://www.apa.org/pi/disability/resources/publications/telepsychology?teb=2

BARNA. (2018, February 27). Americans feel good about counseling. *Research release in culture and media.* https://www.barna.com/research/americans-feel-good-counseling/

Beck-Garcia, A. (2019, May 1). Radical acceptance: Teaching children to "just say okay." https://www.nwfamilypsychology.com/nw-family-radical-acceptance

Bergström, J., Andersson, G., Ljótsson, B., Rück, C., Andréewitch, S., Karlsson, A., Carlbring, P., Andersson, E., & Lindefors, N. (2010). Internet-versus group-administered cognitive behaviour therapy for panic disorder in a psychiatric setting: A randomised trial. *BMC Psychiatry, 10*(1). doi: 10.1186/1471-244x-10-54

BetterHelp. (n.d.). FAQ—Get answers to common questions about counseling. https://www.betterhelp.com/faq/

Bulhuis, N. (2017). The difference between biofeedback and neurofeedback. https://www.neurocorecenters.com/blog/difference-between-biofeedback-and-neurofeedback

CACREP. (2020). Find a program. https://www.cacrep.org/directory/

Child Mind Institute. (n.d.). Dialectical behavior therapy (DBT) for teens and young adults. https://childmind.org/center/dialectical-behavior-therapy/

Clarke, J. (2020, February 29). Become the expert of your own life through narrative therapy. https://www.verywellmind.com/narrative-therapy-4172956

Curry, T. (2018, December 31). Critical race theory. https://www.britannica.com/topic/critical-race-theory

Gladding, S. (2009). *Counseling: A comprehensive profession* (6th ed.). Merrill-Pearson.

Granholm. E., Ben-Zeev, D., Link, P. C., Bradshaw, K. R., & Holden, J. L. (2012). Mobile assessment and treatment for schizophrenia (MATS): A pilot trial of an interactive text-messaging intervention for medication adherence, socialization, and auditory hallucinations. *Schizophrenia Bulletin, 38*(3), 414–425. https://doi.org/10.1093/schbul/sbr155

Grohol, J. M. (2019, June 19). An overview of dialectical behavior therapy. https://psychcentral.com/lib/an-overview-ofdialectical-behavior-therapy/

Hall, K. (2012, July 8). Radical acceptance: Sometimes problems can't be solved. *Psychology Today*. https://www.psychologytoday.com/us/blog/pieces-mind/201207/radical-acceptance

Harris, R. (2011). Embracing your demons: An overview of acceptance and commitment therapy. https://www.psychotherapy.net/article/Acceptance-and-Commitment-Therapy-ACT

Hayes, S. (n.d.). About ACT. https://contextualscience.org/about_act

Kail, R. V., & Cavanaugh, J. C. (2016). *Human development: A lifespan view* (7th ed.). Cengage Learning.

Kaplan, D. M., Tarvydas, V. M., & Gladding, S. T. (2014). 20/20: A vision for the future of counseling: The new consensus definition of counseling. *Journal of Counseling & Development, 92*(3), 366–372. doi: 10.1002/j.1556-6676.2014.00164.x

Kliem, S., Kröger, C., & Kosfelder, J. (2010). Dialectical behavior therapy for borderline personality disorder: A meta-analysis using mixed-effects modeling. *Journal of Consulting and Clinical Psychology, 78*(6), 936–951. https://doi-org.proxy112.nclive.org/10.1037/a0021015.supp (Supplemental)

Mayo Clinic. (2019, February 6). Biofeedback. https://www.mayoclinic.org/tests-procedures/biofeedback/about/pac-20385664

MBCT. (n.d.). About MBCT. http://www.mbct.com/about-mbct.html

Myers, J. E., & Young, J. S. (2012). Brain wave biofeedback: Benefits of integrating neurofeedback into counseling. *Journal of Counseling and Development, 90*(1), 20–28. https://www.onlinelibrary.wiley.com/doi/abs/10.1111/j.1556-6676.2012.00003.x

National Alliance on Mental Illness. (2020). Mental health by the numbers. https://www.nami.org/mhstats

National Board for Certified Counselors. (n.d.). Required training distance credentialed counselor. https://www.cce-global.org/credentialing/doc/training

Nelson, C. (2017, January 22). Theraplay. https://www.attachementtraumanetwork.org/theraplay/

Novotney, A. (2017). A growing wave of online therapy. *Monitor on Psychology, 48*(2). http://www.apa.org/monitor/2017/02/online-therapy

Peake, J. M., Kerr, G., & Sullivan, J. P. (2018). A critical review of consumer wearables, mobile applications, and equipment for providing biofeedback, monitoring stress, and sleep in physically active populations. *Frontiers in Physiology, 9*, 743. https://doi.org/10.3389/fphys.2018.00743

Psychology Today. (2020). Mindfulness-based cognitive therapy. *Psychology Today.* https://www.psychologytoday.com/us/therapy-types/mindfulness-based-cognitive-therapy

Ratts, M., Singh, A., Nassar-McMillan, S., Butler, K., & McCullough, J. (2016). *Multicultural and social justice counseling competencies.* American Counseling Association.

Snow, W. H., Lamar, M. R., Hinkle, J. S., & Speciale, M. (2018). Current practices in online counselor education. *The Professional Counselor, 8*(2), 131–145. doi: http://dx.doi.org/10.15241/whs.8.2.131

Stoler, D. (2014, October 4). What is neurofeedback? Psychology Today. https://www.psychologytoday.com/us/blog/the-resilient-brain/201410/what-is-neurofeedback

The Theraplay Institute. (2020). What is theraplay? https://theraplay.org/what-is-theraplay/

United States Department of Education (Ed.). (2020, March 4). College Accreditation in the United States. https://www2.ed.gov/admins/finaid/accred/accreditation_pg12.html

Venngage (Ed.). (n.d.). Cross' five stage model of racial identity development. https://infograph.venngage.com/p/179730/cross-five-stage-model-of-racial-identity-development

Wisniewski, L., & Ben-Porath, D. (2015). Dialectical behavior therapy and eating disorders: The use of contingency management procedures to manage dialectical dilemmas. *American Journal of Psychotherapy, 69*(2), 129–140. doi: http://dx.doi.org/10.1176/appi.psychotherapy.2015.69.2.129

## Credits

# What's in This Book for You: Teacher and Student Resources

Kaye Cole, PhD; Noréal F. Armstrong, PhD; Jacqueline Kroemer, MA; and Jessica Pourhassanian, MS

## Learning Objectives

After reading this chapter, you should be able to
1. Provide resources and tools for extended learning.
2. Apply knowledge and skills from information learned in previous chapters.
3. Demonstrate an understanding by reviewing key concepts and key terms.

## Introduction

This chapter will provide the counselor and student with additional learning opportunities and resources to expand on course readings and classroom assignments. Textbooks often offer great foundational material, but the counselor educator and student are left to find supplemental tools to support classroom learning. A collection of experiential activities, chapter reviews, and resources associated with each chapter follow. Our aim is to provide a well-rounded and all-inclusive text that meets both counselor educator and student needs.

# Key Terms Review

## CHAPTER 1

1. _____ is the physical, cognitive, emotional, and social changes that occur in a person's life.

2. A relationship between two variables that represents the likelihood of one occurring with the other is called a _____ and does not determine cause and effect.

3. There are various ways to use the scientific method; _____ unobtrusively watches and records behavior while the _____ deliberately changes the independent variable to observe the dependent variable.

4. _____ refers to all of the genetic and biological aspects of human development, while _____ refers to all of the social and environmental aspects of human development.

5. _____ explores ways the environment acts upon genetic expression. The interaction of biological and environmental forces creates _____, the idea that people vary in how sensitive they are to particular experiences.

## CHAPTER 2

1. When an individual acquires new knowledge and integrates it into preexisting cognitive constructs, that person is using the process of _____.

2. _____ is used when an individual changes the cognitive structure to include the new knowledge.

3. Erikson's _____ theory maintains that personality is influenced by society and develops via crisis or critical alternatives at each developmental stage throughout an individual's life.

4. _____ theorists, such as B. F. Skinner, believe that environment controls behavior, while theorists of _____, such as Albert Bandura, believe that individuals are active contributors to learning and learn through observation and imitation.

5. Bronfenbrenner discusses _____, which includes the various systems of context affecting an individual's development. These systems include microsystem, mesosystem, exosystem, macrosystem, and chronosystem.

## CHAPTER 3

1. A group of people who identify with one another based on a common purpose, need, background, or other similarities is referred to as _____.

2. _____ are assumptions an individual believes about his self or herself and the surrounding world, typically influenced by family values and personal experiences.

3. _____ is a term used to discuss the multiple identities (gender, sexual orientation, ethnicity, etc.) that encompass an individual and explore how those multiple identities influence various forms of oppression toward that individual.

4. _____ is a concept in which the focus is on the goals and needs of the individual while _____ places higher value on the goals and needs of the group.

5. By acknowledging the multiple identities (i.e., age, values, beliefs, religion, etc.) and personal dynamics of both the client and the counselor, the counselor demonstrates _____.

## CHAPTER 4

1. A person's capacity for emotional, affectional, and sexual attraction to—and intimate and sexual relations with—individuals of a different or same gender, or more than one gender, is a person's _____.

2. _____ is a term that describes individuals that broaden commonly held definitions of gender, including its expression, associated identities, and/or other perceived gender norms in one or more aspects of their life.

3. A term referred to as _____ is used to describe an ideology that not only privileges heterosexuality but also actively degrades and punishes any alternative, non-heterosexual constellations of relationships, identities, and behaviors.

4. A person with a gender identity congruent with the born or assigned gender has opportunities that transgender or gender-nonconforming are not given; this concept is referred to as _____.

5. _____ is a negative attitude about behaviors, individuals, or groups based on—or related to—their perceived sexual orientation, perceived gender identity, gender role, or gender expression.

## CHAPTER 5

1. _____ is referred to as the space between a child's ability to perform a task with help and the ability to perform it independently.

2. Skills that a child develops at a particular age are called _____.

3. There are three types of attachment: _____ is an attachment style in which a child has little reaction toward the caregiver, _____ is an attachment style in which a child has confidence in the caregiver to provide appropriate nurture and comfort, and _____ is an attachment style in which the child exhibits attention-seeking behavior but refuses the caregiver's attempts to comfort.

4. The _____ model focuses on the fit between a parenting style and the child's disposition.

5. The model cited in question 4 involves three types of child: the _____ child adapts easily to new circumstances and has a generally stable mood; the _____ child has irregular patterns and reacts negatively to new situations, crying frequently; and the _____ child can have some negative reactions to new situations but can accept them through repeated exposure and generally has regular patterns.

## CHAPTER 6

1. The changing of sensory input information into a form the system can cope with for storage is called _____.

2. The _____ consists of three distinct networks: alerting, orienting, and executive attention.

3. _____ is the process of where, how long, how much, and what kind of information is kept for later retrieval.

4. _____ involves unique or specific major experiences or events that the child can recall on his or her own at some point in the future.

5. Cognitive and sensory assessments that conjunctively process information of our environment are referred to as _____.

## CHAPTER 7

1.  The _____ of parenting style is based on the warmth response, emotional climate, or level of positivity of the parent, while the _____ of parenting style describes the parent's level of demands or power over the child's behaviors.
2.  _____ is a consequence that increases the likelihood of a behavior recurring whereas _____ is a consequence that decreases the likelihood of a behavior recurring.
3.  _____ occurs when parents may end up unwittingly reinforcing the behavior they wish to discourage.
4.  _____ is the genetic blueprint the child inherits from the biological parents.
5.  The world the child is exposed to and learns to navigate through is often referred to as the child's _____.

## CHAPTER 8

1.  The psychological virtue _____ is characterized by an individual's ability to relate to others and form genuine connections.
2.  _____ is to become different in the process of growth and to be aware of what makes someone different.
3.  Changes in behavior, cognition, values, language cultural activities, personal relationship styles, and beliefs that a cultural minority goes through as it encounters the dominant culture is _____.
4.  _____ is the socialization process by which individuals learn and acquire the cultural and psychological qualities of their own group.
5.  The conscious sense of self we gain from social interaction is referred to as _____.

## CHAPTER 9

1.  _____ is an individual's own self-awareness and ability to self-reflect on experiences, values, and ideologies.
2.  The ability to perceive, understand, use, and regulate emotions in oneself and others is referred to as _____.

## CHAPTER 10

1. _____ is the accumulation of knowledge, facts, and skills acquired throughout a life.
2. The capacity to think logically and solve problems in novel situations, independent of acquired knowledge, is referred to as _____.
3. As individuals age, they gradually lose senses such as sight, _____, hearing, and _____.

## CHAPTER 11

1. The theory that elderly people remember positive things better than negative or neutral things is referred to as the _____.
2. The ability of the brain to undergo biological changes, _____, ranges from the cellular level (i.e., individual neurons) all the way to large-scale changes involving cortical remapping.
3. _____ refers to the rich tapestry of diversity in social practices that different cultures exhibit around the world.

## CHAPTER 12

1. The final stage of the life span that occurs either after age 65 or following the diagnosis of a life-limiting illness is referred to as _____.
2. The term _____ refers to terminal injuries or diseases that will likely result in death within 10 years.
3. When someone is experiencing an unpleasant emotion involving multidimensional concerns of an existential origin, provoked on contemplation of death of self or others, that person is experiencing _____.
4. _____ refers to matters related to existence and the meaning of life.

## Reflective Questions/Discussion Post Prompts

The following are questions that require critical thinking. These questions are designed to help in applying the information from the chapters.

## CHAPTER 1

1. Using what you have learned in this chapter, describe the importance of the interaction of nature and nurture.
2. Define and discuss these concepts: multidirectional, multicontextual, multicultural, and plasticity.
3. Why is differential susceptibility important when considering a person's coping mechanisms and resilience?
4. Considering Bronfenbrenner's ecological system, reflect on who you would place within your microsystem?

## CHAPTER 2

1. What theoretical perspective on human development do you relate to most? Why?
2. How would you help a 67-year-old surgeon who is preparing to retire and is struggling in the crisis between integrity and despair? How would you help the surgeon attain virtue at that stage?

## CHAPTER 3

1. What is your current worldview and what personal dynamics or experiences would you bring into the counseling relationship?
2. Why it is important for clinicians to be aware of an individual's culture when considering that person's life-span development?

## CHAPTER 4

1. Serenity is 21 and a junior in college. She has dated boys since high school because that's what you're supposed to do; however, she was kissed by a girl from her biology class and she felt different than she had when kissed by boys. She is unsure what is happening. How would you help Serenity? What do you want to consider?
2. Consider the various developmental stages. How can the intersections of race, gender, and sexual orientation play a role in progressing through those stages? Explain both positive and negative roles.

## CHAPTER 5

1.   Think back to your childhood. When were you able to master certain skills (e.g., brushing your teeth, tying your shoelaces, writing your name, etc.)? Who was in your life to help with your social interactions? Share who you learned from the most (e.g., parents, teachers, siblings). Do you help others in the same way you were helped, or do you use a different style of scaffolding?
2.   From reading this chapter, what could be some reasons a child might develop insecure–avoidant attachment? How would you help the parents and child?

## CHAPTER 6

1.   How would knowing the cognitive milestones of a 4-year-old help to support a parent who was anxious about the child's development?
2.   How would you use scaffolding to help children who are struggling to express themselves through speaking?

## CHAPTER 7

1.   Think back to your 10th birthday. What was important to you and who did you want around? How did that birthday prepare you for early adolescence?
2.   Looking back on your middle childhood years, how would you classify yourself: follower or leader? Do you still function in that role today? If not, what changed? If yes, what kept you in that role and has it benefited you?

## CHAPTER 8

1.   What problems do you believe will arise in young teens if current cell phone and social media usage continues in an upward trend?
2.   How would you help teens overcome their illusion of invulnerability and imaginary audience thinking if these were detrimental to the teen's development?
3.   Think back to your adolescence. What were your initial thoughts about death and dying?

## CHAPTER 9

1. According to this chapter, what was cited as a support to help young adults who have not formed long-term romantic relationships and are feeling marginalized or inadequate? In our current health situation and use of virtual resources, how would you create space for that support?
2. After reading about Piaget's proposed fifth stage of cognitive development, known as postformal operational thinking, share your thoughts on whether you believe it is a valid position. What are your thoughts on it being a reflective stance on the quest for meaning versus a natural standard of determining human moral maturity?
3. What images of death do you see in your daily life? On TV and in movies? On social media? In music?

## CHAPTER 10

1. What are your feelings about aging and getting older? How do you perceive the aging process and who influenced your beliefs?
2. Every generation has a moment in time that has shaped its generation (WWII, Great Depression, MLK, Jr. assassination, Kennedy assassination, and 9/11). Now the COVID-19 pandemic has affected every generation in very different ways, with culture playing a role. How have the effects of COVID-19 affected middle-aged adults compared with other age groups, and how has race played a factor? How might you prepare to help a client who is middle-aged and Black cope with all that's going on? How are you coping?
3. Think of a list of expressions and euphemisms that are used when people talk about death. How might these keep people from facing the reality of death?

## CHAPTER 11

1. Share your thoughts about programmed aging theory—that aging and death are "hardwired" into all organisms.
2. Explain your thoughts on Carol Gilligan's argument that androgyny, or the incorporation of both masculine and feminine voices, is the best way to reach one's full potential as a human being.

3.  Discuss some of the emotional changes that you can expect to encounter in middle adulthood as it relates to death and dying.

## CHAPTER 12

1.  If you learned your exact death date, what things haven't you done or believe you would want to do before that time? How would knowing the date change how you currently live your life?
2.  What are some of the negative stereotypes you have heard or seen about older adults? After reading this chapter what are some strengths of older adults that can help present them as valuable to society?
3.  What advice might one give to a younger person about living a meaningful life?

## CHAPTER 13

1.  Explain how virtual counseling can be used to continue forward with the 20/20 Vision for counseling. What are some ways in which the counseling profession can serve its clients using technology?
2.  In the midst of the pandemic, face-to-face counseling has been done through social distancing and the wearing of masks. What do you believe could or would be lost in a session due to the use of masks? What could you do to adapt for those changes or losses?

## Experiential Activities

The activities that follow are options to provide extended and applicable learning opportunities for students, a "what's in this book that for me" tool to help students retain and apply the information through action and demonstration of skills. The authors have used many of these activities and found them to be successful.

1.  **Genogram**—Have the students create a diagram (or genogram) that represents the biological, cognitive, psychological, social, and environmental aspects of their lives. Bronfenbrenner's ecological system model can be used if desired.

2.  **Letter to Your Younger Self**—Write a one- to two-page letter to your adolescent self. Think of all the things you know now and how they have shaped who you are.

3.  **Personal Time line**—Create a time line from your earliest childhood memories and mark a major event every 5 years that affected your development. Then reflect on what feelings develop as you create your time line. Are there any patterns? Is there something you want to know more about? Are there any unresolved issues in your life?

4.  **Naturalistic Observation**—Take an hour and go to the park or at the next family gathering sit and watch the kids play.* Record what you witness and connect your natural observations to behaviors shared in the stage theories. Record the date, time, location, age, and gender of the children. Address what was present or absent regarding the age expectations.

    *This activity can be stretched out over a semester and include multiple observations to see growth over time.

5.  **Interviews**—Focus on parents and their 12- to 14-year-old children to see how their relationships have changed. Do they argue more and over what? Interview a counselor, nurse, or others who work with older clients to learn about the behaviors they observe and what needs should be met. Conduct generational interviews to observe their different developmental experiences and views on counseling.

6.  **Book Reviews**—Use the books cited later in the chapter, or other books of your choice, and write a review on the content and how it relates to human development. You may also take one book, assign a chapter to each student, and process their reviews in class.

7.  **Create a Case**—Ask students to select a chapter they enjoy or find interesting and have them create a case study with reflective questions. The case study needs to address one to three key components of the section they have chosen.

8.  **Create Exam Questions**—Students are assigned a chapter and will create five to 10 questions that could be used on an exam. They will review the course objectives from the syllabus and make sure the questions they create would address the learning objectives. The questions can be short answer, multiple choice, fill in the blank, matching, or a combination.

9.  **Child's Play**—Take different childhood games (e.g., Hangman, Memory, Win-Lose-or-Draw*) and apply the contents of the chapters to the games. After a correct guess or match is made, the person who guesses correctly must be able to define or accurately discuss the concept.

    *Jeopardy is another game that can be used to review key topics before an exam. The professor can create the initial game and then students may create their own as a way to study.

10. **Matching Game**—Create three to five sets of flashcards on the theories and the theorists who created them. Give each pair or group of students the cards, set the timer, and let the students try to match all the theorists with the key components of their theory. The pair or group to correctly match all cards first or before the timer sounds wins. (This game can be used with other developmental concepts.)

11. **Create a Game**—Students may choose an age group and develop an age-appropriate game for the group that teaches a concept key to that developmental stage. For example, an "I statement" game to help adolescents communicate their feelings.

## Case Studies

The following are case study prompts. You can add more to the case and/or create discussion questions about the cases. The cases align with the topics in chapters 3 through 12.

- Henry Park is an Asian American car salesperson in South Carolina. He is friendly, a hard worker, and has been top seller of the month three times. As the COVID-19 pandemic reached peak levels, he struggled to sell a single car in the last few months. Consumers would enter the lot, not look in his direction, and wait to engage until another salesperson approached.

- Barry and Joseph have been happily married for 2 years. Joseph's nephew has been staying with them for 6 months, since his mother, Joseph's sister, went to jail on narcotics charges. In their Alabama community, the school-age students are predominately White. Barry and Joseph decided they wanted to adopt Malik, but the family advocate asked if they were ready to help Malik navigate being the only—or one of a few—Black males in the school with two fathers in a rural, conservative city in Alabama. Barry and Joseph did not quite know how to respond.

- Jeffrey and Richard are 6-year-old twins in the first grade who have had class online for the past month. Jeffery enjoys seeing his peers on the screen and playing reading and math games on his tablet. Richard is less focused, not getting his work done, and his grandmother caught him playing a Cars video game instead of doing his work.

- Yolanda is 11 and loves being part of both the 6th grade band and cheer team. Since being stuck at home for the last 3 months, Yolanda has been less active, not talking as much and staying in her room. She shared with her friends on FaceTime that "life sucks" because she can't attend band or cheer practice and she is bored being home all day. One of her friends said, "Well, it seems like you haven't missed a meal; your boobs are so big now." Embarrassed, Yolanda got off the call and ran to look at herself in the mirror.

- Jasmine is frustrated because her parents are trying to force her to marry after her 19th birthday celebration. Jasmine has been looking at schools in London because Mulan goes there, and she and Mulan became very close and intimate before she graduated and moved away. Jasmine isn't sure what is going on, but she knows she wants an opportunity to find out.

- Latoya, a 26-year-old public relations rep and event planner, is preparing to move back in with her parents. She works for an elite event planning agency, but since the pandemic hit has been unable to plan or secure any large contracts. She is also worried about her parents, who are in their mid-50s and work in the medical profession. Latoya feels moving home will be best for her and her parents.

- Triton, a 43-year-old White male with six daughters, is struggling to connect with them as he used to. He works hard to keep them safe and has plans for each of their futures. Triton stays busy focusing on them, but he has not taken time to focus on himself. His wife died tragically and unexpectedly 5 years ago, and now his energy goes to his daughters (even if they don't always want it).

- Clarice, a 75-year-old Cherokee and Black woman, has worked as a registered nurse for more than 40 years. Currently, she is a part-time nurse on a college campus. She works remotely from home 3 days a week and goes to campus 2 days a week. Clarice loves what she does but has been recently thinking of retiring. She is unsure what she would do if she stopped being a nurse, and adding to the situation, her daughter Charletta calls multiple times a day to check on her and ask where she has been and what is doing to stay safe. Clarice wants to be able to talk with Charletta without feeling interrogated.

- Memphis is a physical therapist in Las Vegas. Recently, while at work, he contracted COVID-19 and became very ill. He is now in the ICU on a breathing machine and can only see his family through FaceTime. The doctors are doing all they can to help him recover and to make him comfortable. Most days, Memphis lies in bed and thinks back over his life, his accomplishments, his regrets, and he wishes he had more time. He wonders, *did I do enough?*

## Journal Topics

### CHAPTER 1

Explain why it is important that Bronfenbrenner's approach includes the context of socioeconomic status (SES). What makes a person's SES limiting or advantageous?

### CHAPTER 2

Which stage of development do you relate to more and why?

There have been many detractors of Freud's psychosexual stages. What do you think about the stages and have you witnessed any of the behaviors in yourself or family members?

### CHAPTER 3

How can the intersectionality of race, gender, age, and religion affect child development? Share positive and negative developments.

### CHAPTER 4

How would you handle learning that someone close to you or in your family was questioning their sexuality or gender expression?

### CHAPTER 5

As you have read up to this chapter, if you haven't had children but are thinking about it, what concerns do you have? What would help to put you at ease?

### CHAPTER 6

How would you feel if your child or a child you were close to wanted to dress up for Halloween as Black Widow and the child was male?

### CHAPTER 7

Which method, abstinence or sex education, do you believe should be taught in schools? How do you feel about it starting with middle school (ages 11–13)? If tasked to create the content, what would you include?

### CHAPTER 8

What issues did you struggle with in high school and early college? How was your body image during that time, and how did your social networks influence how you saw yourself?

### CHAPTER 9

An increasing number of people are going to vocational schools, learning a trade, or working more in blue-collar jobs. Do you believe that going to college is as valued and as beneficial as it is advertised to be? If you went back, would you do things the same way regarding your educational path?

### CHAPTER 10

If you have children, how has your relationship with them changed as you've gotten older (middle to late adulthood)? If you do not have children, how has your relationship changed with your siblings and parents?

### CHAPTER 11

Explain whether it would be harder for you to see yourself getting older or watch your parents getting older, and why. What feelings, thoughts, or fears do you have about older age? What are you looking forward to about getting older?

### CHAPTER 12

How would you handle helping someone cope with terminal illness?

### CHAPTER 13

As 2020 was filled with a global pandemic, severe racial injustices, a national mobilized movement for change, and political unrest, how does the counseling profession develop space for solutions? What changes would you like to see as the counseling profession moves forward, and how does your knowledge of human development aid in that process?

## Internet Resources

This section provides links to podcasts, YouTube videos and channels, websites, counseling, and other disciplines' websites that address the various topics discussed in the chapters. It also offers information on where to seek services and helps to develop a "toolbox" to enhance your skills within the profession.

### TOPICS COVERED THROUGHOUT THE CHAPTERS

309: Dr. Wendy Chung: Hunting Down Genes that Cause Human Disease
    https://www.peoplebehindthescience.com/dr-wendy-chung/

Adverse Childhood Effects (Nadine Burke Haris, TED Talk)
   https://www.ted.com/talks/nadine_burke_harris_how_childhood_trauma_
   affects_health_across_a_lifetime?language=en
Career and Job Resources
   https://youth.gov/youth-topics/youth-employment/career-exploration-
   and-skill-development
Commission on Sexual Orientation and Gender Identity
   https://www.americanbar.org/groups/diversity/sexual_orientation/
Domestic Violence Support
   https://www.dvrc-or.org/safety-planning/
The effect of isolation on neural functioning
   https://www.youtube.com/watch?v=i3DoIOc3KhY
Kohlberg's Theory of Moral Development
   https://www.simplypsychology.org/kohlberg.html
LGBTQ Youth Resources
   https://www.cdc.gov/lgbthealth/youth-resources.htm
The power of genetics (nature/nurture)
   https://www.youtube.com/watch?v=uXIW_m0lo0U
Preventing Adverse Childhood Experience
   https://vetoviolence.cdc.gov/apps/aces-training/#/#top
SAIGE (ACA Counseling Division—Society for Affectional Intersex, and Gender
Expansive Identities)
   https://saigecounseling.org/
Working with Teen Grief
   https://americanhospice.org/grieving-children/someone-you-love-has-
   died-a-book-for-grieving-children/

## Resources from the "ISMs" Perspectives

The resources that follow provide information to assist with the process of human
development for the different ISM perspectives.

### MULTICULTURAL

13 Amazing Coming of Age Traditions From Around the World
   https://www.globalcitizen.org/en/content/13-amazing-coming-of-age-traditions-
   from-around-th/

Administration for Native Americans
>    https://www.acf.hhs.gov/ana/resource-library
Asian and Pacific Islander American Health Forum
>    https://www.apiahf.org/about/
The Association of Multicultural Counseling and Development
>    https://multiculturalcounselingdevelopment.org/

## PODCASTS

1619 (*The New York Times*)
>    https://www.nytimes.com/2020/01/23/podcasts/1619-podcast.html
About Race
>    https://www.showaboutrace.com/
Code Switch (NPR)
>    https://www.npr.org/sections/codeswitch/
Intersectionality Matters! (Hosted by Kimberlé Crenshaw)
>    https://podcasts.apple.com/us/podcast/intersectionality-matters/id1441348908
Momentum: A Race Forward Podcast
>    https://www.raceforward.org/media/podcast/momentum-race-forward-podcast
Nice White Parents (Serial and *The New York Times*)
>    https://www.nytimes.com/2020/07/30/podcasts/nice-white-parents-serial.html

## DIVERSITY

The Civil Rights Project/Proyecto Derechos Civiles
>    http://civilrightsproject.ucla.edu/
>    Helps renew the civil rights movement by bridging the worlds of ideas and action
>    to be a preeminent source of intellectual capital within that movement and to
>    deepen the understanding of the issues that must be resolved to achieve racial
>    and ethnic equity as society moves through the great transformation of the 21st
>    century.
DACA
>    https://www.uscis.gov/archive/consideration-of-deferred-action-for-childhood-ar-
>    rivals-daca
Immigration Equality
>    https://immigrationequality.org/
>    The nation's leading LGBTQ and HIV-positive immigrant rights organization.
>    Through direct legal services, policy advocacy, and impact litigation, it advocates

for immigrants and families facing discrimination based on their sexual orientation, gender identity, or HIV status.

https://www.hrsa.gov/sites/default/files/culturalcompetence/servicesforhispanics.pdf

*The Lemon Grove Incident* (YouTube)

https://www.youtube.com/watch?time_continue=1&v=Uu9dxMMLGyU&feature=emb_title

National Network for Immigrant and Refugee Rights

http://www.nnirr.org/

Works to defend and expand the rights of all immigrants and refugees, regardless of immigration status, by using popular education, creating dialogues, and monitoring intergovernmental bodies.

## RACE AND DISCUSSIONS REGARDING RACE

A Conversation with Latinos on Race

https://youtu.be/tLLCHbCgJbM

A Conversation with Native Americans on Race

https://youtu.be/siMal6QVblE

A Conversation with Police on Race

https://youtu.be/5Funraox29U

A Conversation with Whites on Race

https://youtu.be/xXow7olFyIM

Facing History and Ourselves

https://www.facinghistory.org/

Founded in 1976, Facing History and Ourselves is a nonprofit international educational and professional development organization whose mission is to engage students of diverse backgrounds in an examination of racism, prejudice, and anti-Semitism to promote the development of a more humane and informed citizenry. Offers resources, study guides, and classroom activities on topics related to immigration.

Helm on White Racial Identity Development

https://youtu.be/b7XduE2Q9-Y

Intersectionality (TED Talk by Kimberlé Crenshaw)

https://www.youtube.com/watch?v=akOe5-UsQ2o

Islamophobia killed my brother. Let's end the hate. (TED Talk by Suzanne Barakat)

https://www.youtube.com/watch?v=XiEQmcZi8cM

People, Principles, and Practices—Cultural Humility
    https://www.youtube.com/watch?v=SaSHLbS1V4w&t=1164s
Racism in America: A History in Three Acts
    https://youtu.be/QaqW0lDlDgo
White Privilege (TED Talk by Peggy McIntosh)
    https://youtu.be/e-BY9UEewHw

## GENDER

Gender and Adolescence: Global Evidence (GAGE)
    https://www.gage.odi.org/
INCITE!
    http://www.incite-national.org/
    Women of Color Against Violence, a national activist organization of radical feminists of color, fosters a movement to end violence against women of color and our communities through direct action, critical dialogue, and grassroots organizing.

## SEXUAL ORIENTATION

Resources, articles, links, advocacy websites, and webinars to help students gain more information and be aware, and perhaps even leave a space for them (counselor educator/student) to add their own local resources for the area where they live.
Bisexual Resource Center
    https://biresource.org/
    International organization providing education about and support for bisexual and progressive issues.
Campus Pride
    https://www.campuspride.org/
    Helps develop necessary resources, programs, and services to support LGBT and ally students on college campuses across the United States.
Gay & Lesbian Alliance Against Defamation (GLAAD)
    https://www.glaad.org/
    For more than 25 years, GLAAD has worked with news, entertainment, and social media to bring culture-changing stories of LGBT people into millions of homes and workplaces every day.
Gay, Lesbian, Straight Education Network (GLSEN)
    https://www.glsen.org/
    Strives to assure that each member of every school community is valued and respected regardless of sexual orientation or gender identity/expression.

Gender Spectrum

https://www.genderspectrum.org/

Provides an array of services designed to help families, schools, professionals, and organizations understand and address concepts of gender identity and gender expression.

How Trans Kids and Their Parents Decide When to Start Medical Transition

https://youtu.be/QD720mHFqW0

Human Rights Campaign

https://www.hrc.org/

Advocates on the behalf of LGBT Americans, mobilizes grassroots actions, etc.

National Center for Transgender Equality

https://transequality.org/

The National Center for Transgender Equality (NCTE) is a 501(c)3 social justice organization dedicated to advancing the equality of transgender people through advocacy, collaboration, and empowerment.

SAIGE (formerly ALGBTIC)

https://saigecounseling.org/

What are the different types of sexuality?

https://www.healthline.com/health/different-types-of-sexuality#a-c

## ABLEISM

Association on Aging with Developmental Disabilities

https://www.agingwithdd.org/

I'm not your inspiration, thank you very much (TED Talk by Stella Young)

https://www.youtube.com/watch?v=8K9Gg164Bsw

Overcoming Ableism

https://youtu.be/X1xnyVCBYNQ

## AGEISM

Association for Adult Development and Aging

http://www.aadaweb.org/

I'm 17 (TED Talk)

https://youtu.be/0OkOQhXhsIE

Let's End Ageism (TED Talk)

https://www.ted.com/talks/ashton_applewhite_let_s_end_ageism?utm_source=tedcomshare&utm_medium=social&utm_campaign=tedspread

## CLASSISM

Labanowski, Phyllis (2013). *Class action: Sound of wealth* [YouTube video].
http://www.classism.org/sound-wealth/?hc_location=ufi

Public Broadcasting System. (2017, June 5). Chasing the dream: Poverty and opportunity in America. *For millions, underemployment is a new normal* [TV series]. USA: PBS.
http://www.pbs.org/wnet/chasing-the-dream/stories/millions-underemployment-new-normal/

Public Broadcasting System. (2017, September 18). Chasing the dream: Poverty and opportunity in America. *Despite promising census figures, not everyone is bouncing back from recession* [TV series]. USA: PBS.
http://www.pbs.org/wnet/chasing-the-dream/uncategorized/despite-promising-census-figures-not-everyone-bouncing-back-recession/

YouTube/politizane. (2012, November 20). *Wealth inequality in America* [YouTube video].
https://www.youtube.com/watch?v=QPKKQnijnsM&t=10s

## Books to Read

What follows are books related to or about different aspects of human development. Please challenge yourself to read one or two and add to the list with books you encounter along the way.

*The boy who was raised as a dog: And other stories from a child psychiatrist's notebook—What traumatized children can teach us about loss, love, and healing* (paperback, Bruce D. Perry)
https://www.amazon.com/Boy-Who-Raised-Psychiatrists-Notebook-What/dp/0465094457/ref=zg_bs_11162_7?_encoding=UTF8&psc=1&refRID=HE6GH-CPNCDPDY9E405JJ

*Childhood disrupted: How your biography becomes your biology, and how you can heal* (paperback, Donna Jackson Nakazawa)
https://www.amazon.com/Childhood-Disrupted-audiobook/dp/B010EC119M/ref=zg_bs_11162_23?_encoding=UTF8&psc=1&refRID=HE6GHCPNCDP-DY9E405JJ

*The deepest well: Healing the long-term effects of childhood adversity* (paperback, Nadine Burke Harris, MD)
https://www.amazon.com/Deepest-Well-Long-Term-Childhood-Adversity/dp/132850266X/ref=zg_bs_11162_8?_encoding=UTF8&psc=1&refRID=HE6GH-CPNCDPDY9E405JJ

*How we change (And ten reasons why we don't)* (Ross Ellenhorn) https://www.amazon.com/How-We-Change-Reasons-Dont/dp/006296111X/ref=tmm_hrd_swatch_0?_encoding=UTF8&qid=&sr=

*How to be an adult: A handbook for psychological and spiritual integration* (paperback, David Richo)

https://www.amazon.com/How-Adult-Psychological-Spiritual-Integration/dp/0809132230/ref=zg_bs_11162_24?_encoding=UTF8&psc=1&refRID=HE6GH-CPNCDPDY9E405JJ

*Leaning In: A student's guide to engaging constructively with social justice content*

https://www.researchgate.net/publication/279539507_Leaning_in_A_student's_guide_to_engaging_constructively_with_social_justice_content

*Uniquely human: A different way of seeing autism* (Barry M. Prizant)

https://www.amazon.com/Uniquely-Human-Different-Seeing-Autism/dp/1476776245/ref=zg_bs_11162_9?_encoding=UTF8&psc=1&refRID=HE6GH-CPNCDPDY9E405JJ

## Summary

As counselor educators and counseling students, the aim of this chapter was to provide embedded resources for extended learning opportunities. The expectation is that this chapter will provide tools, ideas, resources, and spark ingenuity in learning life-span development. Gaining an understanding and awareness of how development works, what influences development, and developmental outcomes is the foundation from which your skills will grow and be used in the counseling profession. The tools provided in this chapter allow for the exploration and application of the concepts explained within this book. We hope that as you finish reading, you are assured that *what's in this book is for you.*

## Key Terms Answer Key

### CHAPTER 1

Answers: (1) human development; (2) correlation; (3) observational method, experimental method; (4) nature, nurture; (5) epigenetics, differential susceptibility or sensitivity

### CHAPTER 2

Answers: (1) assimilation; (2) accommodation; (3) psychosocial; (4) behaviorism, social learning theory; (5) interconnecting systems

## CHAPTER 3

Answers: (1) culture; (2) beliefs; (3) intersectionality; (4) individualistic, collectivist; (5) cross-cultural competence

## CHAPTER 4

Answers: (1) affectional/sexual identity; (2) gender expansive; (3) heterosexism; (4) cisgender privilege; (5) sexual orientation, gender identity prejudice

## CHAPTER 5

Answers: (1) zone of proximal development; (2) developmental milestones; (3) insecure-avoidant, secure, ambivalent-resistant; (4) goodness of fit; (5) easy, difficult, slow to warm-up

## CHAPTER 6

Answers: (1) encoding; (2) attention network approach; (3) storage; (4) episodic memory; (5) attention

## CHAPTER 7

Answers: (1) warmth dimension, control dimension; (2) reinforcement, punishment; (3) negative reinforcement trap; (4) heredity; (5) environment

## CHAPTER 8

Answers: (1) fidelity; (2) differentiation; (3) acculturation; (4) enculturation; (5) ego identity

## CHAPTER 9

Answers: (1) identity; (2) emotional intelligence

## CHAPTER 10

Answers: (1) crystallized intelligence; (2) fluid intelligence; (3) presbyopia, presbycusis

## CHAPTER 11

Answers: (1) positivity bias; (2) neuroplasticity; (3) cultural variation

## CHAPTER 12

Answers: (1) end of life; (2) life-limiting illness; (3) death anxiety; (4) existential concerns

9 781793 525994